KU-256-631

SERIES PREFACE

series preface

To understand the rapidly changing world in which we live, the study of geography is essential. Yet the nature and importance of a geographic perspective can easily be misconstrued if geography is seen simply as a set of changing patterns and arrangements. Like the world around it, the discipline of geography itself has undergone sweeping changes in recent decades as its practitioners have confronted and developed new concepts, theories, and perspectives. Placing the contributions of geographic research within the context of these changes is critical to an appreciation of geography's present and future.

The *Human Geography in the Making* series was developed with these considerations in mind. Inspired initially by the influential 'Progress Reports' in the journal *Progress in Human Geography*, the series offers book-length overviews of geographic subdisciplines that are widely taught in colleges and universities at the upper division and graduate levels. The goal of each of the books is to acquaint readers with the major issues and conceptual problems that have dominated a particular subdiscipline over the past two to three decades, to discuss and assess current themes that are shaping the evolution of the subdiscipline, and to highlight the most promising areas for future research.

There is a widely recognized gap between topically focused textbooks and narrowly defined scholarly studies. The books in this series move into this gap. Through analyses of the intellectual currents that have shaped key subdisciplines of geography, these books provide telling insights into the conceptual and empirical issues currently influencing research and teaching. Geographic understanding requires an appreciation of how and why ideas have evolved, and where they may be going. The distinguished contributors to this series have much to say about these matters, offering ideas and interpretations of importance to students and professional geographers alike.

Alexander B. Murphy
Series Editor
Professor of Geography
University of Oregon

FORTHCOMING TITLES

Making Political Geography

JOHN AGNEW

Department of Geography, UCLA

A member of the Hodder Headline Group
LONDON
Distributed in the United States of America by
Oxford University Press Inc., New York

First published in Great Britain in 2002
by Arnold, a member of the Hodder Headline Group,
338 Euston Road, London NW1 3BH

http://www.arnoldpublishers.com

Distributed in the United States of America by
Oxford University Press Inc.,
198 Madison Avenue, New York, NY10016

© 2002 John Agnew

All rights reserved. No part of this publication may be reproduced or transmitted in any
form or by any means, electronically or mechanically, including photocopying, recording
or any information storage or retrieval system, without either prior permission in writing
from the publisher or a licence permitting restricted copying. In the United Kingdom such
licences are issued by the Copyright Licensing Agency: 90 Tottenham Court Road,
London W1T 4LP.

The advice and information in this book are believed to be true and accurate at the date
of going to press, but neither the author nor the publisher can accept any legal
responsibility or liability for any errors or omissions.

British Library Cataloguing in Publication Data
A catalogue record for this book is available from the British Library

Library of Congress Cataloging-in-Publication Data
A catalog record for this book is available from the Library of Congress

ISBN 0 340 75954 2 (hb)
ISBN 0 340 75955 0 (pb)

1 2 3 4 5 6 7 8 9 10

Production Editor: Wendy Rooke
Production Controller: Martin Kerans
Cover Design: Terry Griffiths

Typeset in 10/14.5 Gill Sans by Charon Tec Pvt. Ltd, Chennai, India
Printed and bound in Great Britain by MPG Books Ltd, Bodmin, Cornwall

What do you think about this book? Or any other Arnold title?
Please send your comments to feedback.arnold@hodder.co.uk

QM LIBRARY
(MILE END)

CONTENTS

PREFACE

In the art exhibition *The Great War of the Californias*, artist Sandow Birk envisages a future in which a war is fought between San Francisco and Los Angeles and their respective hinterlands. The exhibition represents a purported retrospective showing of paintings of the war left by artists. In his Introduction to the exhibition Birk (2000: 17) writes:

> The Great War of the Californias was fought in a thousand places. From Lake Tahoe to Tijuana, in places like Potrero and Pasadena, Bakersfield and Beverly Hills, Telegraph Hill and Tarzana. More than three million Californians fought in, and over 20,000 died in it. Californians killed each other in California towns, along California beaches, in California skies. In the two days of fighting at the battle of Van Nuys, 2000 died in a mere forty minutes.

Of course, the exhibition is a satire. But it is a satire of particular interest to the making of political geography. Political geography is about the geographical distribution of power, how it concentrates and how it shifts between places over time. Wars have been one of the ways in which power is redistributed, not often to the benefit of those who start them. In this case, the war is about the long-running competition between San Francisco and Los Angeles for which city would be dominant in California. In such paintings as *The Bombardment of the Getty Center* (cover), in which the massive edifice (and art gallery) on the western hill above the 405 Freeway in west Los Angeles comes under fire from northern artillery, Birk not only uses familiar (to filmgoers and TV watchers) and apparently peaceful California to paint scenes redolent of medieval and early modern warfare but, in his commentary, draws attention to the dramatic social inequalities and ethnic differences that could, under certain circumstances, erupt into open warfare as the various differences are swept into a territorial frame of reference pitting northern against southern California. Los Angeles has had its own local 'wars,' of course. The most recent one was the riots of 1992. So, as with most good satirists, Birk has a serious purpose. He wants to point out the historical contingency of political identities and the way these can be redefined territorially even in the seemingly most unlikely of situations.

This understanding is not one that has always prevailed in the study of 'political geography.' As a modern field of study it came about in the 1890s as an 'aid to statecraft' on the part of the Great Powers of the day. Contemporary national political identities and reason-of-state were taken as givens. The 'needs' of territorial states and the role of relative location on the earth's surface and the resources available in driving and determining the outcome of competition between them were the main concerns of the field. Lurking behind the history of political geography is the history of thinking about how nature relates to nation-state as inherited from the eighteenth-century European Enlightenment and the early nineteenth-century Romantic reaction against it. If the idea of 'levels of development' associated with different national territories comes from eighteenth-century Enlightenment thought, then that of hierarchies of national territories on a racial-natural basis competing with one another for domination comes out of nineteenth-century German idealism.

This intellectual genealogy long dominated the field. Until recently, most political geographers have been either cameralists (advocates of state-based economies) or imperialists. There are still some of each around, even if many advocates of cameralism now think of themselves as on the political Left rather than on the nationalist Right. Changing times can produce strange bedfellows. But over the past twenty years liberal perspectives, pitting states against markets, and social perspectives, looking to a plurality of forms of governance, have tended to become more influential. Of course, disputes between cameralists (both nationalist and state socialist), imperialists, liberals, and romantic localists have deep roots in modern political thought. Finally, however, political geography has come to share in the debates, even if often without much consciousness of the historical longevity of the discourses now in play.

But it is not only the range of implicit political projects informing the field that has changed. The intellectual attitude has moved one hundred and eighty degrees. Since the 1960s a more independent and critical approach has begun to develop, acknowledging the need to question rather than actively serve the particular interests of the 'home state' of the political geographer. At the same time, the empirical scope of the field has widened to consider questions about the origins and spread of political movements, the links between places and identities, and geographies of nationalism and ethnic conflict. We have gone from states (particularly *my* state) are everything to the political is everywhere. This intellectual leavening of the field has simply transformed political geography from a peculiarly state-centered field to one interested in the range of ways in which geography intersects with 'the political' broadly construed: from the material and discursive construction of states and their interrelations to the connections between places and political identities.

The geopolitical context of the time has been crucial to the making of political geography over the past one hundred years. This is the basic premise of the book. The field has not evolved simply as the result of an internal dynamic, as one 'paradigm' simply replaced another because of intellectual fancy or academic competition. It is not that such considerations have been absent. But they have been relatively less salient to the making of the field than the nature of the world that political geography has claimed to directly report on and interpret. The time of modern political geography's founding in the 1890s was one of burgeoning inter-imperial rivalry between a set of Great Powers – Germany, Britain, France, the United States, Russia, and Japan – that reached its twin peaks in the two world wars. This period gave rise to the political geography that privileged the role of physical geography in determining or conditioning state prospects and limits. The Cold War of 1945–89 with its emphasis on global ideological competition between two models of 'modernity' – the democratic capitalism of the United States and the state socialism of the Soviet Union – initially produced a diminished interest in the study of political geography. The field as it had existed before World War II did not seem to offer much food for thought in the new circumstances. Of course, the period did encourage a 'freezing' of political boundaries and a seemingly permanent standoff between the two sides. Ideology not geography was what mattered. As the Cold War slowly eroded, however, political geography underwent something of a revival in the United States and elsewhere. The chapters that follow attempt to tell this story about the making of political geography.

As I was writing this book the suicide-attacks by agents of the militant Moslem *al-Qaeda* terrorist network on the New York Trade Center and the Pentagon building of the US Department of Defense in Washington DC were followed by the US government's declaration of war on 'international' terrorism. Many Americans have reacted by flying the national flag as a symbol both of their threatened identity and as a sign of their mobilization and support of a military response to the terrorist acts. These events seem to portend the emergence of a geopolitical context in which states, however mighty, confront shadowy networks of discontented and fanatic groups following this or that objective, often of a religious or ethnic nature. As this feature of a new world (dis)order, and other dimensions of it such as increased flows of money, goods, and people between localities and regions in it, take geographical shape, political geography can be expected to change its shape in order to deal with what has changed. Of course, not all is 'change.' One of the virtues of Sandow Birk's exhibition lies in its story of how disparate ethnic disputes and hot-button political issues tend to get redefined territorially. Even in a heavily networked world, therefore, identities and interests can continue to take territorial form. Indeed, the US response to the terrorist attacks of 11 September 2001 has been to 'go after' the rogue states that shelter the leaders of terror networks, in particular Afghanistan. Even networks of global activists need local territorial anchors.

A number of people helped me to get started or to bring this book to completion. Alec Murphy asked me to do it. I hope that I have delivered more or less what he had in mind. Laura McKelvie thought that my prospectus made reasonable sense. Subsequent editors at Arnold, particularly Liz Gooster, have kept up interest and prompted me to keep working. My research assistant in winter and spring quarters 2001, M. Troy Burnett, helped enormously with research on and writing up the vignettes in Chapter 2, showing why political geography still matters, and with summarizing the content of textbooks from the interwar period that I refer to in Chapter 3. I am deeply appreciative of all he did for me. I know that he gave up considerable 'good surf' in order to work on this book! My UCLA colleague Michael Curry found a copy of the March 2000 *American Philatelist* in an airplane seat pocket and gave it to me because it contained an article on the stamps of Nagorno-Karabagh, the territory disputed by Armenia and Azerbaijan in the former Soviet Union. This topic is now the subject of one of the vignettes in Chapter 2. Another UCLA colleague, Tom Gillespie, taught me about 'ecological hotspots' and why preserving them matters to maintaining global genetic diversity. UCLA Professor Emeritus Benjamin Thomas talked to me about teaching political geography in the United States during and after World War II. He also kindly gave me many textbooks from that era. Many of my departmental colleagues at UCLA, particularly Nick Entrikin, Allen Scott, Denis Cosgrove, Michael Shin, Glen MacDonald, and Dave Rigby, provided support and encouragement. Other colleagues at UCLA and elsewhere have also encouraged my endeavors: particularly Scott Waugh, Ivan Berend, Mick Mann, Jacques Lévy, Carlo Brusa, Mabel Berezin, Luca Muscarà, Ed Soja, Miles Kahler, Eric Helleiner, Carol Medlicott, Michael Heffernan, Stuart Corbridge, Anssi Paasi, Jim Duncan, Jo Sharp, James Sidaway, Jim MacLaughlin, Peter Meusburger, Ferruccio Trabalzi, David Newman, Gearóid Ó Tuathail, and Mark Bassin. Chase Langford, the UCLA departmental cartographer, drafted many of the figures and prepared all of them for publication.

I would have done very little on this book if I could not have counted on the love and friendship of three remarkable people. My daughters, Katie and Christine, both currently college students at different campuses of the University of California – Santa Barbara and Irvine, respectively – always advise me to 'keep the students in mind' and diverted me from finishing this sooner because of their own projects. Finally, Felicity gave me good advice on all sorts of things, provided me with sources I have found useful, and sustained me through rough patches. It was her desire to see Sandow Birk's exhibition at the Laguna Art Museum in Laguna Beach, California in June 2000 that made me aware of his brilliant satire. Beyond that, she has reminded me how satire can offer insight into even the most mundane of matters, including political geography. Humor and seriousness can go hand-in-hand. All told, therefore, the 'external context' has counted as much in the writing of this book as it has in the making of political geography.

John Agnew
Los Angeles CA
Martin Luther King Jr Day, 21 January 2002

INTRODUCTION

The commonsense meaning of political geography is the study of how politics is informed by geography. For a long time this meant trying to show how the physical features of the earth – the distribution of the continents and oceans, mountain ranges, and rivers – affected the ways in which humanity divided the world up into political units such as states and empires and how these units competed with one another for global power and influence. Today the dominant meaning has changed considerably. On one side, geography is now understood as including social and economic differences between places without necessarily ascribing these to physical differences. On the other, politics has been broadened to include questions of political identity (how social groups define themselves and their political objectives) and political movements (why did this movement or political party start here and why does it have this or that geographical pattern of support?). Even more fundamentally, 'geography' is itself now thought of as the selection and ranking of certain themes and issues – from the naming of the continents and the division of the world into regions to the identification of certain regions as more or less 'strategically' important – rather than a set of objective facts beyond dispute. In this understanding, knowledge cannot be readily separated from power. Those with power, the ability to command others, are able to define what counts as geography. From this point of view, the meaning of political geography is completely reversed: it now becomes the study of how geography is informed by politics.

This book is a critical and necessarily selective survey of how and why political geography has changed as it has accumulated these varied meanings. The 'making' in the title, therefore, is of vital importance. It signifies the focus on the people, historical contexts, and scholarly works that have produced the various meanings of political geography down the years. Political geography is also not just a 'branch' of the field of Geography, as if the field emerged fully formed in the late 1800s with a complete set of internal divisions. It has been 'made' through the ways in which the world's actual geography has been implicated in the practice of politics over the past one hundred years by all students of politics, including many who have also been influential practitioners. Political geography, then, is a set of scholarly and political ideas about the relationship of geography to politics and vice versa that have roots in a number of fields, particularly in geography and political science, but also in sociology, anthropology, ethnic studies, and international relations. The task of this book is to trace the development of these ideas, portray some of the important authors and their academic and political influence, identify some of the crucial philosophical and theoretical issues within political geography today, and suggest some of the substantive themes of emerging significance in the early twenty-first century.

Today, a whole variety of what can be considered 'public issues' of great import and publicity have profoundly geographical aspects to them. Often, knowing or identifying these geographical aspects helps to make greater sense out of otherwise mysterious situations and events than simply reciting the 'facts' as they are frequently presented. This is what contemporary political geography is all about. To take some public issues from the daily news in September 2001 and emphasize their geographical aspects:

▨ The selection of the World Trade Center in New York City and the Pentagon outside of Washington DC as targets of terrorist action on 11 September 2001 was not random. Neither was the method of attacking these sites. In the first place, the sites have a deep symbolic significance as, respectively, seats of global finance and of the US Department of Defense. Such sites are not scattered randomly but located in major economic and political centers. In the second place, the terrorists hijacked airplanes flown by major American carriers (American and United, also deeply symbolic of the terrorists' animosity to the 'United States' as an entity in world politics) from multiple airports (Dulles in Washington DC, Boston, and Newark, to increase the prospects that some would get through to their targets) headed to Los Angeles and San Francisco and thus carrying heavy loads of fuel that would accelerate the bomb-like potential of the planes hurled at their targets. Inspired by a hatred of 'America' as a geopolitical abstraction in a religious cosmology associating the United States with the personage of Satan, the terrorists constitute a shadowy network of like-minded individuals, notwithstanding the existence of territorial bases to their operations in such chaotic countries as Afghanistan and the Sudan, and financial sponsorship from elements close to the government of Saudi Arabia and other 'conservative' Moslem states. The terrorists thus understood both the symbolic significance of where they struck and the best geographical strategy to achieve their goal. Of course, they also represent a challenge to the established vision of world politics as largely international, i.e. with conflict always occurring between identifiable territorial states. They think

2

in terms of 'Islam' and 'the West' and not in terms of furthering the interests of this or that state. An important result of the enormity of the acts in the American popular imagination will be to encourage a reinforcement of national border controls and limit the openness of American society through increased government surveillance, given that the terrorists operated from within the United States prior to their strikes. The idea of a 'war against terror' has become the organizing phrase for US foreign policy, justifying both narrowing of the legal rights of foreign aliens resident in the US and substituting for the Cold War as a basis for military planning. Problematically, however, the phrase tends to see terrorism outside of any specific political context, so that, for example, the Saudi sponsorship of fundamentalist Islam and the occupation of Palestinian territory by Israel, vital aspects of why the US faces a terrorist threat in the first place, receive little or no sustained attention because any change in US policies towards Saudi Arabia or Israel would disturb significant political interests in the United States: in particular, the oil lobby, heavily represented in the White House, for Saudi Arabia, and the Jewish lobby, heavily influential in American electoral politics, for Israel.

In the Ardoyne neighborhood of north Belfast, Northern Ireland, a crowd of local Protestants (politically loyal to Britain) hurled insults at small Catholic schoolgirls escorted by parents (presumably Irish nationalists) as they walked to the first day of school. The girls' school is on the edge of a Protestant enclave in a predominantly Catholic area. The fight was about defending communal identity by defining clear boundaries between adjacent groups. The scene of much inter-communal violence over thirty years of conflict, Protestants are a shrinking minority in this area as more affluent Protestants move out to Belfast's suburbs and socially mobile Catholics, usually with larger families, move in. The local Protestants face the prospect of losing their ability to hold the line between the two groups and thus perpetuate their own identity. Ethnic conflicts and struggles over political identities are closely bound up with controlling territories and maintaining boundaries.

Libby, Montana is literally a town that is choking to death. Hundreds of people are suffering from the effects of the asbestos that the town's mine produced down the years; whether they worked there or simply breathed the air around metal tailings from the mine. Asbestos disease relentlessly destroys the lungs of those afflicted. This is the latest in a stream of public health disasters associated with living in a place with a particular industrial poison. As in so many other

3

cases, most notoriously Love Canal in Niagara Falls, NY, a single company profited from the mine and then left town, neglecting to clean up on the way out. In Libby it is the W.R. Grace Company. Who should now pay for the clean up and the health costs of the victims? Grace? The US federal government? The state of Montana? Most public goods and, in this case, public 'bads' are distributed unevenly. Libby has one very serious public bad. There is a more general principle at work: some places have many good public services and few bads, other places have the reverse, often because of histories of economic exploitation and social deprivation.

Three Republican senators announced that they would not seek re-election to the US Senate: Gramm of Texas, Helms of North Carolina, and Thurmond of South Carolina. As they leave office, the three men symbolize the geographical shift in American politics that carried the Republican Party to dominance in the south and weakened it elsewhere, particularly in the north-east and on the west coast. All former Democrats, they represent the ways in which the federal civil rights legislation of the 1960s and the growth of a national welfare state led to a reversal of a 'solid south' for an increasingly federalist Democratic Party and the rise of a southern Republican party committed to opposition to civil rights and to the powers of Washington DC. If Thurmond's politics were essentially those of a racial segregationist and Helms' of opposition to cultural pluralism in any shape or form, Gramm's politics were geared to the message of smaller-scale national government (except on military spending!) rather than race or cultural issues. The messages, however, appealed to similar predominantly white constituencies in a still distinctive American south, if with something of a generational twist from the ancient Thurmond of the old 'cotton south' to the much younger Gramm of suburban Texas. Politicians are elected geographically, by people concentrated in similar places with similar histories, so it should be no surprise that understanding electoral politics benefits from being thought about geographically.

Responding to a lobbying campaign by Mexican President Vicente Fox, US President George W. Bush announced that he was willing to consider granting 'permanent residency' to some three million Mexican nationals who were living in the United States but who had entered the country illegally. This statement produced controversy about the role of the Mexican president in an American 'domestic' issue and why Mexican nationals, as opposed to illegal immigrants of other nationalities, should receive special treatment. After the attacks of 11 September 2001, however, the whole question of how to deal with illegal immigration was put on hold. Nevertheless, this case draws attention to some larger political questions, such as the degree to which there can be entirely domestic issues in an increasingly interdependent world, the role of illegal immigrants in helping economic growth in rich countries, such as the United States, and retarding it or helping it in the typically poorer countries from which they come, and the relative privilege that should be given to neighboring countries as opposed to those further away with fewer historic ties.

These are all examples of important public issues that can benefit from a geographical framing. The framing not only allows for an integration of facts into a more meaningful story but also identifies how crucial geographical factors can be in thoroughly understanding political phenomena – from global terrorism and ethnic conflicts to the politics of environmental degradation, American party politics and decisions about granting amnesty to illegal immigrants. The trick in doing so is to think in terms of maps; of maps that not only locate but that also join together the places and regions inherent in the various stories. The map can be in the mind's eye, on paper, or on a computer screen. There is a map that brings together the facts of the terrorist bombings of 11 September 2001. There are also maps that show who lives where in north Belfast, where public goods and public bads are to be found around the United States, who votes for whom where in the US, and which immigrants live where in the US, where they came from and under what legal conditions.

The various public issues, however, can be examined in a wide variety of ways. Maps are invariably selective. The map relationships to emphasize must be selected on some basis. As we shall see, political geographers have done their selecting in widely varying ways. The making of political geography is largely a story of how they have gone about doing so and how this has affected what they have decided to study.

The four main chapters of this book cover the following ground. Chapter 2 introduces the making of political geography in four ways: in terms of how it has been made by authors with very particular relationships to concentrations of power, how the emphasis on different subject-matter and different theoretical perspectives has evolved from the late nineteenth century to the present, how different meanings of the 'political' have informed it down the years, and why political geography continues to matter in the early twenty-first century. In Chapter 3, 'The Historic Canon', some of the classic works in political geography from the 1890s to World War II are given pride of place. I concentrate on some of the 'big names' of the period and their influence, attempting to place both ideas and influence in the context of the time and the inter-imperial rivalry that characterized the period. A further section considers the crisis the dominant ideas faced as this period ended and was later replaced by the Cold War. Considering the selective retention of certain older themes during the Cold War brings the chapter to a close.

Chapter 4, 'The Revival', examines the key themes and perspectives in a new political geography that began to emerge in the 1960s. This expanded beyond the traditional focus on national states, their boundaries, and the global contexts in which they found themselves, to a more general interest in boundary-making as the process whereby power is expressed geographically at whatever geographical scale – local, regional, national, global – this occurs. From this point of view, political geography was redefined as the study of political practices producing boundaries, and of the impact of these boundaries on the power and welfare of different social groups. Certain important theoretical statements and empirical case studies are used to highlight the new meaning given to political geography.

Three 'waves' of perspectives, representing distinctive philosophical and political positions, are seen as having swept successively across the intellectual landscape: spatial analysis beginning in the 1960s, political-economic perspectives in the 1970s, and postmodern perspectives in the late 1980s and 1990s. At the same time, the empirical scope of what was understood as 'political geography' was also expanding from the geopolitics and spatiality (internal geography) of states (the classic concerns) to geographies of social and political movements, ethnic conflicts and nationalism, and place and the politics of identity. Each new 'wave' seemingly brought with it new subjects of study. An attempt is made to tie the waves to the intellectual and political fluidity at the end of the Cold War, the huge social changes in Europe and North America in the 1960s and 1970s, and the recent emergence of a more globalized world in which established theories of politics and society seemingly offer less intellectual purchase than they once did.

Finally, Chapter 5, 'The Horizon', identifies three issues that beckon on the intellectual horizon: the question of power and geographical scale in a globalizing world; the global politics of the physical environment; and the question of moral choice in the geographical organization of politics. A number of empirical case studies and descriptions of particular books are used to provide examples of the type of analysis the new topics can elicit. I do not mean to suggest that other issues, such as those examined in Chapter 4, are now of lesser importance, only that these three seem to offer the greatest challenge in the political context of the early twenty-first century. Political geography has never been anything if not a reflection of its times.

HOW POLITICAL GEOGRAPHY
IS MADE

In this chapter I want to offer four different perspectives on how political geo-graphy can be considered to have been 'made,' particularly over the past one hundred years. These raise general issues necessary to a full understanding of what follows in subsequent chapters:

1 I argue that knowledge is always situated in specific historical–intellectual con-texts and power relationships that color both approaches and interpretations but that political geography as a term meaningfully refers to the mediating effects of geography on politics;

2 I provide a brief history of the sub-field and the varied perspectives and themes that have been adopted so as to orient the reader to the subject-matter of subsequent chapters;

3 I survey the different meanings that have been given to the qualifier 'political' and suggest that across most of these there is a definite distinctiveness to what is political and, hence, that a separate political geography makes sense;

4 I establish why the relationship of geography and politics matters in the con-temporary world and, hence, why you should be interested in this book. I use five vignettes drawn from contemporary settings around the world to make some specific points about how the relationship of geography to politics still counts, if not more than ever.

Power and knowledge

Political geographers, like many other social scientists, have become increasingly sensitive to the charge that they always look at the world from specific social and geographical 'positions' – such as American, white, male, gay, and Catholic (and so on). Even as they endeavor to offer theoretical coherence and empirical evidence for the perspectives they bring to bear on particular situations, they cannot in good faith claim to be totally disinterested or impartial. In the world of human making there is no singular 'view from nowhere' that can be invoked to justify this or that perspective as better than another. This does not mean that all knowledge claims are thereby equally valid. Seeing knowledge as produced in historical-geographical contexts does not entail a different claim: that all knowledge is simply relative to this or that historical-geographical context or social position. The point is that we should be alert to the contextual biases built into any and all knowledge claims.

At one time, however, a strong naturalistic view of knowledge did prevail almost totally, and the first generation of political geographers – such as Friedrich Ratzel in Germany and Halford Mackinder in England – used it to mask their profoundly nationalistic viewpoints. That said, they lived in an era when total devotion to one's nation was largely taken for granted by the upper middle-class academics who wrote most political geography in Western Europe and the United States. The historical-geographical context matters, therefore, in understanding how political geography has been 'made' down the years, just as it does for other fields.

More specifically, it is clear that upper-middle class European and American men have long dominated the entire enterprise. Indeed, the rise of 'intellectuals' as a class of people in Europe and North America is associated with the professionalization, commercialization, and legitimization of knowledge on the part of powerful institutions (states, universities, businesses) that were and largely still are dominated by white men from privileged social backgrounds. It is only within the past thirty years that white men of other social-class origins, women, people from post-colonial settings (such as India and Africa) and smaller European states (such as Finland and Ireland), and other outsiders (including people from places such as Australia, China, and Japan) have made inroads into the Inner Temple of academia in general and the study of political geography in particular. Figures, in no particular order of preference, such as Jim MacLaughlin, Nuala Johnson, Gearóid Ó Tuathail, Anssi Paasi, Susan Roberts, Laura Pulido, Simon Dalby, Colin Williams, Joanne Sharp, Eleonore Kofman, Sallie Marston, Sanjay Chaturvedi, Sankaran Krishna, Xiodi Wu, Lynn Staeheli, and Katharyne Mitchell are representative of this leavening of the field by people whose life experiences and backgrounds are very different for one reason or another from those of the figures who founded the field and of those who initiated its later revival.

This is important for two reasons. First, it means that, until recently, understandings of such key concepts in political geography as power, boundary-making, and territoriality have reflected the understandings and practices of those long in command within the world's Great Powers such as France, Germany, Britain, and the United States. At one and the same time that they have claimed the mantle of 'objective reality' and 'science' for their accounts, they have also served different national interests with which they have explicitly aligned themselves. The growth of political geography elsewhere, for example in countries such as Italy, Russia, and Japan, if not without its novelties and differences of emphasis, nevertheless tended to follow the intellectual tracks laid down by the currents of thought emanating from higher up in the global hierarchy of states.

The combination of claim to objectivity with serving a national interest has had a specific foundation. This is the implicit claim to offer a 'view from nowhere.' This is the idea that the whole world can be known totally from beyond the particular geographical and intellectual location of the person making the claim. But as the philosopher Thomas Nagel (1986: 25–8) has pointed out, there can never be complete objectivity; there is always an 'incompleteness' to objective reality. In other words, objective reality does not exhaust reality. Rather, 'any objective conception of reality must include an acknowledgment of its own incompleteness.' The solution for Nagel is to 'enrich the notion of objectivity' by adding the views of oneself and of other selves so as to incorporate the insights of subjectivity. As Nagel concludes: 'to insist in every case that the most objective and detached account of a phenomenon is the correct one is likely to lead to reductive conclusions. I have argued that the seductive appeal of objective reality depends on a mistake. It is not a given. Reality is not just objective reality.' So, even though acknowledging the prospect of knowing that is not completely subjective, Nagel is suggesting that the quest for complete objectivity is a fruitless one. There can never be a view from nowhere that is not also, and profoundly, a view from somewhere. The history of political geography certainly provides support for Nagel's argument.

Widening the social origins of those studying the field, however, opens up the potential range of geographical and intellectual locations from which the problems of the field can be studied. Indeed, it also opens up the possibility of redefining the kinds of problems that the field studies. Moving away, for example, from an exclusive focus on states as if they have always been and still are the sole fount of power in everyday life, we can expect to see a distinctively different set of 'subjectivities' entering the field, thereby 'enriching' objective reality in new ways, beyond that of the national interests that once reigned supreme – given the lower attachment of many new recruits to this or that national interest, particularly of the Great Powers of the day.

The second reason why wider recruitment into the ranks of political geographers matters is that political geography has long presented itself as a problem-solving activity, to be called on by those in seats of power to help resolve their dilemmas. This technocratic impetus was there from the start. A technical or control impulse characterized the natural and social sciences from their beginnings as university disciplines in the late nineteenth century (Stanley, 1978). It was never without challenge. Within late nineteenth-century Europe, for example, radical thinkers such as Peter Kropotkin and Elisée Reclus provided the basis for a critical approach to political geography. But this proved out of touch with the times, a period of intense national and inter-imperial rivalry, and unattractive to those intent on professionalizing Geography and other fields, such as Political Science, within the expanding university systems of the Great Powers. Attracting government and business support for the new fields required providing such institutions with problem-solving capacity, not criticizing their activities and wherewithal. Only recently have 'minor figures' such as Reclus and Kropotkin been rediscovered and accorded significant respect. Unfortunately, the tendency is to laud their intellectual independence and political radicalism without attending to the serious problems with many of their ideas (see, for example, Miller (1986) on the problems with Kropotkin's social analysis).

It is the rise of critical perspectives in social theory – initially associated with the sociology of knowledge and some varieties of Western Marxism, but later expressed most forcibly in feminism and some types of poststructuralist philosophy – that have led away somewhat from the problem-solving focus on states and hagiography of the founders. In particular, feminist and other thinkers have opened up for discussion such issues as reason versus affectivity (emotion) in human action and notions of an homogeneous (presumably masculine) national public upon which much discourse in political theory has long relied (e.g. Young, 1987). From this point of view, problem-solving should involve the ability to specify whose problems are given pride of place but also, much more importantly, how those problems are defined and addressed. Feminist and other critical thinkers, therefore, have questioned the idea of problem-solving as an academic focus without prior attention being given to the ways in which it is done and for whom.

What was lacking until recently has been an appreciation of the relationship of knowledge to power. We have learned from such writers as the French philosopher Michel Foucault (e.g. 1980) and the Palestinian-American literary theorist Edward Said (e.g. 1978), that knowledge consists of 'discourses' or sets of ideas, terms, and connecting phrases that arise in distinct historical-geographical contexts (such as Vienna in the 1890s, Paris in the 1970s or Los Angeles in 2001) and that persist because they are adopted by others and become part of a 'common sense' that defines a discipline or field of study (such as political geography). This is not to say that all knowledge production can be read off from the social and geographical backgrounds of its producers. Since the European Enlightenment of the seventeenth and eighteenth centuries there have always been currents of thought that challenge and threaten dominant conceptions of knowing. For a much longer time there have always been 'outsiders' critical of the intellectual status quo. A long-standing feature of modern intellectual history, therefore, has been a 'suspicion' of established knowledge claims and the social interests such claims uphold. The social construction of knowledge in particular historical-geographical contexts is not the same as social determination *tout court*. From this point of view, indeed, some claims are better than others and there can be progress in political geography (Bassett, 1999).

Discourses are both enabling and disabling: they allow us to construct research projects, for example, but they also direct our minds in certain directions rather than in others. Within the Anglo-American social sciences in general, for example, particularly since World War II, thinking with geographical concepts has not had widespread support. At the same time, down until the 1960s, political geography was largely devoted to examining the creation of the world political map and the emergence of Great Power spheres of influence without much, if any, attention to its political-theoretical assumptions. This was the dominant discourse, reflecting the times in which it arose: the new world of states at the end of European colonialism and the day-to-day operation of the Cold War. It is only with the recruitment of people into the field from a wider range of backgrounds, the emergence of a globalizing world economy, and the ending of the Cold War that new perspectives have found acceptance. The very political and social instability of the current world encourages the sort of intellectual experimentation that has increasingly characterized political geography in the recent past.

To reiterate, this is not to say that authorship and intellectual innovation are totally determined by the time and place in which an author is situated. Figures like Kropotkin and Reclus strongly suggest the limits of contextual explanation. It is more that contexts tend to impose limits on what can be thought and written. Even many late nineteenth-century anarchists and socialists found colonialism not only acceptable but also praiseworthy for the possibility of 'progress' that it brought to regions they thought of as 'backward' and benighted. Today, Western intellectuals tend to reject the singularly biological basis to race, whereas many of their early twentieth-century counterparts found this idea not only acceptable but absolutely fundamental to their understanding of the world. In a somewhat different vein, disputes within Islam over the treatment of women and non-Moslems pose difficulties for those in Europe and North America who believe that Western capitalism or modern statehood are the singular sources of oppression in the world. In the face of global environmental crises it has become popular in some circles to argue for a less human-centered understanding to economic development, incorporating other species into calculations about economic development and its effects. These are all examples of how historical-geographical contexts condition the possibility of different kinds of knowledge-seeking, and limit exploration of the ideas that can be used in that task.

Despite the history of contending perspectives and discursive 'breaks' because of contextual influences, there is a degree of coherence to the term 'political geography' that has persisted down the years and from place to place. This coherence has three dimensions to it. One is a persisting focus on a common set of concepts – particularly boundary, territory, state, nation, sphere of influence, and place – even as these concepts have been endowed with changing meanings and applied in different ways (for example, within rather than just between states). One can plausibly claim that interest in and use of these concepts predates the adoption of the term political geography itself. Hence it is the concepts, and not the label that packages them together, that constitute the field as such. Certainly, such luminaries in the history of political thought as Aristotle, Sun Tzu, Machiavelli, Hobbes, Montesquieu, Madison, Herder, Rousseau, Hegel, Marx, and Gramsci addressed questions of statehood, citizenship, and the geographical distribution of power. They can be thought of as proto-political geographers (among other things, of course). But there is nevertheless the sense that since the late nineteenth century an academic division of labor has evolved – producing among others a niche called 'political geography' – which has become institutionalized in university courses, academic organizations, conferences, and academic journals.

The second dimension is a theoretical focus on trying to discover the ways in geography (defined in various ways, from the physical geography of the world to the distribution of ethnic groups and economic resources) mediates between people, on the one hand, and political organization, on the other. There is a persisting tendency to insist that politics cannot be adequately understood without understanding the geographical contexts in which it takes place, from global geopolitics at one end of the scale to local politics at the other. What has been understood as 'the geographical' has undoubtedly changed down the years. At one time it was understood almost entirely in physical terms, whereas today the sense is almost entirely of the human organization of the earth's surface. Notwithstanding these differences, however, it is clear that a common commitment to placing politics in a geographical framework has remained constant.

Finally, there is a sociology to academic sub-fields manifested in professional organizations (such as the Political Geography Specialty Group of the Association of American Geographers or the Political Geography Committee of the International Political Science Association) and journals devoted to their subject-matter (such as *Political Geography* and *Geopolitics*). This reflects the way in which university graduate training is organized to induct students into 'areas of knowledge' by preparing them to work, publish, and teach in a given sub-area. In this understanding, political geographers constitute a sort of 'intellectual tribe,' sharing certain norms of academic practice – how research is done, how articles are written, whom the articles are written for – that differ from those in such adjacent areas as 'international relations,' 'cultural geography,' and 'economic geography.' Given the marginal status of Geography in general, and political geography in particular, in higher education in many countries the 'disciplining' of students into the field is possibly less problematic than in ones that are more dominant. Nevertheless, there is still a danger of encouraging certain views at the expense of others and restricting intellectual innovation (Luke, 2000b).

So, even when perspectives differ and writers use different terms to label what they do, a coherent field of political geography can be defined. Increasingly, disciplinary labels are seen as problematic. Indeed, you may be using this book in a course with a quite different title such as 'Politics and Place' or 'Geopolitics.' Be that as it may, if you are concerned with the intersection of geography and politics you are doing political geography or some aspect of it!

The history and language of political geography

The term *political geography* in contemporary usage, like so much of the terminology and labels in the social sciences, dates from late-nineteenth century Germany. Arguably, the term was first coined in print by the French *philosophe* Turgot in 1750. This is the beginning of the period in European intellectual history when the modern social sciences began to emerge and when 'the study of the underlying forces that shape our will substituted for the idea of human agency that lay at the heart of the now superseded political sciences' (Wokler, 1987: 327). But it is to the German geographer Friedrich Ratzel in 1885, in an article on the 'new political map of Africa,' that the history of the sub-area of academic geography known as political geography is usually traced. Ratzel published the first book with political geography in its title (*Politische Geographie*) in 1897. Only recently unified politically, Germany was the center of attempts at rationalizing social knowledge in the interests of state development through the establishment and state support of universities as research rather than as simply teaching institutions. Other Great Powers, such as England, France, and the United States, rapidly followed suit. In the United States, universities such as Johns Hopkins University in Baltimore and the University of Chicago were directly modeled on the German prototype research university with an emphasis on narrow specialization and the training of postgraduate students as future researchers.

As the study of and writing about the earth as a whole, Geography is an old field but it was professionalized within the university relatively late. Only in Germany were there well-established chairs (or professorships) in Geography in the mid-nineteenth century (Sandner, 1994). England, the United States, and France acquired their first Geography departments only in the last two decades of the nineteenth and first decade of the twentieth century. Consequently, the identification and practice of sub-fields also came late. In Geography this was complicated by the fact that many of its proponents tended to see it as an 'integrative' field and resisted breaking it down into specialties, even if this seemed necessary for the purposes of research. In France, for example, Vidal de la Blache resisted the idea of separate geographies, each with their own qualifier. For him there was one Geography or none at all. Though there was a long-established tradition in German-speaking Europe of 'state geography,' as opposed to a 'regional geography' based on natural divisions, devoted to showing how social as well as natural features were bound up with but often contradictory to existing geographical patterns of statehood, its naturalizing of the state was incomplete. Only with Ratzel does 'the state take possession of geography and become its supreme object.' (Farinelli, 2001: 44). In the sub-dividing of geography Ratzel was the first to identify a separate political geography. Even as he did so, however, Ratzel was championing the geography of the state as the centerpiece of geography as a whole. In this intellectual world the political was not a separate sphere but the central one associated completely with statehood. Ratzel is thus a theorist for his time. One in which a new 'aristocratic–bourgeois state,' to use Farinelli's term, was in the ascendency in the organization of knowledge in general, not just in relation to self-confessed Geography. Of course, this was also the time of a reinvigorated European colonialism, related in large part to German attempts at 'catching up' with Britain and France in empire building following the recent unification of Germany and defeat of France in the Franco-Prussian War of 1870.

The space, or area occupied by the state, and its position on the world map were seen by Ratzel as the key concepts of his 1897 book. Rooted in a particular space, a state expresses both a material relationship to its space through the 'soil' (an idea that the German chancellor Bismarck used freely to argue for German unification) and a spiritual relationship through the peculiarities of the occupying national group. States can only thrive, however, if they expand into other territories to express their vitality and their higher 'cultural level.' To Ratzel, the size of a state is one of the measures of its cultural level. Whether war is inevitably the mechanism of expansion is not made clear. Nevertheless, Ratzel's entire approach is premised on the idea that a state's position or location in relation to other states makes it more or less vulnerable to the expansion of other states. A state such as Germany is thus more vulnerable than an England because it is surrounded on all sides by other states. The combination of German vitality and geographical vulnerability produces the need to expand.

Though Ratzel and like-minded thinkers saw their writing in 'scientific' terms, as reflecting natural processes or laws that lay beyond human command, they also saw their work as serving the goals of the particular states in which they lived. Thus, for Ratzel the need was to offer a 'scientific' account of why Germany required a larger space than that it currently occupied. To Halford Mackinder, in England, the need was to use a global model pointing out certain 'natural facts' about the distribution of the continents and oceans to represent the threat from Germany and/or Russia in the heartland of Eurasia to the vulnerable British Empire scattered largely around its fringe. This fusion of a claim to scientific objectivity with particular national purpose was to characterize political geography throughout the period of intense inter-imperial rivalry between Britain, France, and the United States on the one side and the rising Powers of Germany, Japan, and Italy on the other. The geopolitical ideas of Ratzel and Mackinder were of greater appeal to the latter than to the former because they provided something of a broad guide to action for those attempting to challenge the geopolitical status quo.

The term 'geopolitics' first arose in this context. Invented by the Swedish political scientist Rudolf Kjellén in 1899, geopolitics referred to the harnessing of geographical knowledge to further the aims of specific national states. If Kjellén was concerned to dispute the claim of Norwegian nationalists (Norway was part of Sweden until 1905) that the mountain spine down Scandinavia constituted a natural boundary between two distinctive peoples by arguing that seas and rivers were much more significant, the term geopolitics came to be applied by German thinkers in the 1920s and 1930s, most notoriously Karl Haushofer, to formal models of Great Power enmities based on their relative global location and need to establish territorial spheres of influence to feed their urge to expand. Through this formalization, Ratzel's idea of states as organic entities came to inform, if hardly to direct, German foreign policy after the Nazi accession to governmental power in Germany in 1933. After World War II the association with the Nazis gave the word geopolitics a negative connotation. Though used informally to refer to the geographical structure of international relations in the 1950s and 1960s, it has only been since the 1970s that the word has re-entered political geography. Today it is used to refer to the ways in which foreign policy elites and mass publics construct geographical images of the world and use these to inform world politics.

There was a current of thinking, largely developed in the United States after World War I, but also present in France and elsewhere, that took a more pragmatic view of the purpose of political geography than that of German *Geopolitik*. In this perspective, the need was to identify political-geographic problems (such as colonialism, the protection of minorities, international co-operation, raw materials, and national boundaries) and carefully detail their worldwide incidence and significance for world politics. The American Isaiah Bowman was the great advocate of this task for political geography. This was a form of state geography in which few if any questions were asked about statehood *per se* (in this sense Ratzel is a more interesting thinker, whatever one thinks of his ideas) but much attention was paid to the pressing practical problems of the time in a frame of reference drawn largely from US President Woodrow Wilson's outlook on national self-determination and the need for international collective-security institutions such as the League of Nations. If in later years Bowman liked to distinguish political geography from geopolitics, it is rather because he saw political geography as a state geography than as a geography of the state. Afraid of the double meaning of 'political' in political geography (it could mean a perspective from a particular political standpoint as well as an enumeration of the conditions under which politics is practiced), Bowman hewed to enumerating the conditions so as to better portray his work as non-partisan and scientific.

Bowman's fear that geopolitics would taint political geography, however, proved well founded. Though American political geographers like Bowman, Richard Hartshorne, and others, were actively involved in providing the US war effort during World War II with their brand of geographical synthesis, political geography emerged from the war years doubly tainted. As the US government began its very own brand of geopolitical reasoning with the onset of the Cold War with the Soviet Union, open talk of geopolitics was associated with the worst excesses of Nazi expansionism. This served to ghettoize political geographers, who had nothing to say in response, even as diplomatic historians and political scientists invented their very own geopolitics without actually using the word (based on such ideas as 'containment' of the Soviet Union, 'the domino effect' connecting events at a distance from the United States to the homeland, and 'national security' to identify an interest beyond that of any particular Americans). It also served to encourage a retreat by geographers in general from engagement with political issues, even of the relatively benign form engaged in by Isaiah Bowman. Though courses in political geography continued to be taught in the United States and elsewhere, and textbooks modeled largely on Bowman's continued to be published, little or anything that could be described as empirical research or critical thinking about the geography of the state or politics more generally appeared during these years. Certainly in the United States, and elsewhere in the English-speaking world, political geography became the 'wayward child' that the cultural geographer Carl Sauer said it was in the 1950s and the 'moribund backwater' that the economic geographer Brian Berry described it as in the 1960s. In a sense, of course, a kind of unexamined but influential 'geopolitics' (if not political geography) did live on: in the practices of foreign-policy elites in the United States and around the world.

The exception who helps to prove the rule was Jean Gottmann, a French-trained geographer of Ukrainian-Jewish background. At the time, however, his work had little if any influence in the English-speaking world. His brilliantly perceptive 1952 book, *La politique des Etats et leur géographie*, is based on a model of state development that Gottmann was to develop throughout his later career. He saw the political partitioning of the world as the result of the interaction between forces of external change (*circulation*) which move people, goods, ideas and information, and the territorially-based beliefs and symbols (*iconographies*) that build group identities and create communities. The relative balance between these sets of forces determines the degree to which a 'system' of states is open or closed. This historical approach to political geography was out of favor at the time because of the overwhelming emphasis given by dominant figures, such as Hartshorne and Stephen Jones, to the seeming perpetual functions performed by national boundaries and the obsession with distinguishing what was 'geographic' from the 'historical,' presumably studied by non-geographers. In 1961 Gottmann published his *magnum opus*, *Megalopolis*, a book in which he argued that the balance was beginning to shift historically from national states to city networks as the basis for political geography.

Gottmann long remained an iconoclastic figure. Without a permanent university appointment in either France or North America for many years, he engaged in a long period of movement to and fro across the Atlantic. His very mobility and life experience probably explain the critical approach he brought to his political geography. Unlike so many political geographers, he was not a prisoner of national horizons. His exposure to social and political theory also contributed to a much richer understanding of political-geographical ideas than that of any previous self-confessed political geographer.

It is fair to say that Jean Gottmann was political geography's first real intellectual. Yet, by the late 1960s he was no longer alone as a theorist of political geography. The period 1965–70 marks the beginning of a revival of interest in political geography as more than a descriptive recital of particularities about boundaries and state characteristics. The revival initially had two elements: one was a focus on using electoral data and electoral districting to explore claims about how space mattered to political behavior (particularly the so-called neighborhood effect or impact of local voting traditions on electoral choice); the other was an interest in the historical geography of European state formation. The participants came from a variety of academic backgrounds and found common cause in such forums as the Committee on Political Geography of the International Political Science Association.

By the early 1970s, figures such as Kevin R. Cox, David Reynolds, and Richard Morrill in the United States, Ron Johnston in New Zealand (later in England), Peter Taylor in England, Paul Claval (in France), Stein Rokkan (in Norway), and Jean Gottmann (finally settled at Oxford University in England) were establishing a 'new' political geography by distancing themselves from much of what had come before and seeing their endeavor as integrating political geography into the 'mainstream' of social science. Much of this new political geography was modeled closely after the *spatial analysis* that swept through Geography in the English-speaking world in the 1960s. It was based on searching for geographical patterns and theorizing about their origins. Much of the theorizing drew from social-psychological thinking about political intentions (as in voting studies) or the comparative sociology of state formation (as in Rokkan's work on Europe). What was particularly striking, however, was the departure from a strict focus on national states to consider geographies of boundary-making within states, electoral geographies (although the French tradition of electoral sociology had taken an ecological approach to election results since the early 1900s it had, at its origins, tended to correlate outcomes with unchanging local features such as geology and soils), and geographies of conflict between social groups. It can be seen, therefore, both as a reaction to the political and social upheavals of the 1960s and the need to address these in a manner acceptable to current canons of scholarship.

This was not to last in dominating political geography. The development of a 'radical' geography in response to both the Vietnam War and the civil rights struggles of the late 1960s produced a critique of spatial analysis as politically conservative, theoretically limited, and Eurocentric. In its place came *political-economic* perspectives drawing on Karl Marx and a range of other thinkers (particularly the American sociologist Immanuel Wallerstein), claiming to find the roots of political territoriality in the history of the capitalist world economy and global competition between the Great Powers. Not only figures associated with radical geography, such as Yves Lacoste, Richard Peet, David Harvey, Doreen Massey and Neil Smith, became influential, but also established figures in political geography, such as Peter Taylor and Kevin Cox, adopted various political-economic perspectives and put them to work in their research. What they shared in common was a critical view of contemporary world politics and society as unequal and hierarchical, a desire to communicate with critical social theorists in other fields about the importance of political-geographical mechanisms such as boundaries and core–periphery relationships in creating and maintaining the structures of inequality, and a commitment to political activism, if often in the classroom rather than extending into the world at large.

By the late 1980s the sense of philosophical certainty and political commitment associated with the political-economic perspectives met with increased resistance. This was partly a product of more conservative times in countries such as Britain and the United States where post-1960s political geography was best rooted but also of increasing skepticism about the possibilities of top-down political change and 'all-knowing' theorists telling people what 'really' matters. A diffuse but nonetheless important reaction set in. Plausibly labeled '*postmodern*,' to signify perspectives that reject the modernist enterprise of social theory without knowing subjects and the idea of unsituated objective knowledge, this wave has had both direct and indirect effects in political geography. On the one hand, it has stimulated research attuned to the experiences of diverse groups (as, for example, in Paul Routledge's research on Indian villagers protesting against a government military facility) and the languages in which political disputes take place (as in Gearóid Ó Tuathail's examination of American discourse over the Gulf War). On the other, it has encouraged more modernist researchers to take the role of discourse and language more seriously, in rhetorical and communicative as well as representational roles. This is apparent, for example, in Agnew and Corbridge's (1995) book on the history of geopolitics as put into practice by political elites.

Contemporary political geography is a mix of all three of the waves that have washed over the sub-field since the 1960s. It is an infinitely more complex picture than in previous eras when dominant perspectives were easy to identity.

This reflects the vast expansion of universities and the incentives to establish 'new' approaches and distance them from established ones. But it is also due to the intellectual vitality of political geography, which has passed from a singular focus on statehood and formal geopolitical models as timeless truths to a wider range of subject-matter concerning the politics of territory and boundary-making under distinctive historical and geographical conditions.

The meaning of the 'political'

Politics is about struggles for power to exercise control over others and self, satisfy interests, and express or gain recognition for identities. That much is widely accepted, if with wide differences over whether to emphasize control, interests or identities. What is less agreed upon is how the political originates and how important it is in relation to other 'dimensions' of human life such as the economic or the cultural. Until recently, political geographers seemed rather agnostic or casual about the nature of the political. They have tended to see states as the singular source and focus of power and to see power as the ability to coerce others, but without much if any explicit discussion of where they might stand beyond this bland acceptance of conventional wisdom among journalists and many politicians. Few political geography textbooks pay any attention to the meaning of the political and proceed seemingly oblivious of the need to critically examine the very qualifier they insist on putting in front of geography.

In practice, *statist* or *liberal* conceptions have prevailed. The former sees the (national) state as the singular source of identities and interests with persons as the agents of the collective enterprise represented by the state. Politics is a deadly serious business in which the political is the arena of authority in which absolute decisions are made and control is exercised. If the early-modern English political theorist Thomas Hobbes is one of the authors of this perspective, its clearest expression in the twentieth century appears in the writing of the German legal theorist Carl Schmitt. In his view, the essence of the political lies in distinguishing 'friends' (those associated with a particular 'form of existence') from 'enemies' (adversaries of this way of life who would negate it given the chance) (Schmitt, 1996). Both totalitarian, as in Nazi Germany and Stalinist Russia, and national-security politics, such as that on either side during the Cold War, rested on this meaning of the political. But one can recognize elements of it in the geopolitics emanating from the works of Ratzel and Mackinder. A potentially more benign version of this would be the civic nationalist or patriotic claim of 'love of one's country' as the essence of the political, requiring as it does a clear sense of who is inside and who is outside the common project (Viroli, 1995).

A logically similar, if politically more pluralistic, conception of the political is found among so-called *communitarians*. From this point of view, politics is about associating with others to express identities and pursuing the common interests that such identities then define. In this case it is the socio-political group (and its expression in distinctive institutions) rather than a state as such that is usually the object of affection, meaning, and belonging. Much of the literature on multicultur-alism in contemporary social science rests on this meaning given to the political, notwithstanding the 'liberal' politics (usually involving government assistance to this or that group) that often accompanies it (e.g. Young, 1990).

The main target of both the statist and communitarian perspectives down the years has been the liberal one. In this understanding, the political should never be about control or identity but rather about procedures for discussion and com-promise between the distinctive interests of different individual persons and the factions in which they coalesce. Associated classically with such theorists as John Locke and James Madison, the American philosopher John Rawls is perhaps its most distinguished contemporary exponent (e.g. Rawls, 1971). Interests are seen as emanating from society and hence the state has come into existence to manage and adjudicate between private interests. Politics, therefore, is necessary but should not become too 'serious,' otherwise it undermines the ability to manage divisions within society. It is about who gets what and where but, above all, how. The liberal perspective, however, has fragmented. On the one side, are those who stress the primacy of individual economic motives and interests in politics and, on the other, are those, such as some liberal feminists, who stress the pluralism of socially created differences that empower some groups (such as men) more than others. Spatial analysis in political geography tends to rest on liberal assumptions about both statehood and the primacy of individual economic motives.

Increasingly, however, the 'classical' views have been challenged from two different directions. One perspective, associated with the political-economic critique that became important in political geography in the 1970s, tends to conceive of the polit-ical as supplementary or complementary to the economic which, in the 'last instance' is seen as determining of the nature of modern, capitalist society. The dominance of capitalists as a class within states and in conflicts between states for capital accumu-lation at a global scale is seen as making the world go round. Politics is sees as the price that has to be paid for bringing other classes into 'public life' and thereby legit-imizing national statehood and the international contests such statehood engenders.

Though frequently casting the political as simply 'functional' for the economic, in the hands of some theorists (such as the English sociologist Michael Mann) this perspective has opened up to consider the relative autonomy of statehood from singular class imperatives and the emergence of bureaucratic groups with their own identities and interests. Two giants in the history of social thought now appear as engaged rather than alienated: Max Weber, the sociologist of bureaucracy, complements Karl Marx, the economic theorist of capital accumulation.

The second direction is more radical in departing from both the classical views and the political-economic critique. Its major difference lies in seeing power as enabling as well as coercive. From this point of view, the political is the capacity for agency: the ability to act, resist, co-operate, and assent, as well as the ability to control, dominate, co-opt, seduce, and resent. In this understanding the political is no longer reducible to the economic, coercive activities by some over others, or states and their conflicts. Rather, the political exists whenever power is exercised in struggles over collective goods and identities, including the language that is used and the experiences or examples that are given a privileged position, reflecting the intellectual dominance of Europeans, men, white women, or whomever. From this point of view, articulated most forcibly in Joan Scott's (1992: 37) argument about the need to understand 'experience' as always pre-interpreted by the terms used to express it, any kind of social research 'entails focusing on processes of identity production, insisting on the discursive nature of "experience" and on the politics of its construction. Experience is at once always already an interpretation *and* in need of interpretation. What counts as experience is neither self-evident nor straightforward; it is always contested, always therefore political.'

At first sight this might seem like expanding the concept of the political almost to the point of meaninglessness. When everything is political, nothing is political. But it can be rescued in any of three ways, drawing variously on such twentieth-century political/social theorists as Antonio Gramsci, Hannah Arendt, Michel Foucault, Gilles Deleuze, and Bruno Latour. One is by emphasizing that historical configurations of power give rise to *hegemonies* (mixes of coercion and consent) exercised by dominant social groups or states (depending on the context). The widespread availability of power, therefore, never guarantees its equal distribution. Historical bias is built into its geographical distribution from place to place (see, for example, Agnew and Corbridge, 1995). A second solution is to envisage the world as engaged with only indirectly through the *discourses* that provide the logic and language for practical reasoning. Such discourses are by definition hegemonic, they provide the direction and meaning to life, but they can also be challenged insofar as the magic of their words is identified and exposed as biased in favor of this or that state or social group. It is this larger definition of power, and particularly the concern for the operation of power through public discourse and in the action of different groups in relation to hegemonic projects, that characterizes the postmodern perspectives that became important in 1980s political geography (see, for example, Ó Tuathail, 1996). The term 'postmodern' is not without ambiguity. What is most at stake, however, is the idea that the very process of defining the terms in which the political is addressed is itself political (Butler, 1992: 7; also Scott, 1992). Third, and finally, power can be thought of as implicit in the practices of *actor-networks* that connect, entrain, and shape all social activities. In so-called actor-network theory, power is the resource that networks provide to actors (human, animal, and technological) to make networks serving business, associational, and political purposes work (see, for example, Thrift, 2000). The relational practices and performances that make up political networks, therefore, constitute the political in this solution to the narrowing of the political from the realm of everywhere to something more specific. Whether we might not well be back here with a substantively liberal understanding of the political is open to question.

Does 'political' geography still matter?

The world is undoubtedly a 'smaller' place than it used to be, in the sense of the relative ease with which information, money, goods, and people can now whiz around the world. Although few places on the earth's surface have been totally out of touch with those elsewhere since the fateful expansion of Europeans into the rest of the world beginning in the late 1400s, the interlocking of places today through economic and cultural transactions is both more intensive and more important in people's everyday lives. In the world of the Internet, CNN, global production chains, and interconnected world financial markets the 'old world' of contending empires, nationalist politics, and so on is often portrayed as about to fade into the sunset (van Creveld, 1999). But does the 'time–space compression' of the world about which we now hear so much also signify the imminent collapse of the political boundaries that still mark the world map, decreased hostility between social groups over the spoils of political and military dominance, increased equality between places in the global distribution of power, and the demise of territorially based political identities? Or is it more that the world's political geography is currently experiencing a set of stresses from economic and technological change that affect the meaning and roles of territory, boundaries, spheres of influence, ethnic geographies, and place-based politics? In this historical context, which conception of the meaning of 'the political' outlined earlier makes most sense to you? Are the classical statist and liberal views losing their theoretical grip? Bear these questions in mind throughout the following pages.

In the rest of this chapter I use five vignettes or stories to explore some issues that are desperately important in the contemporary world, and which all have important political-geographical elements to them. They are ones that are constantly in the newspapers, even if the particular situations chosen to illustrate the general points they make are possibly idiosyncratic or exotic to the reader. My purpose here is to show how situations that you may not have thought about previously as political-geographical ones can be thought of fruitfully in this way. Far from dying out in the Internet world, questions of political accessibility, boundary-making, and self-expression and identity-creation through territorial control are very much alive and kicking.

What is clear across all of the vignettes is that political geography still matters enormously in people's lives, if often differently from in the past. Take, for example, one of the major problems of contemporary American society, the issue of drug addiction and the illegal trafficking that services it. One can argue that legally available alcohol, tobacco, and prescription drugs are all harmful when abused, and that were the same status to be given to currently illegal stimulants this might lead to a more 'rational' approach to reducing addiction and its largely negative social effects. Be that as it may, official policy in the United States since the Nixon presidency of 1969–74 has been to pursue a 'war on drugs' through both domestic advertising campaigns against the dangers of drug abuse and attempts at reducing the importation of drugs into the country. Reducing access to illegal drugs such as heroin and cocaine through reducing the supply and raising prices is therefore one of the main features of the US policy. This relies on the idea that if only supplies can be stopped before they arrive in the United States then drug use can be curtailed. The boundaries of the United States thus become the 'front line' in the war against drugs.

The drug problem is an immense one and an important feature of the globalizing world economy, missed by those who focus relentlessly on national statistics of legal trade to argue that the world economy is still an international rather than a globalizing one. The problem has a number of dimensions that deserve to be identified before the vignette itself is described:

■ The international illicit drug business generates as much as $400 billion in trade annually according to the United Nations International Drug Control Program.

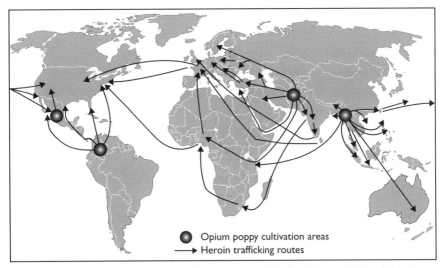

Figure 2.1 World heroin trafficking routes. Colombia, Mexico, Pakistan/Afghanistan, and Thailand/Burma are the main supply areas. The United States, Canada, Australia, and Western Europe are the main demand areas, although addiction rates have increased recently both in source areas and along smuggling routes.
Source: *UNDCP (1997)*

That amounts to 8 percent of all international trade and is comparable to the annual turnover in textiles, according to the study. *Source:* United Nations Office for Drug Control and Crime Prevention, *Economic and Social Consequences of Drug Abuse and Illicit Trafficking* (New York, NY: UNDCP, 1998), p. 3.

According to the United Nations, profits in illegal drugs are so inflated, that three-quarters of all drug shipments would have to be intercepted to seriously reduce the profitability of the business. Current efforts only intercept 13 percent of heroin shipments and 28–40 percent* of cocaine shipments. (*At most; the UN Office for Drug Control and Crime Prevention notes that estimates of production and total supply are probably understated by reporting governments.) *Source:* United Nations Office for Drug Control and Crime Prevention, *Global Illicit Drug Trends 1999* (New York, NY: UNDCP, 1999), p. 51.

According to the United Nations, illegal drugs create enormous profits – a kilogram of heroin in Pakistan costs an average of $2720, but sells for an average of $129,380 in the United States. *Source:* United Nations Office for Drug Control and Crime Prevention, *Global Illicit Drug Trends 2000* (New York, NY: UNDCP, 2000), p. 165.

■ It costs approximately $8.6 billion a year to keep drug law violators behind bars. *Sources*: Bureau of Justice Statistics, *Profile of Jail Inmates 1996* (Washington, DC: US Government Printing Office, April 1996), pp. 1 and 4; Bureau of Justice Statistics, *Prisoners in 1996* (Washington DC: US Government Printing Office, 1997), pp. 10–11; Criminal Justice Institute, Inc., *The Corrections Yearbook 1997* (South Salem, NY: Criminal Justice Institute, Inc., 1997) [estimating cost of a day in jail (i.e. prisoner on remand) to be on average $55.41 a day, or $20,237 a year, and the cost of prison to be on average about $64.49 a day, or $23,554 a year].

■ A study by the RAND Corporation found that every additional dollar invested in substance abuse treatment saves taxpayers $7.46 in societal costs. *Source*: Rydell, C.P. and Everingham, S.S., *Controlling Cocaine, Prepared for the Office of National Drug Control Policy* and the United States Army (Santa Monica, CA: Drug Policy Research Center, RAND Corporation, 1994), p. xvi.

■ 'The heavy toll drug abuse exacts on the United States is reflected in related criminal and medical costs totaling over $67 billion. Almost 70 percent of this figure is attributable to the cost of crime.' *Source*: Office of National Drug Control Policy, *National Drug Control Strategy 2000 Annual Report* (Washington DC: US Government Printing Office, 2000), p. 66.

■ A 1998 report by the National Institute on Drug Abuse (NIDA) and the National Institute on Alcohol Abuse and Alcoholism (NIAAA) estimated the economic costs of alcohol abuse in the United States to be $148.02 billion in 1992, 80 percent ($119.32 billion) of which were due to alcohol-related illness (including health care expenditures, impaired productivity and premature death). In contrast, illegal drug abuse cost a total of $97.66 billion in 1992, of which less than 40 percent ($38.71 billion) was due to drug-related illness or premature death. This figure includes $4.16 billion in HIV/AIDS and Hepatitis treatment costs. *Source*: National Institute on Drug Abuse and National Institute on Alcohol Abuse and Alcoholism, *The Economic Costs of Alcohol and Drug Abuse in the United States, 1992* (Washington, DC: US Department of Health and Human Services, May 1998), Table 1.1, p. 1.3 and Table 4.1, p. 2.4.

■ In 1969, $65 million was spent by the Nixon administration on the drug war; in 1982 the Reagan administration spent $1.65 billion; and in 1999 the Clinton administration spent $17.7 billion. *Sources*: U.S. Congress, *Hearings on Federal Drug Enforcement before the Senate Committee on Investigations, 1975 and 1976* (1976); Office of National Drug Control Policy, *National Drug Control Strategy,*

1992: Budget Summary (Washington DC: US Government Printing Office, 1992), p. 214; Office of National Drug Control Policy, National Drug Control Strategy 2000 Annual Report (Washington DC: US Government Printing Office, 2000), p. 94, Table 4.1.

- Recent estimates indicate that Colombia repatriates $7 billion in drug profits annually, which is nearly as high as the total legitimate exports for Colombia, which were $7.6 billion in 1993. *Source*: Trade and Environment Database (TED), TED Case Studies: Columbia Coca Trade, Washington DC: American University (1997), p. 4.

- It is estimated that Colombian narcotics cartels spend $100 million on bribes to Colombian officials each year. *Source*: Trade and Environment Database (TED), *TED Case Studies: Columbia Coca Trade* (Washington DC: American University, 1997), p. 4.

- In 1993, 98 percent of Bolivia's foreign exchange earnings from goods and services came from the coca market. *Source*: US Congress, Office of Technology Assessment, Alternative Coca Reduction Strategies in the Andean Region, F-556 (Washington DC: US Government Printing Office, July 1993).

As a result of the increased openness of the US to foreign goods and people, US national boundaries are increasingly porous (Flynn, 2002). One of the US Custom Service's top priorities is to interdict illicit narcotics – a daunting task when one considers that all the pure cocaine to feed America's annual coke habit could be transported in just fifteen 40-foot-long containers. But nationally, 16.4 million trucks and more than 5 million loaded 40-foot containers entered the United States in 1999, and trade is expected to more than double in the next two decades. In the year 2000, of the 16,000 containers transferred from ships in US ports, only 500 or so were inspected. Furthermore, more than 2.7 million undocumented immigrants have succeeded in entering the US simply by walking, swimming, or riding across the Mexican and Canadian borders. How can all of this cargo and all of these people possibly be searched for illicit drugs?

Vignette One: *Drug traffickers have no respect for national boundaries* illustrates both the rise of a new actor in world politics, the drug trafficker, and the challenge this actor and the drug business pose to the world's established national boundaries, using a review of the film *Traffic* (2000). In this case the boundary still matters, but as a challenge to be overcome surreptitiously and behind which affluent users are clustered, rather than as a barrier that can only be breached militarily.

vignette 1

Drug traffickers have no respect for national boundaries

The hip and polemical film Traffic (2000) artfully asks: exactly where is the front line in the drug war? Where has the line between the protagonists and the antagonists, good and bad, ally and enemy, been drawn? Is it the militarized line that nominally separates the United States from Mexico, as is popularly imagined? Or is the battle front circumscribed on a more personal scale, in the family, with the line drawn at the bathroom door?

Steven Soderbergh, an avowed social critic, in this movie, a spin-off a British production of the same name, critically explores America's 25-year-long war on drugs. He clearly makes the statement that current efforts and strategies are ineffective and futile, for not only is the demand for illegal drugs at an all-time high but the supply chains seem infinite and ubiquitous, difficult to identify and impossible to eradicate.

William Weld, the former governor of Massachusetts, in a cameo appearance as an ambiguous political figure in the film, offers some wisdom about the nation's drug problem: 'You'll never solve this on the supply side.' Weld's comment at a Washington DC cocktail party to the new 'drug czar', played by Michael Douglas, is suggestive of one of the movie's central themes: that despite spending almost 18 billion dollars the US war on drugs is a failure, and that it has failed mostly because the supply can never be effectively cut off, no matter how much money and blood go into the effort. 'It's an unbeatable market force,' according to the fictional character Eddie Ruiz – the mid-level dealer who agrees to become an informer after caught by federal agents. 'It's a lot easier to get than alcohol' is the mantra of the young characters, including Caroline Wakefield, the 16-year-old addict whose father ironically happens to be the newly appointed drug czar.

Yet none of these stark realities is fully admitted as the film's drug czar pursues the national policy of border fortification, enhanced import and customs security, and militarized interdiction. Simultaneously, Soderbergh reveals the futility of the putative war down to the trench level, as the idealist San Diego detective, played by Don Cheadle, tirelessly pursues the suppliers, including a wealthy 'businessman' living in a posh San Diego suburb, even after witnessing the assassination of his partner as well as a key informant.

On the other side of the divide, Mexico is depicted in broad sepia tones as that dark place where corruption flows unimpeded and where an honest cop is *about as rare as moderation in a crack house. Yet, one Tijuana cop, played by Benicio del Toro, somehow manages to remain incorruptible and even heroic, as he doggedly battles the drug cartels and the complicit government. Despite seeing his friend and partner murdered, and his own life dangling on the razor's edge, his selfless and pragmatic approach is ultimately vindicated when, at the end of the film, a little league baseball field is illuminated through his 'sincere' efforts. The symbolism of that lighted field amidst the dark chaos of the drug war is a powerful message for those, back in the real world, who advocate a less combative approach.*

In numerous interviews, Steven Soderbergh, the movie's director, insists the movie wasn't made to change drug policy, but he also thinks that the time is ripe for change, and that the movie will help the process along. 'I feel absolutely that it's in the air right now,' Soderbergh told a reporter, as Traffic neared the $60-million box-office mark after just six weeks.

He's right about the timing. Strange things are happening in the drug-policy realm that seemed politically impossible just a short time ago. Nine states have now passed ballot measures legalizing the use of marijuana for medical purposes. New York's Republican governor, George Pataki, has proposed lightening up on the state's draconian drug-sentencing laws. The recently departed national drug czar, General Barry McCaffrey, urges that we stop calling the anti-drug campaign a 'war,' reinforcing the remark of Michael Douglas' character in the closing scene of the film: 'I don't know how you wage war on your own family.'

If the futility of the war on drugs calls the meaning of national boundaries into question there are other contemporary political situations that appear to validate their continuing significance and appeal to varied groups, even when on closer attention the opposite may be the case. Vignette Two: *Why Israel and Palestine Cannot Coexist on the Same Territory* examines one of the world's most intractable conflicts, paying particular attention to the difficulty of establishing 'statehood' for Palestine without providing contiguous territory over which a new state could have sovereignty. Yet, the economic reality of the situation is that a new 'Palestine,' wherever it is located, will be dependent on Israel for a wide range of services and much employment for its population. Perhaps the only way out of the impasse in the long run is for both sides to accept a single state within which power would be shared? As yet, however, we are very far from that eventuality.

vignette 2

Why Israel and Palestine cannot coexist on the same territory

Edward Said, the noted literary scholar and Middle East commentator, offers a frank account of the demoralizing aspect of the seemingly immutable and intractable Israeli–Palestinian conflict. In his opinion, it is mostly about the inability to understand and embrace each side's narrative or story about why they claim the same territory:

> We [Palestinians] were dispossessed and uprooted in 1948, they [Israelis] think they won independence and that the means were just. We recall that the land we left and the territories we are trying to liberate from military occupation are all part of our national patrimony; they think it is theirs by Biblical fiat and dias-poric affiliation. Today, by any conceivable standards, we are the victims of the violence; they think they are. There is simply no common ground, no common narrative, no possible area for genuine reconciliation. Our claims are mutually exclusive. Even the notion of a common life shared in the same small piece of land is unthinkable. Each of us thinks of separation, perhaps even of isolating and forgetting the other…. (Said, Edward, 'Palestinians under siege', in the London Review of Books, 14 December 2000).

This sobering commentary suggests that the Oslo Accords and the resulting 'peace process', predicated on an anachronistic political-geographic fix to inter-mingled populations claiming the same territory, has done more damage to the peace and reconciliation efforts in general and to the aspirations of the Palestinian people in particular. In Said's estimation the occupation of Gaza and the West Bank of the Jordan has gone on too long (since 1967) and the peace talks have dragged on with too little to show for them. The Palestinian goal, if it were even independence, seems no closer, and the suffering of ordinary people has gone fur-ther than can be endured. Consequently, the outside world continues to witness the vicious circle of stone throwing in the streets and the renewed support and revival of the Intifada, as well as retrenched Israeli exceptionalism and expansion-ism under the banner of Zionism. Furthermore, media misrepresentation has made it almost impossible for the American and European publics to understand the geographical basis of the events, in this, the most geographical of contests.

The only hope, according to Said and others, is to keep trying to rely on an idea of co-existence between two peoples in one land. This co-dependency idea *allows for deliberative and discursive forms of democratic participation that is not pre-determined by membership in separate, delineated territorial states. It is a way of confronting the problem within political spaces as opposed to across boundaries and borders – the latter having been the modus operandi of the twentieth-century state-centric world. The immutability of the conflict suggests that a new, less state-centered, critical perspective is required – one that does not privilege the state and the discourse of solving sovereignty issues by territorially dividing up the world. Yet, because each side is 'territory mad,' determined to have exclusive rights to the territory of the other, no real solution is in sight. The fiction of Palestinian sovereignty inscribed in the Oslo Accords is visible to all but the most cynical Israeli and most naïve American politicians.*

With the election of Ariel Sharon as Prime Minister in February 2001, achieved in part as a result of the absolute boycott of the election by Israeli Arabs, the political mood within Israel in general and the 'peace process' in particular has reflected despair, overt acrimonious separatist sentiments by Palestinians, and the further entrenchment of and justification for a state permanently under martial law. In other words, popular opinion, on both sides of the conflict, is such that complete partition into separate political territories, no matter how untenable, as will be shown, is the preferred solution. One is prone to challenge this underlying logic by wondering if it is possible or feasible to address and solve one of the oldest ethnic conflicts by merely drawing the appropriate territorial boundaries.

So, what specifically of this vaunted and much celebrated 'peace process' that at its core has tried to territorially divide the region? What has it achieved and for whom? Why, if indeed it was a peace process, have the miserable and desperate condition of the Palestinians and the loss of life become so much worse than before the signing of the Oslo Accords in September 1993? What does it mean to speak of peace if Israeli troops and settlements are still present in large numbers? For instance, according to the authoritative Report on Israeli Settlement in the Occupied Territories (RISOT), *the rate of settlement building has doubled since 1993 and more than 195,000 Jews live 'illegally' and against the dictums of the Accords in Gaza and the West Bank. Before Oslo supposedly 'forbade' this, the figure was 125,000. Furthermore, the RISOT report does not factor in the 150,000 Israeli-Jews who have taken up residence in Arab East Jerusalem under the rubric of Former Deputy Mayor of Jerusalem Abraham Kehila's doctrine of 'Judaification.' Kehila is quoted as saying in 1993: 'I want to make the Palestinians open their eyes to reality and understand that the unification of Jerusalem under Israeli sovereignty is irreversible.' Has the world been deluded or has the rhetoric of 'peace' through boundary-making exemplified by the Oslo (1993), Cairo (1994), Taba (1995), Wye (1998), and Sharm-el-Sheik (1999) agreements been essentially a gigantic fraud?*

To begin with, some facts. In 1948 Israel took over most of what was historical or British mandated Palestine, destroying and depopulating 531 Arab villages in the process. Two-thirds of the population was driven out – forming the origin of the four million refugees of today. The West Bank and Gaza, however, went to Jordan and Egypt respectively. Both were subsequently lost to Israel in 1967 and remain under its control to this day, except for a few areas that operate under a highly circumscribed Palestinian autonomy – the topographical specifications of these areas were decided unilaterally by Israel, as the Oslo process specifies. In other words, Israel took 78 percent of Palestine in 1948 and the remaining 22 percent in 1967. It is only that 22 percent that is in question now, and it excludes West Jerusalem, which had been conceded in advance to Israel at Camp David.

What land, then, in accordance with the hopes of the peace process, has Israel returned? According to Edward Said: 'it is impossible to detail in any straightforward way – impossible by design.' It is part of Oslo's design that even Israel's concessions were so heavily encumbered with conditions, qualifications and entitlements that the Palestinians could not feel that they enjoyed any semblance of self-determination. As the influential New York Times *columnist and Middle East expert Thomas Friedman remarked, 'Israeli propaganda that the Palestinians mostly rule themselves in the West Bank is fatuous nonsense. ... Sure, the Palestinians control their own towns, but the Israelis control all the roads connecting these towns and therefore all their movements.'*

It is the constructed geographical map of the peace process that most dramatically shows the distortions that have been developed and have been systematically disguised by the calculated discourse of peace and bilateral negotiations. The Oslo strategy was to re-divide and subdivide an already divided Palestinian territory into three sub-zones–A, B, and C, in ways entirely devised and controlled by the Israeli side. 'Palestinians themselves,' Said notes, 'have until recently been mapless.' They had no detailed maps of their own at Oslo, nor were there any individuals on the negotiating team familiar with the geography of the Occupied Territories to contest decisions or to provide alternative plans. Subsequently, this lack of geographic knowledge coupled with Israel's claims of biblical manifest destiny created the non-contiguous territorial arrangement. The resultant tensions have likewise justified the Israeli Defense Forces continued control.

In the lexicon of the three sub-zones (see Figure 2.2), A refers to the area of full Palestinian self-rule, B to partial Palestinian self-rule, and C to Israeli Security and Civil Control. The map reveals that not only are the various parts of Area A separated from each other, but that they are surrounded by area B and, more vitally, Area C. In Area B, Israel has allowed the Palestinian Authority to help police the main village areas, near where settlements are constantly under construction. Despite the nominal sharing of police powers, Israel essentially holds all the security cards in Area B. In Area C, it has kept all the territory for itself, 60 percent of the West Bank, in order to build more settlements, open up more roads and establish military staging grounds. Jeff Halper views this cleverly intended set up as a 'matrix of control from which the Palestinians would never be free.' (see Halper, Jeff, 'The road to apartheid', in News from Within, and 'The 94 percent solution: a matrix of control', in Middle East Report, vol. 216, Fall 2000).

The Gaza component of Area A is much larger mainly because, with its arid lands and overpopulated and rebellious masses, it was considered a liability for Israeli settlement, which was happy to jettison all but the best agricultural lands. The closures and encirclements mandated by the three sub-zones have intentionally turned the Palestinian lands into besieged pockmarks on the map.

In October 2000, Amira Hass, a correspondent for the Israeli newspaper Ha-aretz in the Palestinian territories, succinctly summarized the situation, using the language of South Africa under apartheid:

> More than seven years have gone by, and Israel has security and administrative control of 61.2 percent of the West Bank and about 20 percent of the Gaza Strip (Area C), and security control over another 26.8 percent of the West Bank (Area B). This control is what has enabled Israel to double the number of settlers in ten years, to enlarge the settlements, to continue its discriminatory policy of cutting back water quotas for three million Palestinians, to prevent Palestinian development in most of the area of the West Bank, and to seal an entire nation into restricted areas, imprisoned in a network of bypass roads meant for Jews only. During these days of strict internal restriction of movement in the West Bank, one can see how carefully each road was planned: so that 200,000 Jews have freedom of movement and about three million Palestinians are locked into their Bantustans until they submit to Israeli demands.

Furthermore, added to Hass's observations is the fact that the main aquifers for Israel's water supply are under the occupied West Bank; that the

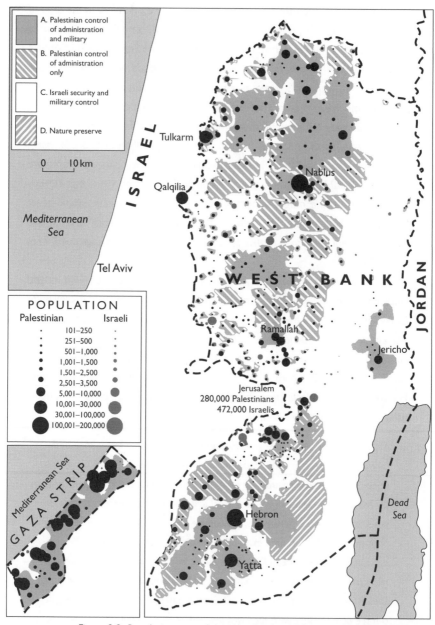

Figure 2.2 Population map of the West Bank and Gaza, showing Palestinian and
Israeli settlements and the three zones of the Oslo Accords.
Source: redrawn from Margalit (2001: 22)

'entire nation' of Palestine excludes the four million refugees who are categorically denied the right of return, even though any Jew anywhere in the world enjoys an absolute right of return at any time; that restriction of movement is as severe in Gaza as it is on the West Bank; and that Hass's figure of 200,000 Jews in Gaza and on the 'West Bank enjoying freedom of movement' does not include the 150,000 new Israeli-Jewish inhabitants who have been brought in to 'Judaize' East Jerusalem.

To exacerbate the conundrum, the slow pace of the unfolding peace process is justified by the US and Israel in terms of safeguarding the latter's security; whereas, one hears nothing about Palestinian security or protection from a colonizing aggressor. 'Clearly,' Said concludes, 'as Zionist discourse has always stipulated, the very existence of Palestinians, no matter how confined or dis-empowered, constitutes a racial and religious threat to Israel's security.'

In conclusion, the understanding of the world political map, as promulgated in Cold War rhetoric and propaganda from 1947 to 1989, was of a set of fixed entities made up of self-contained, territorially distinct and contiguous states that could be arbitrarily used as 'chess pieces,' 'dominoes,' or 'billiard balls' in the bi-polar game of ideological warfare between the US and its allies on the one side and the Soviet Union and its allies on the other. Whatever ethno-territorial conflicts emerged during this period – for example, Pakistan–India, Czechoslovakia–Hungary, Yugoslavia, Palestine–Israel, and conflicts in pretty much all of post-colonial Africa – were either suppressed by linking them to the over-riding global conflict or addressed using a formula of redrawing the borders – partition, i.e. simply changing the lines on the map to fit the demands. It was believed, via the doctrine of self-determination of nations, that territorial conti-guity of all ethnic–nationalist claims was not only possible but feasible. All that was needed to fit all the disparate groups in the world into neat, bounded and distinct pockets was a map and the political wherewithal to make the 'reality' conform to the map. Inherited from the older European imperialism, this non-chalance about remapping to achieve territorial contiguity still defines the dom-inant approach of the Great Powers, not least the United States, to resolving ethno-national conflicts: in the Middle East, the former Yugoslavia, and elsewhere.

Now, at the beginning of the third Christian millennium, it appears that sim-ple de-territorializing and re-territorializing of the world's ethno-national cleav-ages along the lines of the state-centered sovereignty paradigm no longer works and absolutely does not provide a lasting framework for social justice, if it ever really did. This is partly a result of the inability to define and categorize,

de facto and de jure, the aspiring 'nations' as well as the impossibility of circum-scribing neat little contiguous lines around these 'nations.' To assume that every contending group occupies specific, clearly outlined territories was and is fan-tastically tragic. Using the on-going Palestinian–Israeli debacle as an example, efforts to neatly draw boundaries around the two claimants, in accordance with the dominant themes of the Oslo accords and the resulting 'peace process' has proven beyond the imagination of both sides, masking Israel's continued occu-pation and on-going colonization of 'Palestinian' lands and the economic and political marginalization of 'Palestinian' Arabs.
Sources: *Said (2000); Sontag (2001); Malley and Agha (2001); Agnew (1989); Christison (1999); Margalit (2001).*

The Israel–Palestine conflict obviously has its own peculiarities, not the least that Israel is itself a 'solution' to the persecution of Jews in Europe and elsewhere and Palestine had no history as a state before the advent of Israel. The territorial claims in this case are also more than simply ethnic or national given that the religious sites in Jerusalem – the Western Wall for Jews, the Al Aqsa mosque for Moslem Arabs – are symbolically central to the impasse between the two sides. The main weak-ness of the Palestinians is that they do not have a state and Israel is ill-disposed to give them a real one, even if that made sense, as Edward Said suggests it does not. The present 'offer' is for a scattered reservation on mainly barren land. The Israeli journalist Amos Elon (2001: 11) captures the dark irrationality of the situation: 'Israel has been unable to resolve the painful paradox of steadily increasing military power and steadily decreasing national security. The reasons for this continuing paradox are political: the attempt of one people to rule another against its wish.'

The fact is, then, that statehood still counts, if often in paradoxical and counter-intuitive ways. This is why groups from Quebec to Sri Lanka and points in between want their own. It counts because states gain recognition for both national differ-ences that otherwise remain subjugated or unappreciated by others and because the world is still largely organized in terms of states for a wide range of activities, from postal and monetary systems to welfare and military organization. Two vignettes illustrate these contentions. Vignette Three: *Hail Ruthenia!* uses a partic-ular example from Eastern Europe to make the point about national recognition, nascent as the process may be in this case. Vignette Four: *Stamp Collecting Makes the World Go Round* makes the rather different point that statehood exists virtually as well as actually, in the sense that *de facto* recognition of a state-mandated activ-ity, in this case postage stamps, endows a claimant state with a degree of legitimacy.

In other words, statehood is as much about external recognition as it is about internal organization. It is a social as much as a material fact. The example of stamps issued by the Armenian enclave of Nagorno-Karabagh in the Caucacus Mountains of Azerbaijan is used as an illustration of the vitality of the idea of statehood in a global context where it is still highly valued. The strangeness of the two cases suggests, however, that when statehood can be so easily expected or implicitly recognized (if questionably realized), it must differ from the statehood exercised by Great Powers or successful welfare states. Of course, geographical variability in the relative powers of states both within and outside their boundaries has long been a feature of the world political map. As the number of states proliferates it is one that should not be forgotten. We are now up to 193 and still counting.

vignette 3

Hail Ruthenia!

'Sub-Carpathian Rusyns, arise from your deep slumber;' and so begins the anthem of the aspiring Ruthenian nation. The What? Who? Where? The place is 'Ruthenia', located in a wedge-like position surrounded by the Ukraine in the East, Slovakia and Hungary to the west, Poland to the north and Romania on the southern flank. The 'Ruthenians' or 'Rusyns' are a part of the family of east Slavic peoples – akin to Russians, Byelorussians, and Ukrainians – who all of their modern 'history' have been controlled by neighbors. They are mainly farmers or woodcutters in the heavily forested Carpathian foothills, and as Timothy Garton Ash (1999) chides, 'everything about their origins, culture, language and politics is disputed.' Farcical or not, they and their intellectual representatives are clamoring for attention and more autonomy within the current Ukrainian state, itself a recent re-creation. And, with individuals spread throughout the region, as well as the United States, prompting the self-proclaimed moniker of 'the Kurds of Central Europe', the Ruthenian's demands for their own state takes us to the heart of one of the most important problems of contemporary international politics. In the decade following the Cold War, in an environment of re-discovered freedom and political liberalism, suppressed and sometimes only half-formed nationalities have re-emerged and formulated political aspirations all over Europe.

The Ruthenian story is, in every respect, a quintessentially Eastern European one. Yet in Western Europe, as well, there are nationalities, in varying degrees

Figure 2.3 Ruthenia in its regional setting.
Source: Garton Ash (1999: 54)

of formation, that strive for anything from autonomy to statehood – Scotland, Wales, Catalonia, and Basque. Further, such claims are not endemic only to Europe. UNPO, the Unrepresented Nations and People's Organization, maintains a website that lists up to fifty such entities throughout the world; including Abkhazia, Aboriginals of Australia, Alceh and the East Timorese in Indonesia, the Kurds, Tibet, and Kosova. It is a salient issue in dictatorships as well as liberal democracies, with varying degrees of violence. One of the big questions that Ruthenia prompts for Europe is whether the ethnically checkered successor states of the former Soviet Union, might yet go the bloody way of former Yugoslavia and Chechnya.

For most of their modern history Ruthenians lived in the Austro-Hungarian Empire. When the empire was broken up after World War I, they found themselves scattered between Poland, Hungary, Romania, Yugoslavia, and the Soviet Union, but the greatest concentration was in the new state of Czechoslovakia. Czechoslovakia, the most democratic and liberal of those successor states, gave them considerable linguistic and political autonomy, in a province it called 'Sub-Carpathian Rus'. During World War II it, as an appendage of Slovakia, was the pawn of Hitler, the Hungarians, and finally ended up in Stalin's Soviet Union as an oblast, or region, of Ukraine. When the Soviet Union collapsed, it became part of the new Ukrainian state.

What makes the Ruthenian issue particularly significant in contemporary discourse is that the Ruthenians, according to Samuel Huntington's thesis about a coming 'clash of civilizations', straddle two of the great dividing lines in Europe – one religious, the other geopolitical. The religious split is between Western (Catholic or Protestant) and Eastern (Orthodox) Christianity. The Ruthenians worship in either the Orthodox Church and the Uniate (or Greek Catholic) Church, which uses the Eastern rite but acknowledges the authority of the pope. In geopolitical terms, the Ruthenians are on both sides of the new eastern frontier of NATO, with sizable minorities in member countries Hungary and Poland, and soon-to-be-admitted Slovakia. Furthermore, as the European Union continues with its expansionist ambitions, Ruthenia within a few years may well sit directly on that entity's eastern border. It does not take a great stretch of the imagination to envision an independent Ruthenian state, recently separated from a directionless and unstable Ukraine, aspiring for entry into both NATO and the EU.

The Ruthenian situation is still far from that of the Kurds or Kosovars. For now, their demands are for basic minority rights, like education in their own language. They demand that 'Ruthenian' should be an option in the Ukrainian census scheduled for 2001, and that Ukrainian state forestry companies should stop the mechanized stripping of the trees from their beloved hills – symbols, both hills and trees, of their national heritage. They further hope to prevent the Trans-Carpathian oblast from being incorporated into a new, enlarged province governed from Lvov. They also continue to look for more co-operation across the frontiers, in what is already the Carpathian Euroregion. Improvements in Slovakia trying to appease the Eurocrats of Brussels on issues of minority rights will assuredly increase the grievances in neighboring Ukraine.

The twentieth-century history of the Ruthenians, and their experience in the geopolitics of the region, can be perfectly summarized by a popular East European joke. The joke tells the story of an old man who says he was born in Austria-Hungary, went to school in Czechoslovakia, married in Hungary, worked most of his life in the Soviet Union, and now lives in Ukraine. 'Traveled a lot,' comments an interviewer. 'No, I never moved from Mukachevo.' What isn't a joke, however, is the Ruthenian aspiration for statehood within the context of a very *economically and politically unstable region dealing with the ideological residues of the Cold War. The issue of statehood is sure to develop as the Rusyns continue to 'arise from their slumber.'*

Source: *Garton Ash (1999)*

vignette 4

Stamp collecting makes the world go round

Invoking William Shakespeare's rhetorical question, 'What's in a name?' one may similarly ask, 'What's in a stamp?' Only the most naïve would believe that stamps are solely the necessary tax that is paid to process one's mail. Stamps and stamp production are unabashedly infused with political-geographic meaning, and, quite often, are actively produced symbols employed directly, and covertly, as seemingly banal tools in every state's 'nationalizing' project. Stamp designing is rooted in specific places, infused with political and psychological intent and almost always meant to convey territorially specific, quasi-mythical stories and celebratory messages of achievement. The designs may range from the state flag to an indigenous species of plant, a long-dead war hero, a national sporting event, or a popular monument. Whatever the iconography of the particular stamp, the intent is hardly arbitrary.

Correspondingly, the political imagining of stamp production is played out in stamp collecting. Delving specifically into the insular world of the philatelist one finds a 'hobby' directly and indirectly engaged with the more salient and controversial issues of contemporary political geography – state building, ethnic political autonomy, nationalism, international relations, sovereignty. Stamp collectors, in general, believe that stamps should be 'legitimate,' in the sense that they are potentially valuable as a collectible, if they are recognized internationally in practice, even if they are not recognized expressly, as by treaty or international agreement. Fundamentally, this is the same principle of international law that applies to the recognition of nation-states. A nation becomes a state when the international community begins treating it as such. State sovereignty is not simply proclaimed, it is a creative endeavor valorized by reciprocal relations.

Because the philatelic community is always on guard for not just the rare, valuable stamp but also the fake – the illegitimate, non-recognized and non-sanctioned pretender – it plays a role in international political discourse. When examined through a critical political-geographic lens, stamp collecting is revealed to be more than just a benign, leisurely pursuit. It is a highly politicized act that not only lends legitimacy to the modern, territorial bounded state paradigm but also provides a discourse and a forum for the ubiquitous struggle of national secessionist and autonomy movements. In the dialectic of stamp production and collection, the synthesis is a credibility vehicle for autonomous movements and nation-state claims. Having one's stamp officially recognized by the Universal Postal Union (UPU) or the venerable philatelist magazine, Scott's Catalogue, is akin to recognition by the United Nations. Consequently, creating a stamp to 'process mail', with all the requisite semiotics, is one more device employed by aspiring nations seeking sovereignty recognition in the international community. The Nagorno-Karabagh region, high in the Caucaus Mountains, typifies a common scenario played out between the world of international politics and the world of stamp production and collecting.

Nagorno-Karabagh is a fertile but mountainous area of 4400 square kilometers in the southern Caucasus, situated inside what is today internationally recognized as Azerbaijan. The name itself, a Russian–Turkish–Persian compound, is proof of the region's complex and variegated history. It means 'Mountainous Black Garden.' The Karabagh Armenians call the region Artsakh or 'Strong Forest.'

Figure 2.4 Nagorno-Karabagh.
Source: redrawn from O'Lear (2001: 306)

During the Soviet Union era, Karabagh was a semi-autonomous region or oblast, despite being located entirely within the republic of Azerbaijan. When the USSR began to stagger in 1988 Karabagh declared its independence from Azerbaijan, and, subsequently, clamored for diplomatic and institutional recognition from Moscow. Despite the general trend and climate for republic-level partitioning, Moscow thwarted Karabagh's claims for autonomy and instead relegated the issue as an Azerbaijani internal affair. Yet, in 1991, the citizens of Karabagh voted for independence from the USSR, thus exacerbating civil tension. The conflict gradually escalated. The Azerbaijanis besieged Stepanakert, Karabagh's capital, in 1991–92 and occupied most of the region. Then the Armenians, supportive of Karabaghi irredentism, counter-attacked and by 1993– 94 had seized almost the entire region. Some 600,000 Azeri refugees were displaced. A Russian-brokered cease-fire was imposed in May 1994, by which time as many as 25,000 people had died, and countless more been displaced. Under the cease-fire agreement, Karabagh is self-governing and democratically elects a president and an assembly of representatives. It has its own armed forces and a diplomatic 'representative' in neighboring Armenia. Furthermore, it issues visas and prints postage stamps for its mail system (see Figure 2.5).

However, according to the two highly respected philatelist publications, Scott's Catalogue *and* Linn's Stamp News, *this is not enough to make the stamps of Karabagh legitimate, because, 'Karabagh is not a country.' Conventional wisdom in stamp-collecting circles maintains that in order to have a legitimate, internationally recognized stamp, you have to be an internationally recognized 'country.' Hence, aficionados and collectors have rebuked Karabagh's stamps as nothing more than a 'Cinderella.' A label that masquerades as a 'real' stamp from a 'real' country is called a Cinderella – purportedly because it's not what it appears to be, i.e. an ephemeral fantasy.* Linn's Stamp News *publishes a list of phony Cinderella countries, as a warning to collectors. There are about 400 countries on their list, from Alexandria and Atlantis to Zenovia and Zulia; including various former Soviet republics, whose stamp-printing is viewed as nothing more than the pursuit of profit – a scam to acquire hard currency from gullible stamp collectors. However, Matthew Karanian, writing in the* American Philatelist *(Karanian, 2000), argues that because the stamps of Karabagh are used to prepay mailing fees, and because they are accepted by the postal administrations of other countries, the stamps are, in fact, quite legitimate. Further, because they are issued in denominations that are needed to pay actual postal rates, and in reasonable quantities, they do not exploit collectors and,*

Figure 2.5 Nagorno-Karabagh stamp.
Source: *Karanian (2000: 265)*

consequently, should be accorded the respect of non-Cinderella products. For instance, one need only log-on to the Karabagh web page, http://www.sergphil. 8m.com, to test the stamp's viability by requesting a letter to be sent to any address in the world.

To process its mail, Karabagh's only alternative would be to rely upon a foreign postal administration and to use the stamps of a foreign country, such as Armenia or Azerbaijan. However, as stated, for ten years Karabagh has been fighting a secessionist war with Azerbaijan, which, not surprisingly, severely limits postal reliability. Because of the religious connection, Armenian Christianity, Karabagh does get assistance from neighboring Armenia. The mail is trucked to Armenia via a dizzying mountainous road, and from there it is processed as if it were Armenian mail – without, however, the addition of Armenian stamps.

Although it exacerbates tensions with Azerbaijan, the arrangement is perfectly legal and not unique. A similar situation has existed between Turkey and its beneficiary, the Turkish Republic of Northern Cyprus – also a region undergoing a secessionist feud. Although the 'international community' does not recognize Northern Cyprus as a sovereign state, its mail does get delivered. Palestinians also are using their own postage stamps in the occupied territories of Gaza and the West Bank. Mail bearing 'Palestinian Authority' stamps that is internationally destined is sent to and handled by Egypt and Jordan. The 'international community' recognizes the legality of Palestinian stamps, even though Palestine is still not recognized internationally as a sovereign nation-state. Scott's Catalogue even added

these Palestinian stamps to their own catalogue of 'legitimate' collectibles in 2000 –
an event that the New York Times deemed significant enough to report.

Scott's Catalogue *refuses to list Karabagh. The international community*
does not officially recognize Karabagh as a nation-state. It is not a member of
the United Nations, and it has foreign relations only with Armenia – which also
does not 'officially' recognize Karabagh. But the separatist region does have the
international community's de facto recognition of its postal administration. This
results every time its mail gets delivered outside its borders. And, as Karanian
(2000: 266) observes: 'This recognition certainly should advance the cause of
getting Karabagh stamps listed in the stamp catalogues.' And, it is not a great
leap of faith to envision how such recognition contributes to Karabagh's
state-building efforts.
Sources: *Karanian (2000); O'Lear (2001).*

Political geography, however, has increasingly expanded since the 1960s beyond
the concern about the territories and boundaries of states. The contemporary
sub-field is about the geographical distribution of power in general and how this
relates to other geographies such as those of ethnicity, class, gender, and sexual
orientation, and how these geographies produce the politics of identity and
interests. Even as large parts of the world have become more and more integrated, political inequalities between the places occupied by different social groups
have become more rather than less marked. The 'new' world economy privileges
those regions and localities best positioned in relation to other 'nodes of advantage' while other places and their residents are left behind. Within global cities
such as Los Angeles, London, and Paris, as much as in marginalized regions such as
parts of southern Italy or the old textile towns of northern England, are areas of
serious economic and social disadvantage in which many people are trapped by a
lack of empowerment in relation to local and national political institutions as much
as by a lack of employment and employability in the marketplace. One such place
is the subject of the fifth and final vignette: *What Don't Kill You, Make You Stronger.*
This is the area often known as the 'South-Central' of Los Angeles. Through showing the difficulties of life in this area the vignette points to the potential role of
political activism even within desperately poor places isolated from the main
power centers of American society.

This story has wider relevance to the general issue of how power and resistance
are implicated in people's lives within the boundaries of states. In this case the relevant boundaries are those of a neighborhood within a major city. But they could

equally be the boundaries of regions and localities anywhere that affect the life circumstances and prospects of those living within them. Boundaries matter whenever they demarcate differences in power and opportunity between groups of people in relation to markets and governmental institutions. In the Los Angeles Metropolitan Area political power is dispersed across a large number of municipalities, special districts, and public agencies. Within the city of Los Angeles, a weirdly shaped entity that sprawls from the San Fernando Valley in the north to the LA Harbor in the south, the dominant politics is that of ethnicity. The Westside and the Valley are still largely white, the Eastside is now largely Latino, and South-Central, largely African-American since the 1940s, is increasingly Latino. In the 2001 citywide mayoral election a mainly white/African-American candidate (James Hahn) defeated a Latino/white candidate (Antonio Villaraigosa). But electoral politics hides the fact that there are dramatic differences in class and ethnicity across LA's neighborhoods. LA is a highly segregated city with the quality of public services and private prospects largely determined by where one lives. Where one lives, therefore, is not merely incidental to your life. It is how racial, ethnic, and class differences come together to determine the power one can exercise in one's own and in other people's lives. This is the political geography of everyday life for ordinary people.

vignette 5

What don't kill you, make you stronger

'South-Central' is the part of Los Angeles known elsewhere in the city as its most dangerous and deadly neighborhood. In the year 2000, 76 people were killed in the part of South-Central covered by the South-east Division of the LA Police Department (LAPD), including 23 victims under 21 years of age. The lion's share of the homicides in Los Angeles take place in this area. Most of the victims in 2000 were young black men. Overwhelmingly, the deaths were not random but the result of gang initiation killings and disputes between gangs and drug dealers over territory.

Of course, sometimes innocent people just happened to be in the wrong place at the wrong time. In a neighborhood in which regular employment in factories or other workplaces has become increasingly rare, the drug business fulfills a need. Yet, it also has devastating consequences in terms of lives cut short and

Figure 2.6 The streets and local government boundaries of South-Central Los Angeles.
Source: Stewart (2001: 11)

high rates of incarceration in California's burgeoning prison sector. Some facts about the role and impact of illegal drugs in poor city neighborhoods help to put the death toll in South-Central in perspective:

■ In a report funded by the Wisconsin Policy Research Institute, researchers concluded that 'drug sales in poor neighborhoods are part of a growing informal economy which has expanded and innovatively organized in response to the loss of good jobs.' The report characterizes drug dealing as 'fundamentally a lower class response [to the information economy] by men and women with little formal education and few formal skills,' and the report notes 'If the jobs won't be created by either the public or private sector, then poor people will have to create the jobs themselves.' Source: Hagedorn,

John M., Ph.D., The Business of Drug Dealing in Milwaukee *(Milwaukee, WI: Wisconsin Policy Research Institute, 1998), p. 3.*

In a report funded by the Wisconsin Policy Research Institute, researchers concluded that drug-dealing plays a substantial role in the local economies of poorer urban neighborhoods. 'At least 10 percent of all male Latinos and African-Americans aged 18–29 living in these two [surveyed] neighborhoods are supported to some extent by the drug economy.' The report also concluded that 'most drug entrepreneurs are hard working, but not super rich' and that 'most drug entrepreneurs aren't particularly violent.' One-fourth of all drug-dealers surveyed said they encountered no violence at all in their work, and two-thirds reported that violence occurred less than once per month. Source: ibid., p. 1.

In its annual report for 1998–99, the French organization Observatoire Geopolitique de Drogues (Geopolitical Drug Watch) writes of the US: 'Inmates are even less likely to find a job after than before serving a sentence, and, if nothing changes, most of them are doomed to unemployment for life ... and are likely to go back to prison.' Source: Observatoire Geopolitique des Drogues, The World Geopolitics of Drugs 1998/1999 *(Paris: OGD, April, 2000), p. 133.*

The same organization also points out the deeper economic impact from the eventual release of American drug felons: 'According to some estimates some 3.5 million prisoners will be released between now and 2010, and an additional 500,000 each year thereafter. Such a large-scale release of unskilled people – most of them cannot even read and write – will have a negative impact on wages, which are already low in deprived urban areas, due to a massive influx of men desperate to get a job; especially, since the reform of the welfare system in 1996 severely reduced felons' access to welfare money.' Source: ibid., p. 133.

Typically, descriptions of neighborhoods such as South-Central stop there. Areas like this are the by-word for social pathology. But during the same period when 76 young men and boys were killed in 2000, 'nearly 200 students were graduating from Locke High School, kids were splashing in inflatable plastic pools, God's music sweetened the air above churches along Broadway, and beats dropped loud and heavy from the windows of passing cars. People went to work, ran their businesses, raised their children, planned their future. And an old man took his horse for a walk down Avalon Boulevard. "It's all love around here," says 21-year-old William Henagan Jr, an aspiring videographer. And danger. "What don't kill you make you stronger," he says of his experiences. "That's the way I look at it."' (Stewart, 2001: 10).

There is, then, a paradox at work. As Jocelyn Stewart reports from the neighborhood, life there produces a 'wild mix of images, the best and the worst of people, a river in the desert.' But what she sees above all is people still chasing 'progress,' which means trying to better themselves and their families both individually and collectively. The older inhabitants settled in the area because of discrimination in jobs and housing that kept them out of other districts. Though restrictive covenants, documents that barred selling houses to members of designated groups (Jews, blacks, etc.), were banned in 1948 in California, South-Central was by then largely African-American and remained so thereafter: isolated and ghettoized within the larger city and metropolis. In the 1960s, riots and the closing of factories, such as those of General Motors and Goodyear in nearby suburbs, undermined the local economy. Between 1970 and 1985 70,000 blue collar jobs left the area. This is when drugs came in; local gangs captured the business and served as distributors to the rest of the city and its suburbs. The negatives of the drug business and the war on drugs concentrated in neighborhoods like South-Central. Crack cocaine created a new local market in the 1980s. Gangs grew larger and more violent as the profits increased. More and more young men went off to prison, leaving their absence a palpable feature of the area. But a sense of community persists for some, particularly for those who can connect to older traditions of service and public involvement. Some plant gardens, others advise boys without fathers. The massive immigration from Latin America has also revitalized the neighborhood. Though, as Stewart notes: 'In this now-mixed community, Latinos and African-Americans sometimes settle into cold silence, sometimes erupt in open hostility. But there is also as much common ground' (Stewart, 2001: 16). As a result, there has been a dramatic increase in political action, as people 'gather to fight problems, not each other.' The local Community Coalition has spent the past ten years battling local problems: from watching the spread of liquor stores, trying to force school improvements, lobbying to have crack addicts treated rather than imprisoned, and changing the way in which the neighborhood is policed from a militarized to a communal model.

Still, as everyone in South-Central knows: 'A bullet can find you before you find yourself' (Stewart, 2001: 17). The most fateful question one young man can ask another is 'Where you from, homie?' If the question comes from someone in a gang it is about whose side are you on and what will you kill or die for. But it is also profoundly about geography. It is about living in neighborhoods in which the wider society no longer offers much except policing and demand for the drugs that move through them. The final word goes to Jocelyn Stewart (2001: 35):

> Imagine living in a community best known for its dead and wounded. If you come from here, you know there is much more: those who plant gardens, fix loose bicycle seats and look out for neighborhood children, those who pay respect to the dead by working hard to keep this community alive; body and soul.
>
> If someone asks you to talk about the place you come from, they are the ones you think of: the ones altering the landscape, the ones holding up the sky.

Source: Stewart (2001)

THE HISTORIC CANON

Political geography had a history before the term itself came into use in the 1890s. For example, the seventeenth-century Englishman William Petty's idea of 'political arithmetic' and his 'Political Anatomy of Ireland' can be seen as historical precursors of late nineteenth-century political geography. In mid-eighteenth-century France Anne-Robert-Jacques Turgot used the term 'political geography' to refer to the relationships between the facts of geography, seen as all physical and human features of spatial distribution, and the organization of politics. It is also apparent that many of the great figures in the history of political thought, from the ancient Greeks Aristotle and Thucydides to the early modern Florentine Machiavelli and later writers such as Hobbes, Locke, Montesquieu, Turgot, Madison, Rousseau, Hegel, and Marx, had ideas about political territoriality and the effects of geographical location and access to resources on conflict and war that can be regarded as basic elements of political geography. They picked up on the practical realities facing political elites and offered their solutions in the context of the historical periods in which they lived. Thucydides' great work, *The Peloponnesian War*, concerns the two decades of war between Athens and Sparta (431–411 BC), and forms the first example of use of the opposition between sea- and land-powers that later political geographers such as Halford Mackinder used as a basic organizing principle. The founders of political geography as such, therefore, could draw upon many centuries of relevant thought to inform their research and writing.

What is clear, however, is that their thinking and that of later writers is closely connected to the times in which they wrote. Though they might all like to claim a timelessness to their work, a transcendence of both the present and the situatedness of their knowledge, they were all both limited and stimulated by the general intellectual culture of their historical contexts. This chapter begins with a general overview of the geopolitical context of the period from 1890 to 1945 in which political geography first developed as an academic field. The period was one of intense rivalry between the Great Powers for global power and influence. A second section identifies an important continuity across the period in the naturalized understanding of knowledge that tended to dominate Geography in general and political geography in particular. There are interesting and important differences between countries and over the course of the period in the ideas that tended to dominate among political geographers. So, the selection of figures and works for close attention in the making of political geography in this period must offer a range of viewpoints. Inevitably, however, this chapter cannot deal with all of the writings of the period. An attempt is made to examine what could be called a 'historic canon:' those works and their authors whose intellectual and political influence was greatest during the period and since. But I also pay some attention to ideas and figures whose ideas were less influential. Their experience tells us something about the limits of originality when it fails to connect with the ethos or Zeitgeist of an era and how it is later remembered. But it also suggests that we should not simply consign everyone to the same intellectual box simply because they lived in the same time period.

I designate one group of figures and exemplary texts as founders: Friedrich Ratzel and Halford Mackinder, on the one side, as initiators, and Paul Vidal de la Blache and Elisée Reclus, on the other, as critics. This is followed by 'Wilsonianism and American political geography,' focusing particularly on Isaiah Bowman; 'Space, Race, and Expansion,' with a focus on the German Karl Haushofer and on the creation of an Italian geopolitics; and a final substantive section on 'Geopolitics versus Political Geography,' with discussion of texts by Bowman, Albert Demangeon, Yves Marie Goblet, and Jacques Ancel. A 'Conclusion' sums up the chapter and points the way forward to post-World War II political geography.

The geopolitical context, 1875–1945

The late nineteenth century was both the zenith of European empire-building and the time when new extra-European Great Powers – the United States and Japan – emerged into global prominence. So, not only were the European Great Powers, particularly Britain and France, renewing their colonial activities under stimulus from the colonialism of newly unified Germany and Italy, Europe was no longer the sole center of global imperialism. At the same time, and as noted by the English political geographer Halford Mackinder in 1903, the relatively easy expansion of worldwide empires into 'open spaces' that began with Columbus' voyage in 1492 had come to an end. With the exception of the polar regions, the expansion of any one empire now had to be completely at the expense of the others. More Great Powers and shrinking space for their expansion spelled possible doom for established and up-and-coming alike unless strategies could be fashioned to protect and enhance what they had from the threats posed by the others.

Of course, the 'open spaces' were almost invariably occupied, but by peoples who had succumbed to European deceit, military prowess, and diseases. As a result of this history, such peoples had long been judged the civilizational inferiors of Europeans but now, increasingly, they were also categorized as (natural) racial inferiors too. Into a political atmosphere of intense inter-imperial rivalry, therefore, came a new way of explaining the global political hierarchy based on the increasing acceptance of ideas of environmental and racial determinism. European 'success' was henceforward to be explained in terms of the climatic and/or racial characteristics of Europeans relative to those whom they had conquered or dominated. If in the past Providence had shone down or God had offered a helping hand, now natural characteristics associated with different world regions and the peoples who lived in them were to become popular ways of explaining global political arrangements and offering insights into how best to plan for this or that empire's future success or brilliance.

The enmity between the Great Powers was not based solely on sheer willfulness or the will to power of this or that domestic group, such as the military or armaments manufacturers. The period from 1875 to 1945 was one of fundamental instability in the world economy because of the arrival of new Great Powers wanting to muscle their way into markets controlled by others and the declining capacity of Britain, the main commercial as well as colonial power, to provide its lending services to the world economy without damaging its colonial position. It is worth saying more about this because it provides the historical context in which modern political geography came into being.

The period 1815–75 was one in which Britain held the balance of power in Europe, enjoyed a significant edge in sea-power that allowed it a coercive role in imposing its trade and monetary policies around the world, and sponsored a set of doctrines – comparative advantage, free trade, and the gold standard – that, though appearing universal, benefited influential interests in Britain. This combination of 'European Concert' and British hegemony elsewhere began to collapse after 1870, once other states with powerful economic and military assets began to challenge

Britain. Germany was by far the most important of these. Its capabilities could not be translated into an enhanced global political role without upsetting both the Concert and the global flows of trade and capital centered around Britain. Concurrently, the increased industrial production of the United States and the European states undermined British industrial pre-eminence and led British business and governments into the use of non-tariff barriers and colonial trade to restrict global free trade and price competition. The net result was an erosion of the system of trade and finance centered around Britain and the emergence of a set of competitive imperial states dividing the world into zones based on territorial monopoly.

Another outcome was a polarization of the Great Powers into two increasingly antagonistic groups. One, headed by Britain and France (with tacit American support), was oriented towards maintaining the mix of free trade and imperialism from the previous era. The other, headed by Germany, was concerned with expanding its colonial possessions and challenging British financial dominance. This division was apparent by the 1890s and gained its most famous expression in the 'Anglo-German naval rivalry,' or race between Britain and Germany to see who could build the most and the biggest battleships the fastest.

Inter-imperial economic rivalry was powerfully fueled by the growing nationalism of the period. The extension of railway systems around national capitals, the increased role of governments in economic activities, and the growth of mass elementary education conspired to produce an enhanced sense of nation-states as 'communities of fate.' State boundaries seemed to define natural units whose geographical limits were the product of differences in national 'vitality' and 'capability.' This vision did not go unchallenged by, for example, the growing socialist and anarchist movements of the period. Class more than nation was their putative central category. Even they, however, often succumbed to the pervasive nationalism by organizing nationally and seeing empire as a positive rather than a negative phenomenon for their industrial-world constituencies. 'Socialism in one country' was well under way before the Russian Revolution of 1917 and the subsequent use of the term as a defense of empire within the future Soviet Union.

The late nineteenth century saw a huge expansion and enlargement of the world economy through the new imperialism (Wolf, 1982). Regions inside and outside of Europe became specialized in the production of specific raw materials, food products, stimulants (coffee, tea, opium, etc.), and manufactured goods on a scale unparalleled in world history. Regional industrial specialization in Europe, Japan, and the United States was stimulated by regional specialization in raw material production elsewhere. The worldwide economic depression of 1883–96, due among other things to decreased profitability in manufacturing as new producers flooded the global marketplace, encouraged a spurt of investment in raw material production. By 1900 not only was most of the world formally bound into colonial empires (as in India, SE Asia and Africa) or under commercial domination by one or more of the Great Powers (as in China and Latin America), but more and more of the world's resources were drawn into a geographically specialized world economy. Bananas in Central America, tea in Ceylon (Sri Lanka), and rubber in Malaya are just three examples of intensive regional commodity specialization from this period.

This was also a period of dramatic technological change. From 1880 to 1914 'a series of sweeping changes in technology and culture created distinctive new modes of thinking about and experiencing time and space' (Kern, 1983: 23). Such innovations as the telegraph, the telephone, the automobile, the cinema, the radio, and the assembly line compressed distance, truncated time, and threatened social hierarchies. The global spread of railroads and the invention of the airplane were perhaps the most important challenges to conventional thinking and practice about time and space. The sense of a 'closing world,' therefore, was neither illusory nor purely the product of the renewed efforts at colonialism.

With hindsight, World War I can be seen as an almost inevitable outcome of the competitive relationship between Germany on the one side and the dominant Powers, such as Britain, on the other. Perhaps the war could have been avoided if militarist attitudes and the nationalism of the time had been weaker. The possibility of engaging other Powers as allies encouraged an initial recklessness in the principal combatants that was regretted once the industrialized killing of the war became apparent. Japan and Italy looked for whatever advantage they could find between them, finally tilting away from Germany for a spell. The United States, with its gargantuan national economy, remained divided in its approach to the conflict. Initially joining in the search for colonies during the Spanish-American War of 1898–1900 and finally siding with Britain in 1917, the United States after World War I became divided between those – most importantly President Woodrow Wilson – advocating an internationalism based on accepting the need to negotiate rather than fight over national differences, and those, dubbed 'isolationists,' who counseled American withdrawal from an active global role.

The lessons of World War I, however, were neither well taught nor readily learned. World War II can be seen as a repeat of World War I for many of the same reasons. The treaties following the cessation of war in 1918, in particular the Treaty of Versailles, resolved few of the tensions that had underlain the conflict. Rather, they added new sources of hostility between the main European powers, particularly in the form of prevalent German resentment that Germany had been excessively punished by economic reparations and territorial losses for its role in starting the war. Moreover, the new states that emerged in Eastern Europe introduced not only greater potential for bilateral alliances (such as France and Poland, Britain and Czechoslovakia) against Germany but also a set of enemies for Germany in a region with significant German-speaking populations and extensive German economic interests.

World War I did produce a number of significant changes in world politics. US intervention had proved militarily decisive. Japan was now recognized as a major Asian power, having already embarked on a strategy of empire building that was to eventually lead to conflict with the US and the European powers in 1941. The collapse of the czarist regime in Russia in 1917 created a new kind of state based on a state-directed economy. The new state saw itself as threatened by and threatening to the capitalist world economy. Neither Japan nor Soviet Russia was readily incorporated into what was left of the British-dominated world trading and financial system in the inter-war period. The United States, after sponsoring the collective security system called the League of Nations in the aftermath of the war, withdrew from its active implementation. All told, therefore, the changes emanating from World War I worked towards rather than away from a future conflict.

The climax came with the remilitarization of the German economy under Nazi rule after 1933. The fact that World War II involved the active alliance of Germany, Italy, and Japan, the three Great Powers with the most autarkic economies and elites most dissatisfied with the global status quo, shows the degree to which inter-imperial rivalry was the governing process behind the advent of the war. Of course, their subsequent defeat by the US, the Soviet Union, and Britain also came to represent the defeat of the colonial approach to global management of wealth and power (see Chapter 4).

Naturalized knowledge

The university field of Geography as whole was invented in the late nineteenth century in part as an offshoot of the growth of national geographical societies devoted to exploration, collecting information about exotic peoples, and the opening up of foreign lands to commerce and/or conquest. The other part of its origins lay in detailed mapping and portrayal of the regions and landscapes of national territories to communicate the material basis of national identity in the burgeoning elementary schools of the era. In this respect, of course, Geography was one of a panoply of subjects with ancient roots that were reinvented under their old names to service the needs of statehood and empire-building: from Anthropology's measuring of physical differences between human groups and Literature's capture of national literary genius to History's telling of distinctive and noble national histories. New fields such as Sociology, Economics, and Political Science acquired their own niches in the national service.

The basis to knowledge was contested in many of these fields, including Geography. Voluntarist understandings of nationhood were still championed, for example, but were increasingly eclipsed by 'blood and soil' conceptions. Idealism of both the transcendental, inherited from Hegel in particular, and the pragmatic varieties, important among Americans, also had their supporters, who often mixed it into accounts that often also had materialist elements, borrowed from either biology and/or political economy. Notions of 'will,' 'spirit,' and 'consciousness' on the part of collective nouns such as nations, classes, and races also co-existed with the claim that such entities are in fact mental constructions rather than real phenomena. There were widespread fears among dominant classes of racial and social 'degradation;' the sense that the rapid social and economic changes of the nineteenth century threatened the established social order, itself increasingly less aristocratic (landed) and more bourgeois (commercial). An increasingly prestigious and dominant thrust in all of the new 'disciplines,' however, was towards a 'naturalization' of knowledge claims. By this I mean a tendency to want to explain human and social phenomena largely if not entirely in terms of natural processes, either physical and/or biological. In other words, they wanted to explain using processes assuredly not of mental construction that lay outside the questionable 'human' realm in which values, interests, and identities were all subject to divergent interpretations and hence less amenable to 'expert opinion.' Later commentators have often 'cleaned up' the complexities of this period too much. So, though naturalization of knowledge was the dominant thrust, it was frequently combined with other elements to defy simple categorization as 'idealist' or 'materialist.'

Naturalization of knowledge claims had two vital intellectual preconditions. One was the separation of the scientific claim from the subject position of the particular writer. Claims were made to universal knowledge that transcended any particular national, class, gender, or ethnic standpoint. So, even as a particular 'national interest' was addressed, it was framed by a perspective that put it into the realm of nature rather than that of politics or society. This 'view from nowhere' was by no means new but it was very important to the new university fields in supporting their assertion of expertise and relevance to addressing the problems of the age.

The second precondition was preference for the use of arguments drawn from the natural sciences to explain social and political phenomena. Thus, the principle of natural selection as proposed by Charles Darwin filtered down into popular culture and into fields such as Geography largely in terms of the idea of 'survival of the fittest.' This not only encouraged organic conceptions of nation-statehood (the state as a type of organism) but also ideas about racial competition, degradation, and dominion. Much of what passed for Social Darwinism, however, was inspired by the older evolutionary ideas of Jean Baptiste Lamarck. These were both more open than Darwin's reliance on variation over extended time periods to the direct effects of the physical environment on social processes and, crucially, to the impact of 'will' or intervention in creating more successful organisms. This allowed for the packaging of seemingly contradictory elements into a single study, such as races as biological categories arrayed according to their superior 'consciousness' for which there was no natural basis whatsoever. Such ideas were widely shared among elites, not least the new academic ones, across all of the Great Powers.

Modern political geography arose in the conjunction between the practical needs of state- and empire-building, on the one hand, and the extension of environmental and biological ideas to the realm of world politics, on the other. Political geography, therefore, exhibited both of the traits of the naturalization of knowledge. In the first place, as its proponents argued for how physical geography directed state- and empire-formation, they also set themselves up as problem-solvers for their own states and empires. Thus, Mackinder provided both a global geopolitical model but was concerned primarily with the implications of the model for the future of the British Empire. That the latter may well have inspired the former rather than vice versa never seems to have occurred to him or anyone else at the time, or to some since. Second, by transposition from evolutionary biology, the European territorial state acquired the status of an organism with its own needs and demands. But this idea had older and quite different roots. German idealist philosophers from the late eighteenth and early nineteenth centuries, such as Fichte and Hegel, had regarded the state as a being or entity with a life of its own. It was but a short step from this to Ratzel's conception of the state as an organism, a step made possible by the spread of ideas from biology into the emerging social sciences in the 1890s. What lent this further plausibility was the sense that states were involved in a struggle for survival in a geopolitically 'closed' world where one state could now benefit only at the expense of others.

The entire cultural atmosphere of the period conspired to favor the naturalized view of politics and society and made the *physical* in geography especially attractive as a source of explanation of state character and behavior. Four features of the period's dominant strands of thinking in political geography are directly connected to the historical context, both political and intellectual: the harmony of state and nation, natural political boundaries, economic nationalism, and the determining character of location and/or environmental conditions.

The late nineteenth century was a time of severe social dislocation in Europe. At one and the same time there were massive flows of people within Europe and across the globe, an explosion of urbanization, increasing capital mobility undermining local financial circuits and disrupting established patterns of investment, and strong movements of revolt against these shifts and their impacts in the form of workers' and women's suffrage organizations. One response to this was to try to recreate at the national scale the local social harmony that had supposedly prevailed in past times. Just as sociologists, such as the Frenchman Emile Durkheim, argued for a national moral order to replace dying religious and local ones, political geographers in Germany, France, and Britain all participated in the attempt to give the contemporary state an organic character by connecting it to the nation. A mythic community, in which every social stratum knew its place and duty to the whole was projected onto the nation, served as the ideal upon which to build a more stable geopolitical order. An organic local past was to be recreated in the national present. In this order there was no room for cultural differences within the boundaries of states. Every 'race' was seen as requiring its proper place. Jews, being culturally distinctive and scattered around Europe, were particularly problematic in this context and as they were identified increasingly in racial rather than in religious or ethnic terms. The deep irony of Durkheim, the assimilated French Jew advocating a new national moral order, is worthy of particular note. Indeed, the German political geographer Ratzel is often identified as the founder of the ecological theory of race in which Jews are seen as the one race most out of place. Sander Gilman provides the following gloss on Ratzel's position:

> In the Near East they were productive (for example, creating monotheism) but in Europe they have no real cultural meaning. The association of place and race is linked in the rationale of the German in Africa or the Jew in Europe. They are presented as mirror images, for while the German in Africa 'heals,' the Jew in Europe 'infects'. (Gilman, 992: 183–4)

This line of thinking, with Jews and other widely diffused and mobile peoples designated as contaminants, was to have devastating consequences after the Nazis gained power in Germany in the 1930s.

But whether or not Ratzel himself can be accused of being a proto-Nazi is another question entirely. His emphasis on external environmental circumstances sets him apart from the genetic racism inherent in the Nazi obsession with the German *Volk*. Even more to the point, Ratzel favored German participation in empire-building outside of Europe, denying that Germany could expand in Europe itself. Of course, this is hardly reassuring for those outside of Europe whose racial inferiority, even if on environmental rather than genetic grounds, condemned them to inferiority relative to their German (or other European) masters.

A second dominant element in the political geography of the time was the idea that each state has or should have 'natural boundaries.' This implied, of course, that not all political boundaries were the proper ones. The territorial status quo that had characterized the Concert of Europe was openly called into question. But it also implied that all of the members of a putative nation or ethnic group had the right to live within the boundaries of their own state. Finally, it opened up the possibility of using natural features to designate the natural area of the state. Swedish conservatives, such as Kjellén, argued against Norway's independence from Sweden on the ground that the Scandinavian mountains were not a natural boundary. Seas and rivers were preferred. The arbitrariness of the classification points up the political uses to which such natural claims were put. The Nazi concept of *Lebensraum* (borrowed from Ratzel), justifying the 'right' of vital peoples (such as Germans) to expand into areas not exploited efficiently enough by their current residents, was used to justify subjugating *Mitteleuropa* (Central-Eastern Europe), and was based in the notion of natural boundaries.

A third element in the political geography of the epoch was economic nationalism. The national economy existed to provide for the national community. Ideas of laissez faire and free trade were seen as antithetical to social stability and as sources of social decay. This perspective was widely shared by emerging political elites across Europe and Japan and, to a lesser extent, in the United States. Two of the founders of political geography, the Swede Kjellén and the Englishman Mackinder, both subscribed wholeheartedly to this element of the 'organic conservatism' of the era. The nation-state (and its empire, where appropriate) was defined as the basic unit for all economic transactions. Individuals and businesses were held to be subordinate to the greater needs of the nation-state. Writers as different in many respects as the English economist Hobson and the English political geographer Mackinder shared organic definitions of national interest as the driving force behind economic growth. To Hobson, however, empire sacrificed the 'home' economy, whereas for Mackinder empire was the means of maintaining the economic basis to military power that was essential to national survival. The Britain that had produced the empire now required it to maintain its global dominance. In the context of the time, Mackinder was probably correct. The long-term problem, of course, was that the discourse of benevolent imperialism rested on the systematic subjugation of vast numbers of people for whom the British maritime empire was anything but an exercise in benevolence. Be that as it may, what Mackinder and others agreed on was the organic unity of a national (-imperial) economy as an entity in itself.

Economic nationalism was by no means new. In the seventeenth and eighteenth centuries, doctrines of 'cameralism' and 'mercantilism' had dominated economic discourse. They saw monopoly structures, such as government trading companies and heavy government regulation, as essential for economic growth. The economic growth in question, of course, was that of the nation. By the nineteenth century mercantilism had transmogrified into imperialism because of the difficulties of achieving sustained economic growth within static territorial boundaries. If Britain and France practiced 'free trade imperialism' (a peculiar combination of restrictive practices within their empires and a high degree of free trade outside it), the upstart powers such as Germany could only grow by initially engaging in policies that protected their industries by sheltering them from international competition. Then they too could grow economically by expanding territorially, i.e. acquiring a colonial empire.

This too was now seen as biological in nature. As frontiers closed in North America and the world's land masses were all brought into the world market, control over territory appeared to be a crucial requirement for economic growth. The idea of a 'closed system' was vital to the plausibility of the biological analogy. Only in such a setting did the zero-sum game of each organic entity competing for a larger slice of the same economic pie make sense. This was what brought nature and nation together. With a 'fixed' nature, each nation could only grow at the expense of the others. That the pie could be made larger as a result of innovation and improved productivity was a minority view that never achieved much popularity until after World War II. Indeed, the Great Depression of the 1930s reinforced the logic of competitive national-imperial economies. The state corporatism that became ascendant in the 1920s and 1930s in Fascist Italy, Nazi Germany, Spain, and Portugal, freed the state from guaranteeing rights for individuals and groups to pursue a 'higher cause:' that of guaranteeing the interests of the state (and its dominant elites).

The final feature of the naturalized political geography that developed from the 1890s onwards was its emphasis on the determining character of location and/or

environmental conditions. The relative success of different states in global competition was put down to absolute advantages of location and to superior environmental conditions. 'Marchland' states (states on the edge of land masses) were
seen as possessing intrinsic advantages over 'inland' states because they had fewer
neighboring states and, hence, fewer potential adversaries. 'Maritime' or sea-
power states were seen as outflanking 'continental' or land-power states in control over the oceans, the main means of global movement. Only the coming of the
railroad had called this into question, according to Mackinder. This was so because
of the relative weight of the Eurasian land mass (or 'Heartland') in relation to the
difficulty of coalescing and policing the 'Insular Crescent' (Mackinder) or 'rimland'
(Spykman) around its edge.

Even those with impeccable anti-naturalist credentials were drawn into the
Zeitgeist (spirit of the age). A case in point is the German philosopher Heidegger
who wrote in 1935 of the German Volk or nation 'trapped' in central Europe:

> We are caught in a pincers. Situated in the center, our Volk incurs the severest pres-
> sure. It is the Volk with the most neighbors and hence the most endangered. With
> all this, it is the most metaphysical of nations. (Heidegger, 1959: 39)

The spatial determinism associated with formal geopolitical models such as that
of Mackinder and later writers such as Spykman, however, was never as popular as
a less specific (or more ambiguous) environmental determinism. From this point of
view, the Great Power potential of states was a function of their industrial
prospects which, in turn, could be traced to their natural resources (particularly
energy resources such as coal) and their ability to exploit them. Some went further
and claimed that this 'ability' was itself 'determined' by climate. From the 1890s until
the 1930s such views were not exceptional. Indeed, they formed the mainstream of
educated opinion in such fields as Geology, Geography, and Biology. Much of the
academic Geography of the period in Germany and the English-speaking world
involved elaborating systems of environmental/geographical accounting; classifying
states and regions in terms of inventories of resources, racial characteristics, economic and political organization, and climatic types. These were widely taught in
schools and became the conventional wisdom about why some places 'developed'
and others lagged behind. Natural attributes determined national destiny.

As we shall see, there were voices that offered criticism of elements of the naturalized discourse upon which political geography was founded and not all voices
always spoke in unison. In particular, some French and American political geographers opposed many features of the conventional wisdom; the French because

of their orientation towards a much more historical and human-centered view of the making of states (reflecting perhaps the revolutionary tradition of 1789 to which they were heirs) and the Americans because of their similar 'exceptionalist' view of their own past and the liberal-democratic ideals that they thought it represented in the world. They tended to have more liberal conceptions of the political and were suspicious of the state-based 'determinism' they saw in the pronouncements of figures such as Ratzel and Mackinder. But the relatively high degree of consensus about the conditioning role of location and the physical environment and widespread acceptance of racial categories and colonialism make it possible to characterize the period in intellectually rather homogeneous terms, certainly as compared to more recent times. There is not a little irony in that a period that brought about two world wars was also one in which there was a wide sharing of basic ideas among political geographers in the different countries that spent so much effort preparing for war and warring with one another.

The founders and their critics

Friedrich Ratzel and Politische Geographie

Friedrich Ratzel (1844–1904), like many university geographers of his generation in Germany and elsewhere, was trained in the natural sciences. He studied at the universities of Heidelberg, Jena, and Berlin. After a career as a journalist, he occupied the chair in Geography at the University of Leipzig from 1886 until his death. He lived through the process of German unification and this experience sets him apart from writers who preceded him and those who came after. As a graduate student he was exposed to evolutionary biology in the lectures of Ernst Haeckel and later established a close friendship with the biologist Moritz Wagner, who emphasized the impact of isolation and migration in the creation of species. Space and environmental determinism, then, were central themes of the biology to which Ratzel was exposed. Not surprisingly, therefore, his major work of 1881, the two volume *Anthropogeographie*, placed his new human geography in a naturalistic framework drawn from Wagner's work. His magnum opus *Politische Geographie* of 1897 was similarly oriented (Livingstone, 1992: 199).

Ratzel, however, was also a newspaper correspondent who traveled widely, not least in North America, and wrote prolifically. At his death he left behind a bibliography of around 1250 items, including 24 books, over 540 articles, more than 600 book reviews, and 146 short biographies (Kasperson and Minghi, 1969: 6). Ratzel wrote on a wide range of topics and tended to write in an aggressive manner without much use of caveats or qualifiers. Like many who fancy themselves as 'writers' more than communicators, he wrote in a style that sacrificed clarity for effect. This has made his work subject to much controversy over the meaning that can be ascribed to terms that he used and the overall nature of his arguments. He was often inconsistent in his statements about a given term, such as 'organism,' for example; sometimes giving a strong biological sense to the term and on other occasions implying a weaker analogy.

Two features of Ratzel's political geography seem clear, however. One is that he proposed to reorganize Geography in its entirety around the geography of the state. In this sense his founding of political geography is a refounding of Geography as a whole. Places, regions, spaces, landscapes, and all the other concepts that were associated with geographical thinking are now subordinated to the state. The state is 'the greatest achievement of man on earth' and the 'climax of all phenomena connected to the spread of life' (Ratzel, 1923: p. iv, p. 2). In this sense his work of 1881, often read as a separate enterprise, inexorably leads to that of 1897. The second is that the 'political' in political geography is restricted to the state. Not for Ratzel the idea that the political pervades society. The 'aristocratic–bourgeois' state (Farinelli, 2001) had come to dominate society and Ratzel acknowledged the tight relationship that thereby existed between geographical knowledge, on the one hand, and statehood, on the other. He was openly acknowledging the role that Geography must play in undergirding the 'new' state in order to be both relevant and legitimate in the eyes of the state-holders. Geographical knowledge must always serve some political project; now was the time of the nation-state.

Something of the flavor of Ratzel's political geography is captured by listing the contents by chapter heading of his *Politische Geographie* (1897) book: 1. The State and the soil; 2. The historical movement and development of States; 3. The basic laws of the spatial development of States; 4. The position; 5. The space; 6. The boundary; 7. The relations between soils and water; 8. Mountains and plains. Unlike most previous political theorists who had regarded states and other polities as legal–political entities, Ratzel, attracted by the biological reductionism that was all the vogue at the time, conceived of the state as strictly analogous to a living organism, whose territory fluctuated over time depending upon its social and demographic vitality.

Ratzel's political geography is usually presented as organized around seven 'laws' of the spatial growth of states. The best version of this perspective in English is a translation of Ratzel's 'Die Gesetze des räumlichen Wachstums der Staaten,' *Petermann's Mitteilungen*, 52(1896), 97–107 (Kasperson and Minghi, 1969: 17–28).

This is more readily understandable than the more extended but elliptical discussion in *Politische Geographie*. Reduced to simple statements the seven 'laws' or tendencies, because that seems to be the sense in which Ratzel is writing, are as follows: (1) the size of a state grows with its culture; (2) the growth of states follows other manifestations of the growth of peoples, which must necessarily precede the growth of the state; (3) the growth of the state proceeds by the annexation of smaller members into the aggregate. At the same time the relationship of the population to the land becomes continuously closer; (4) the boundary is the peripheral organ of the state, the bearer of its growth as well as its fortification, and takes part in all of the transformations of the organism of the state; (5) in its growth the state strives towards the envelopment of politically valuable positions; (6) the first stimuli to the spatial growth of states come to them from outside; (7) the general tendency toward territorial annexation and amalgamation is transmitted from state to state and continually increases in intensity.

Whatever the ambiguities in how Ratzel understood the terms 'law' and 'organism,' it seems undeniable that his vision of the state as an expanding organism was based on the ideal of a *Grossraum* (or large space) as indicative of state dynamism and vitality. Thus he asserted, under the first law, that:

> Just as the area of the state grows with its culture, so too do we find that at lower
> levels of civilization peoples are organized in small states. In fact, the further we
> descend in levels of civilization, the smaller become the states. Thus the size of a
> state also becomes one of the measures of its cultural level. (Ratzel, in Kasperson
> and Minghi, 1969: 19)

By this reasoning Ratzel conjoined naturalistic reasoning about the imperative of bigness with the political goal of German state-building and imperial expansion. Of course, this contradicted the conventional philosophy of the nation-state in its stress on ethnic homogeneity and careful territorial delineation. But it conformed to both the social safety-valve theory of the settlement frontier provided by Frederick Jackson Turner at the same time in the United States and to the imperialist political mood of the 1890s. Following the logic of Malthus on population and resources but combining this with themes current in evolutionary biology, Ratzel used the biological analogy of the state as an organism which, as its population grew, was subject to resource exhaustion, and thus had to expand or die. In other words:

> Ratzel believed he had disclosed the natural laws of the territorial growth of states
> and he happily located the contemporary thrust of the European powers in Africa

as the manifestation of their quest for *Lebensraum* [living space]. Imperial history was the spatial story of a struggle for existence. (Livingstone, 1992: 200)

Ratzel's naturalism can be overplayed. His work was as much inspired by the imperialism of the age and euphoria over German unification as by the intellectual attraction to ideas from evolutionary biology. Naturalism provided a convenient shell in which to wrap what was in many respects a remarkably idealist enterprise. This was a point first made, to my knowledge, by Jean Gottmann (1952). *Politische Geographie* and other works are filled with language that could have sprung from the pages of Fichte or Hegel, notwithstanding the equally frequent use of biological metaphors. For example, Ratzel tries to connect the spatial growth of the state to the development of what he calls popular spatial consciousness or space conceptions; 'organic' has the sense of the individuality of the *Volk* as much as something akin to an organism; and land and people constitute a natural whole once the people (nation) is rescued from its distress (*Not*) (Dijkink, 2001).

Long seen as one of the founders of modern political geography, Ratzel's reputation has suffered through guilt by association with the later German geopoliticians and Nazi expansionism. What connected them was an idealist understanding of the state wrapped in the materialist garb of evolutionary biology. What separated them was the kind of biology they emphasized: the role of external environmental circumstances for Ratzel, genetic racial characteristics for the Nazis.

Mackinder and his geopolitical model

Halford Mackinder (1861–1947) shared Ratzel's interests in presenting geography as a science that explained human phenomena in naturalized terms and in serving contemporary imperialism. In this case, of course, the imperialism was that of Britain, the status quo Great Power, rather than the upstart Germany. Mackinder used the term 'political geography' loosely to refer to human geography in general. This usage is deeply revealing of the degree to which Mackinder, like Ratzel, was committed to a 'useful' geography, 'geography as an aid to statecraft,' that while transcending the nature/culture divide also served the political goal of 'reason of state:' educating the British population about the world they lived in and the political threats its empire faced because of the rise of hostile powers (particularly Germany) and technological changes (such as the coming of the railroad) that challenged the global dominance of a maritime–commercial empire such as the British.

Mackinder was a publicist for academic geography and a national politician as much as a professional university geographer. Educated in biology at Oxford, he had a number of important credits to his name: first academic appointee in geography at Oxford University, head of Reading College (later University) (1892–1903), the first ascent of Mount Kenya (1899), Director of the London School of Economics (1903–08), Conservative-Unionist MP (1910–22), and British High Commissioner to southern Russia during the early part of the Russian Civil War (1919–20). As a figure in the history of geography in general and political geography in particular he is famous mainly for three publications. The first is an address to the Royal Geographical Society (RGS) in London in 1887, entitled 'On the scope and methods of geography,' which makes a strong case for geography as 'bridge' of understanding between natural and human worlds. This sees the whole of what today would be called human geography as political geography, suggesting that it was in service to the state that Geography would overcome its potential bifurcation into two parts. In this respect, Ratzel and Mackinder were equally imperialistic about political geography's position within Geography as well as in relation to world politics.

The second paper, also delivered as an address to the RGS, this time in 1904, and the paper which establishes him as a 'founder' of political geography, is 'The geographical pivot of history.' Revised on a number of subsequent occasions, this paper argues that sea-power was declining in relation to land-power, as a result of the coming of the railroad, and there was now a pivotal area, 'in the closed Heartland of Euro-Asia,' that was likely to become the seat of world power (see Figure 3.1). Only intervention to keep the pivot out of the hands of a continental power could avoid this outcome. Otherwise, the ready accessibility of the rest of Eurasia to the Power controlling the pivot would lead to that Power's domination over the rest of the world. This argument had obvious implications for the sustainability of the British Empire, dependent as it was on control over the world's sea lanes and maritime access to India and elsewhere around the edges of the great Eurasian land mass.

Mackinder's third well-known publication, his book *Democratic Ideals and Reality* (1919), builds a more fully formed political geography. Here Central Europe emerges as crucial to the global balance of power. While this developed his already stated pivot idea into a more expanded 'Heartland' concept, much of the book offered more interesting prognostications about the increasing centralization of political power and the temptation this provided for the rise of 'ruthless organizers' committed to manipulating semi-educated populations for 'non-democratic ends.'

Mackinder is a founder of political geography, even though he himself refused to countenance sub-fields of geography, for several reasons. First, he used physical-geographical conditions, or 'realities' as he saw them, to make strong

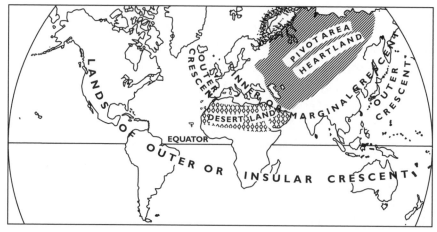

Figure 3.1 Mackinder's 'Heartland' model.
Source: *Mackinder (1904: 424)*

claims about the course and prospects of world politics. His geopolitical model of sea- versus land-power was designed for the ages, even though he used it to make policy prescriptions for the British Empire. This raises the question of the limits of the determinism implicit in the physical 'realities' he described. Indeed, rather like Ratzel, Mackinder used naturalized claims to further a decidedly idealist purpose. In Mackinder's case this was 'warning' about what would happen to the British Empire if nature was allowed to take its course! Mackinder was a reluctant environmental determinist.

Second, Mackinder was a 'man of action.' He was not primarily a reflective scholar. Rather, in all his activities he was a reformer, devoted to the 'cause' of Geography as a subject and to the British Empire as a political-economic project. His writings all have a 'manifesto quality' to them, as noted by his biographer Brian Blouet (1987). His major papers were designed for oral delivery to august gatherings. He managed to boil down his messages to simple axioms, such as his famous adage from *Democratic Ideals and Reality* (1919: 150):

Who rules East Europe commands the Heartland:
Who rules the Heartland commands the World-Island:
Who rules the World-Island commands the World.

This combination of political purpose and simple formulae was important in publicizing Mackinder's ideas, which became better known among politicians and non-geographers than those of other contemporary geographers (Parker, 1982;

Blouet, 1987). Strangely, Mackinder does not receive even a single mention any-where in a book published in 1994 to arouse interest in the founding connection between Geography and empire (Godlewska and Smith, 1994). Yet, there is hardly a better candidate for making this connection come to life than Halford Mackinder.

Finally, Mackinder's ideas, particularly that of the pivot, have seemed to have a prescient quality to them that later generations have found attractive. They take world politics out of the realm of the historically contingent and into the realm of the geographically predictable. Geography trumps history. Not only was the pivot idea picked up by German writers in the 1920s, though put to very different pur-pose than Mackinder would have licensed, but the US policy of 'containing' the Soviet Union after World War II could be seen as finding its 'scientific' basis in Mackinder's Heartland thesis (as in Gray, 1989).

It is a mistake, however, to see Mackinder simply as Ratzel's lost British twin. Even though their views share a common grounding in the biological rhetoric of the time, this is much more muted in Mackinder than in Ratzel. Mackinder was much more oriented to the British Empire as a political–economic concern than as a biological organism (see the previous discussion of economic nationalism). His 'spatial determinism' privileged the distribution of continents and oceans more than climatic or racial characteristics of different areas. Indeed, his emphasis on the pivot could be criticized for ignoring the climatic and resource deficiencies of that region. Thus, in his writings Mackinder largely avoids the extreme environ-mental determinism that Ratzel's American and other disciples (such as Ellen Churchill Semple, Ellsworth Huntington, and Griffith Taylor) made their stock-in-trade. This is not to say that he had anything other than conventional views about race and development. They did not figure prominently, however, in any of his writings. Critics of Mackinder for his 'imperialism,' such as H.J. Fleure, tended to have much more deterministic views of climate and race.

Mackinder also saw himself as a political reformer; using his geopolitical model to proffer political advice to the 'Prince.' That he was hardly a political radical goes without saying. His notion of 'democracy' is hierarchical and paternalistic. But he had an activist view of the state akin to that of social democrats of the time more than to that of the typical conservative. But the statism he espoused was a pecu-liarly English one. Mackinder was active intellectually at a time when attempts were under way in England to avoid both Idealist tendencies to reify the state and individualist (and liberal) tendencies to decry the state altogether (Bentley, 1996: 52–3). The new thinking might acknowledge that the state had its territory and that it needed a large one, even an empire. But it also insisted, as did Mackinder, that states are made up of a patchwork of smaller regions or territories with their own characteristics and that the boundaries of the state provided a 'rampart' behind which social and political goals could be pursued. In this respect, Mackinder was closer to the thinking of Patrick Geddes, Sidney and Beatrice Webb, H.G. Wells, and other English 'Fabian' reformers than to that of Ratzel and his acolytes. Mackinder's context and that of Ratzel were not the same, therefore, however much we might see similar attempts to integrate the physical and the human by using the organic-evolutionary language of Lamarck and Darwin.

The crucial feature of Mackinder's political geography – lost in most discussions of his geopolitical model – was the effort to square two aspects of the British Empire that had become increasingly contradictory by the 1890s. After all, his political geography was directly inspired by the cause of Empire. On one side was the Empire's British aspect: empire as commerce, as maritime power, as democratic or free, and as expansive. On the other was its imperial and transnational aspect: empire as military conquest, as multireligious, as serving Britain, and as based on racial and social hierarchy. Mackinder portrayed the British Empire as a sort of 'community of fate' in which all of its residents somehow did or could share in its fruits. But this position was untenable. There was no way to create an imperial identity that integrated the two versions of empire. An enterprise based on social and geographical inequality could not be turned into an homogeneous entity with an all-encompassing purpose. In emphasizing the role of the Other, of the pivot or Heartland, as an external threat, he missed clearly identifying what it was that might keep the Empire he so dearly loved together as a viable enterprise. That its disintegration might happen more from within than from without because of the untenability of its imperial identity never seems to have occurred to him.

Vidal's critical response

French human geography was founded, it can be said, as a rejection of 'political geography' after the style of Ratzel (Robic, 1994). Yet, in its major early works, such as Paul Vidal de la Blache's *Tableau de la géographie de la France* (1903), the entire focus is on France as a national unit. If anything, Vidal's later work, such as *France de l'est* (1917) is even more concerned with the French national question. What accounts for this seeming paradox?

Vidal's approach is important both as a reflection of the time in which he wrote but also for the alternative conception of political geography he provided. Contrary to Ratzel and Mackinder, who turned human geography into political geography, Vidal did the opposite. Vidal wrote in the aftermath of France's defeat in the Franco-Prussian War and at a time of intense conflict in France between church and state. He seems to have shared the naturalistic approach to knowledge of his German and English contemporaries, even down to a penchant for Lamarckian ideas of evolution (Archer, 1993). He certainly was not, as some recent commentators have alleged, the advocate of the 'humanistic' perspective. But he tended to apply the idea of naturalistic evolution to 'regions' or to 'civilizations,' rather than to states. He also inherited the French tendency, in Dumont's (1983) words, to say 'I am a man by nature and French by accident,' whereas the German variant had become 'I am a man because I am a German.' This is a profound cultural difference and one that accounts, to this day, for differences between France and Germany in conceptions of citizenship, with the latter having a more ethnic and less 'civilizational' (do you speak French?) definition.

The net effect was to realize a conception of political geography antithetical to that of Ratzel. In the first place, Vidal downplayed the importance of national boundaries. Rather, he insisted on the historical contingency and openness of France's boundaries. Indeed, to Vidal, France's peculiarity lay in its fusion of diverse parts rather than as an essential primordial unity. This insight provided the inspiration for the French tradition of electoral geography begun by André Siegfried (1913), one of the founders of modern French political science.

Second, Vidal saw French national identity not in terms of ethnicity or direct environmental constraints but in the fusion of forms of life (*genres de vie*) around national *genius loci*. This historical process is much more than the history of the extension of political power by the state. It is rather the cultural conversion of 'peasants into Frenchmen,' to adopt the title of Eugen Weber's (1967) much later book. In this respect, Vidal is the intellectual descendant of the eighteenth century philosopher Herder who claimed that people bore the 'mark' of the country in which they live (Claval, 1994). Yet, this was not a question of choice. It was how 'nature' manifested itself in human life.

Third, Vidal shared the widespread fear among French elites that France was in decline as a Great Power (Heffernan, 1994). His culturally expansive view of Frenchness, therefore, could be used to sanction colonial expansion. Of course, the task was thus cast as a *mission civilisatrice* more than a conquest.

Finally, in the *Tableau* Vidal prefers the qualifier 'human' to 'political' because he believes that the 'economic' is becoming more important and the idea of separating out the political from other aspects of life thus makes less sense than it once did. So, though Vidal uses 'France' as the milieu for his human geography, he is actively denying the total state-centrism that animates the political geography of Ratzel and Mackinder. Notwithstanding the contextual specificities of his work, Vidal offered the beginning of an enlarged conception of the 'political' – beyond the geography of the state – even as he opposed the idea of a field of political geography as such.

Reclus: human geopolitics?

If Vidal provided a critique of Ratzel's political geography from a French culturalist perspective, there were others who offered more radical perspectives than the dominant views. One such person was Elisée Reclus. A supporter of the revolutionary Paris Commune in 1870, Reclus articulated a much more human-centered geography than that of his contemporaries. In his major work, *L'homme et la terre* (1905–08), he identified 'natural regions,' produced by history, language, and lifestyle (*genre de vie*), that are also riven by social conflicts because of inequalities in wealth and power. Class struggle and the increased consciousness of individuals about their capacity to produce change lead to social change. But it is through human agency that inequalities within and between regions can balance out or create equilibrium. It is from 'human beings that the creative will to construct and reconstruct the world is born' (Reclus, 1905–08: Preface).

Resisting the tendency to reify the state, Reclus was able to offer a perspective that liberated politics from obsession with the state. The weakness of Reclus's geography lay in failing to see that ignoring the state did not undermine it. Recognizing the rise and importance of nation-states in the contemporary world might have made his perspective more persuasive. As an anarchist, however, his normative rejection of the state led him to downplay its analytical significance. At the same time, he was also compromised by his strange defense of French colonialism in North Africa, even as he railed against imperialism in general (Heffernan, 1994). A utopian imperialism thus coexisted with a utopian fixation on a stateless world. This was not a good basis for an alternative political geography, therefore, notwithstanding its critique of the global political status quo.

Wilsonianism and American political geography

Before World War I and in the years following extreme environmental determinism ruled the roost among most American geographers. Figures such as Ellsworth Huntington, Robert De Courcy Ward, and Ellen Churchill Semple represented the establishment in US geography of the naturalized conception of knowledge at its most undiluted (Livingstone,1972). Turner's frontier thesis, about how the experience of the European settlement frontier sweeping across North America had made American society distinctive, echoed this type of reasoning. Ideas of racial hierarchy and the need to restrict American immigration for fear of 'racial degradation' were widely shared among intellectuals and well-established immigrants, particularly those from north-western Europe. American doctrines and laws governing 'race mixing' and eugenics – involving forced sterilization and marriage controls applied to groups deemed 'inferior' – struck the German Nazis as useful prototypes for what they had in mind (Kühl, 1994).

Though popular among the north-eastern elites (and at universities such as Harvard, Yale, and Vassar), because they could be used to justify why 'north-west Europeans' ran everything in the country, these ideas did not always sit well with other features of the 'American experience.' In particular, since the Revolution, with a boost after the Civil War of 1860–64, American political ideology had emphasized two differences between the United States and the Old World (of Europe) that made environmental (and racial) determinism both historically and morally problematic (Rosenberg, 1982).

The first was an emphasis on free commerce and the ideal of a pacific nation. Here were the main ingredients of American exceptionalism: open frontiers, pacific trade, and no standing armies, only militias. Anchored in an individualistic liberalism, this element of popular thought was antithetical to the statism of contemporary Europe. The second was the idea of the United States as a 'social experiment.' If not without powerful contradictions, in particular the virulent racism associated with the history of American slavery, this reflected the view of the United States as a place for 'fresh starts:' people coming from elsewhere and making their lives over or moving around within the country to achieve new beginnings.

Woodrow Wilson, president of the United States from 1913 to 1921, though a white southerner sympathetic to the interpretation of post-Civil War American history in D.W. Griffith's notorious pro-Ku Klux Klan 1915 film *The Birth of a Nation*, was intellectually and politically committed to the vision of American exceptionalism. People, even leading intellectuals, are not always consistent. Wilson was committed to an American 'mission' in the world. He believed that the territorial nature of America was fulfilled, once it had reached the Pacific and defined fairly stable boundaries with Canada and Mexico. America now stood as 'model' for the rest of the world: 'the more democracies there were in the world, the wider America's ideological hegemony would spread. A world dominated by liberal capitalism would be the ultimate shield for the American republic' (Perlmutter, 1997: 32). The most important reflection of this ideology was to be the League of Nations and a world politics based on collective security enforced by international treaties. But Wilson was no political innocent: 'Wilson was one of the first American Machiavellian presidents. He may have seemed naïve, moralistic, and evangelistic, yet he initiated the first American covert actions, and his interventions in Mexico in 1913 and in the Russian Revolution in 1919 demonstrate that this professor of politics from Princeton was no saint' (Perlmutter, 1997: 34).

It is in this context that a truly American political geography began. It is associated above all with the figure of Isaiah Bowman (1878–1950). Chief territorial advisor on the American Commission to the Paris Peace Conference in 1919 and Director of the American Geographical Society, and after 1935 President of Johns Hopkins University, Bowman shifted the focus of political geography from generic, largely speculative arguments about statehood to the empirical structure of state territories. Two influences appear crucial in Bowman's work: the American experience as a model for the world as a whole and the view of World War I as a disaster produced by competitive militarism. In his 1921 book, *The New World: Problems in Political Geography*, Bowman focused on the aftermath of that war and proposed a common framework of analysis for each of 35 countries and world regions (from boundaries and economic conditions to pressing political problems and demography): a gazetteer of politically-relevant conditions around the world. This was as much a recapitulation of the old nineteenth-century state geography suited to the new times as it was a reaction against the environmental determinism of Ellsworth Huntington and other American 'neo-Ratzelians.' In fact, Bowman seems to have been ambiguous about how far to go in abandoning the environmental determinism with which he had been raised at Harvard as a student of William Morris Davis (Livingstone, 1992: 250). But he is important in political geography because for him it was the scientific 'neutrality' of naturalism that was most appealing rather than the specific role of this or that biological factor *per se*. In this regard Bowman is an early American 'policy scientist,' deploying his knowledge as a problem-solver for US 'national interests.'

This inventory approach developed by Bowman became common in textbooks published from the 1920s until the years after World War II, indicating the lasting influence that Bowman had on the field (see, for example, Boggs, 1940; Pearcy and Fifield, 1948). Although written from an American perspective, the focus in Bowman's book on the problems arising from dramatic change in the structural characteristics of states (new boundaries, new ethnic distributions, new communication patterns, etc.) could be seen as practical in nature: offering solutions to real-world problems rather than engaging in theoretical speculation. It thus appealed to the pragmatic imagination of many Americans while fitting into the project of offering a 'new world order' in which problems would be solved rationally (i.e. non-militarily) by the application of systematic knowledge. During World War II Bowman was a strong proponent of rolling back or limiting European colonialism once the war was over (Smith, 1994).

EXTRACTS FROM

THE NEW WORLD (1928 Edition)

To face the problems of the day, the men who compose the government of the United States need more than native common sense and the desire to deal fairly with others. They need, above all, to give scholarly consideration to the geographical and historical materials that go into the making of that web of fact, relationship, and tradition that we call foreign policy. As we have not a trained and permanent foreign-office staff, our administrative principles are still antiquated. Thus even our loftiest intentions are often defeated ... (p. iii)

In the eventual history of the period in which we live, it is reasonable to think that the greatest emphasis will be put not upon the World War or the peace treaties that closed it, searching and complex and revolutionary as their terms proved to be, but rather upon the profound change that took place in the spiritual and mental attitudes of the people that compose this new world. There came into being a critical spirit of inquiry into causes, of challenge to a world inherited from the past, of profound distrust of many existing institutions. The effects of the war were so far-reaching that it was indeed a new world in which men found themselves ... (p. 1)

Love of country does not mean hatred for other countries. Patriotism should mean pride in the works of idealism of one's own country. If it has advanced law and order, regional cooperation, international good will; if it has protected the weak, advanced the arts of peace; if its influence has been beneficent – all of these things one can be proud of. But blind patriotism spoiling for a fight is now one of the most dangerous things in the world precisely because the world is now highly organized and war strikes at the very means and spirit of organization and the cooperative process. (pp. 5–6)

Bowman's general orientation was developed further by others, such as Derwent Whittlesey (at Harvard), Stephen Jones (at Yale), and Richard Hartshorne (at Wisconsin), with the difference that these figures tended to see 'political area studies' more as special cases of regions defined by political processes such as 'the impress of central authority' (Whittlesey) and 'centripetal and centrifugal forces' (Hartshorne) than in entirely descriptive terms. What unites them is antipathy to the deterministic as opposed to the conditioning role of physical conditions and a predilection for American-style commercial expansion as opposed to the territorial imperialism of the Europeans.

But an older environmental determinism lived on in some writing, particularly textbooks, in the use of physical–biological analogies applied to world politics. For example, Samuel Van Valkenburg, Professor of Geography at Clark University in Worcester, Massachusetts, published a textbook in 1939 dedicated to Isaiah Bowman, containing rather positive opinions about the influence of political geography in Germany, even though the author declares himself 'a firm believer in democracy' (p. viii), giving first billing to the 'physical element' in political geography (ahead of the economic and human elements), using France as an 'example' of political geography with an entire section devoted to 'Colonies,' and adapting the Harvard physical geographer William Morris Davis's 'stage theory' of physical-landscape evolution to 'the political pattern of the world.' The stage theory, however, seems largely a descriptive device more than an explanation, even though Van Valkenburg does use the word 'explanation.' After proposing it, he seems to back away from making much of it. One hopes that students noted this signal lack of enthusiasm for what had been proposed.

EXTRACT FROM VAN VALKENBURG

ELEMENTS OF POLITICAL GEOGRAPHY (1939)

Is there an explanation for political stability and instability? The world at present offers many examples of countries that want to bring about political changes, while others seem to be satisfied with the existing conditions and defend the status quo. The terms, 'have countries' and 'have-not countries' are well known, as are also the tendencies of some of the 'have nots' to become 'haves.' This division of states into two groups is not satisfactory because several 'have nots' seem to be perfectly satisfied, while some of the 'haves' claim

(continued)

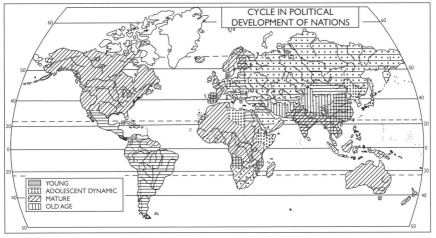

Figure 3.2 Van Valkenburg's 'cycle in political development of nations.'
Source: *Van Valkenburg (1939: figure 2)*

more. The author, perfectly aware of the danger of generalization, neverthe-less has the courage to present another explanation for the interrelations between countries and the changes in the political world pattern. This expla-nation is based on a cycle in the political development of nations, recognizing four stages, namely youth, adolescence, maturity, and old age (see Figure 3.2). After completion the cycle may renew itself, possibly with a change in political extension, while the cycle can also be interrupted any time and brought back to a former stage. The time element (the length of a stage) differs greatly from nation to nation and depends on the character of the state; correspondingly no forecast can be made on the time of shift to a next stage. ... (p. 5)

Space, race and expansion

If the increased physical size of a state was for Ratzel one consequence of greater national 'vitality,' for Rudolf Kjellén (1864–1922), the Swedish political scientist who first coined the word 'geopolitics,' it was the logical outcome of an inevitable compe-tition for power between states. This idea and allied ones, such as the 'geopolitical instinct' that linked national populations to their states, attracted the attention of some geographers in post-World War I Germany. Active in nationalist and later Nazi circles, these geographers formed the so-called school of German geopolitics. This school of *Geopolitik* joined Ratzel's organic conception of the state as refined by Kjellén to Mackinder's global strategic model. This lethal intellectual brew appealed to Karl Haushofer (1869–1946), the leader of the school, and his followers because it offered a simple explanation of Germany's plight after World War I and a seeming solution to it. On the one hand, the terms exacted following Germany's defeat ignored the long-term challenge that Germany posed to Britain and the global status quo. On the other hand, the expansion of Germany as a populous state at the expense of less vital neighbors was justified by its need for *Lebensraum* or living space.

One of the formalized schemes that Haushofer and his colleagues came up with was for combining imperial and colonized peoples within what they called 'pan-regions.' However fanciful in terms of the possibility of overcoming the actual global distribution of power at the time, this mapping did express in extreme form the common assumption that the world was made of racial groupings that could be neatly divided into two 'types' of peoples. The one (the colonized) existed to serve the other (the colonizers) (see Figure 3.3).

The influence of Haushofer and his colleagues is the subject of considerable debate. Although the Nazi takeover in 1933 and subsequent absolute rule gave prestige to *Geopolitik*, its tenets were not exactly at one with the increasingly strident racism and anti-Semitism of the regime. Indeed, *Geopolitik* looked to alliance with the Soviet Union (realized briefly beginning in 1939 but then dashed by the German invasion of the Soviet Union in 1941), saw central Europe in terms of multiethnic federation, and, at least until the 1930s, paid little or no attention to the 'racial question.' These ideas can hardly be seen as lying behind Nazi policy. Indeed, other German geographers, such as Albrecht Penck, can be seen as more important and influential in their emphasis on the need to 'unify' the scattered pockets of ethnic-German settlement to the east, define 'natural' frontiers for Germany more realistic than those of Weimar (post-World War I) Germany, and turn Germany from the 'bourgeois' state it had become into a revitalized *völkisch Reich*. But even Penck did not offer the fatal mix of anti-Semitism, racial purity, anti-Bolshevism (Communism), and *Lebensraum* as a racial concept that Hitler, as the maker and guardian of Nazi thought, came to pursue.

What unified Haushofer, on one side, and Penck, on the other, with the Nazis and other German nationalists, was a resentment about the terms of the Treaty of Versailles and the negative effects they had had on German society, particularly economic reparations and boundary adjustments such as the 'Danzig corridor' in Poland and the return of Alsace-Lorraine to France. They used geographical ideas

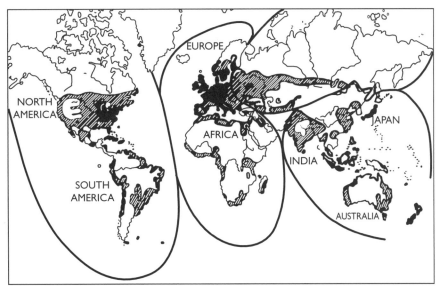

Figure 3.3 Karl Haushofer's pan-region model.
Source: O'Loughlin and Van der Wusten (1990: 3)

to articulate their nationalist concerns. Penck (1916: 227) had put their position most vividly when he wrote: 'Knowledge is power, geographical knowledge is world-power.' Yet Haushofer also believed, like Ratzel and Mackinder before him, that his geopolitical ideas had a more general validity. In this he was a true heir to the strange alliance of naturalized knowledge and idealist intention apparent in Ratzel's political geography. He did not see himself as simply a propagandist for an expansive Germany. Claude Raffestin (2001) plausibly claims that Carl Schmitt's friend–enemy political ontology is basic to the geopolitical cartography engaged in by Haushofer and his collaborators. The use of geometrical symbols and arrows not only reduces places to points on a plane of 'pure politics' (to use a term of Schmitt's) but also universalizes what otherwise would be seen as maps representing Germany's 'unique' situation. With respect to the translation of geography into strategy, the god-like view from nowhere implicit in the maps used by the German geopoliticians represented an attempt to forecast the balance of power between competing states rather than analyze the geographical contexts of these states in their complexity (Raffestin, 2001: 32).

In other countries, such as Japan and Italy, with similar resentments about their global status, analogous forms of geopolitical thinking also developed in the aftermath of World War I. In Italy, the fascist dictatorship of Mussolini was inspired by resentment at the postwar territorial settlement in Europe, the instability of the liberal regime, and the idea of recreating the ancient Roman Empire anew in twentieth-century Italy (Gambi, 1994). 'The new Italy must be prepared confidently to reassert its historic role at the heart of a new Europe' (Heffernan, 1998: 139). Interestingly, it took some time for an explicit Italian geopolitics to develop. In fact, only in 1939 did a journal devoted to Italian geopolitics finally appear. Partly this reflected divisions among leading Fascists over the relative emphasis to place on the Roman heritage and territorial expansion versus the creation of a more self-sufficient Italian national economy. It also reflected the incoherence of fascism as an ideology based as it was more on what it was opposed to – anti-socialist, anti-democratic, anti-parliamentary, etc. – than on what it stood for. But it also represented the fact that Italian fascism aspired to European leadership through the spread of fascism to other European countries. Both German geopolitics and Nazism never had, indeed could not have had, this aspiration.

Unlike German *geopolitik*, Italian geopolitics had a Mediterranean more than a Eurasian and global focus, largely eschewed any kind of racial argument, and tended to emphasize fascism as an ideology that other countries could adopt more than Italian national 'superiority.' What it shared with the Germans was a style of presentation, particularly the use of suggestive maps casting Italian territorial claims in the most positive light, and an affinity for some of the quasi-mystical elements of the Roman past and its imperial heritage of some leading Fascists. One of the main figures in Italian geopolitics, Ernesto Massi, rehabilitated himself within Italian geography after World War II, becoming President of the *Società Geografica Italiana* (Italian Geographical Society). Though he remained active within the Italian neo-fascist movement, he adapted to the 'new Europe' by becoming an exponent of European unification and Italy's place within it. In fact, the old fascist vision of Europe and the new Europe, shorn of colonial enterprise, may not be all that far apart, particularly if the European Union fails to adequately democratize. Massi did not have to change that much at all to find a place for himself in postwar Italian political geography. Haushofer would have had a harder time.

Geopolitics versus political geography

'Geopolitics,' whether that of Mackinder or in later manifestations influenced by Ratzel and Kjellén, was never without its critics. To some the 'orthodox' interpretations were unsound. The Dutch-American political scientist Nicholas Spykman

(1944), for example, reversed Mackinder's logic, arguing that control over the 'rimland' of Eurasia and not the Heartland was crucial. Others saw North America as an emerging global core, particularly with the advent of air-power (e.g. de Seversky, 1950). During World War II there were many calls for the development of an 'American' geopolitics to challenge the German variety pointing to the strategic advantages of an 'insular' North America. Karl Wittfogel (1929–1985), German Marxist and author later of *Oriental Despotism* (1957), had criticized geopolitics for ignoring the economic context of Great Power politics and missing the real significance of 'natural factors' in determining the character of political–economic development. But his goal was to prepare a Marxist geopolitics as an alternative to the nationalist varieties. After World War II a much more influential proponent of geopolitics from an American perspective was Edmund Walsh. He combined his role as a trainer of future American diplomats at the Jesuit-run Catholic Georgetown University in Washington DC with a powerful antipathy to the Russian Revolution and to the 'global march of world communism,' as he saw it. Interpreting the conflict between the United States and the Soviet Union in religious apocalyptic terms, Walsh strove to convince American policy-makers and diplomats that this was no mere conflict of secular Powers but 'a struggle between the two great moral opposites' (Walsh, 1952; quoted in Gallagher, 1962: 142; also see Ó Tuathail, 2000a).

To others, however, geopolitics was a vicious mutation of political geography as such. In France, the many students of Vidal de la Blache were particularly hostile (Parker, 2001). They shared the conviction that states could not be studied in isolation from the rest of the phenomena of human geography (cities, agriculture, trade, etc.) They also saw states as reflective of the nations they claimed to represent and subject to changes in purpose and activity as population movements, trade, and other developments challenged and eroded established boundaries between states. Physical features are likewise subject to change in their roles. To Albert Demangeon (with Lucien Febvre, 1935), for example, for most of its history the Rhine had been a force of unity more than an international frontier. To Yves Marie Goblet (1934) the emphasis on change and fluidity in the world political map meant that it is erroneous to treat existing states as if they are permanent fixtures without paying attention to forces of interdependence bringing about changes in the alignment of nations and states that everyone was aware of but failed to theorize. The diversity of political territorial arrangements both historically and geographically rather than an ideal-type statehood thus needed to be center stage in political geography. Geopolitics denied this variety and justified territorial aggrandizement by large states at the expense of small ones. To Jacques Ancel (1936), however, the term geopolitics should be expropriated for other use. To him it was a branch of political geography rather than something distinctive and separate: 'external political geography.' He took issue with the idea of opposing political geography to geopolitics, arguing that French political geography was deficient in emphasizing the internal structure of states at the expense of examining colonialism, Great Power competition, and the geographical organization of international politics. In many respects Ancel's argument is one that would be accepted by most political geographers today. But at the time he wrote he was very much on his own.

In the United States, Bowman (1942) made great play of distinguishing his 'neutral' and 'objective' political geography from 'crudely partisan' geopolitics. Yet his own political geography was strongly committed to the 'partisan' cause of the United States. Bowman and many other university geographers were actively involved in the American war effort (Kirby, 1994). But the rhetoric of science as the basis to policy prescription was vital to Bowman's career and to his image of geography within the American university. Geopolitics, therefore, had to be denied. Yet in so doing the idea that political geography could have anything systematic to say about world politics was also denied simply because Bowman's political geography had no scope for dealing with the subject matter that geopolitics, however problematically and inadequately, did try to address. Ancel's alternative geopolitics was a possibility. Another was the historicist approach to political geography pioneered by Whittlesey (e.g. 1939). These were anathema to Bowman, however, because they departed from the naturalized claim to knowledge upon which his authority as a 'scientist' rested. Sadly, that was, of course, precisely the authority claimed by Haushofer and his cohorts in Germany. 'The territorial border between science and politics was one boundary Bowman just could not map' (Livingstone, 1992: 253).

Conclusion

Ratzel and Mackinder are a looming presence across the first fifty years of modern political geography. They and their major critics constitute the historic canon upon which more recent political geography has built and against which it has often revolted. There are obvious discontinuities and differences across the writings of the various figures I have identified in this chapter. There are, however, a number of important continuities that also provide an important backdrop to what was to happen in political geography after 1945.

The first is the rather unrelenting focus on territorial states as the geographical units *par excellence* of political geography. Though not without its critics (such as Reclus), the enterprise was largely state-oriented almost to the exclusion of political processes operating at other geographical scales and in other ways. The conception of the political was almost entirely statist, with weaker liberal currents eddying around the edges. The 'hard-nosed,' masculinist, and realist conception of the world is here rooted in the geographical facts of an earth that rewards only those who take what they can.

The second is the merging of a naturalized claim to knowledge, based on various mixes of the 'view from nowhere' and biological metaphors, with the idealist goal of serving one's own nation-state. Perhaps only Reclus and Wittfogel stand out as major examples to the contrary; at least in so far as serving a particular state is concerned. Although, by the 1930s, figures such as Owen Lattimore (e.g. 1940) in the United States and Jacques Ancel in France can be seen as offering much more critical perspectives on the conventional wisdom: Lattimore because he was largely self-taught and brought his intimate familiarity with Central Asia to bear in all that he wrote, Ancel because he hoped to counter Nazi geopolitics with a more 'open' version of geopolitics of his own.

The third is a 'problem-solving' orientation that animated all of the major figures. They aspired to influence policy; to whisper in the ear of the Prince, to paraphrase the Renaissance-era Florentine political philosopher and diplomat Machiavelli. Though geared towards establishing a presence within the new universities of the time, this goal could be served only by appearing 'useful' to *raison d'état*. The prospects for political geography were thus tied to the national flag.

The fourth continuity, and one that distances us today so much from the thinking of the time, was the ready acceptance of the language of racial difference and the possible environmental causes of racial divisions. There was no sense of the social construction of racial differences. The American authors, often so critical of European colonialism for its subjugation of other peoples, nevertheless had blind eyes for the reality of American racism at home and in its colonies (such as the Philippines).

The fifth, and final, is that Europe and, to a certain extent, the United States, are seen as being at the center of the world. The rest of the world is ancillary: bit players or pawns in a world politics driven almost entirely by Great Power competition and inter-imperial rivalries. Of course, the world wars of the period did begin in Europe. But the rest of the world had long figured and increasingly did so in the machinations of the powerful. And it did so not just as a passive object of desire for the powerful but as an active participant in both its victimization and its own incipient liberation.

These continuities were not easily transcended. Indeed, elements of all of them live on today in political geography and beyond: an urge to naturalize knowledge claims to grasp the mantle of science, a Euro-American centered view of the world in which all others are seen as backward when compared to a Euro-American based modernity, and the aspiration to influence national policies to underwrite disciplinary success and gain the ear of political leaders. But as the next chapter tries to show, much also changed after World War II.

chapter 4
REVIVAL

The denial of geopolitics by the political geographers of the victorious powers in World War II such as Isaiah Bowman was to prove doubly problematic. Not only did it sever them from considering 'external political geography,' and thus offering advice about foreign relations to their home or other governments, however distant that advice might be from the designs of Haushofer, it also led to a renewed disavowal of the 'political' in political geography, leading to a renewed emphasis on projecting an aura of technical expertise in describing boundary disputes in great detail rather than offering critical perspectives on the great issues of the day. Theory, the Germans had proved, was dangerous. Associating theory with 'speculation' and the politicization of the field, political geography thus rapidly sank into intellectual irrelevance and political obscurity.

Fade-out

As the United States took on a global political role, therefore, American political geographers refused the opportunity to either actively participate in the expanded horizons or provide the intellectual resources to review and critique what rapidly became the American popular wisdom in world affairs. Elsewhere was no better, if not worse. In the Soviet Union political geography did not formally exist, even as a 'practical' political geography was practiced by the political leaders and the higher echelons of the Communist Party in both subduing unrest within the country and stamping out dissent in its new sphere of influence in Eastern Europe. In Western Europe the concern with re-establishing Geography as a university subject led to both disavowal of its association with international politics and a focus on the 'problem-solving' role of the discipline in relation to regional and urban 'problems' that could be addressed technocratically rather than politically.

The political tenor of the times played an important part in the eclipse of political geography. Between 1945 and 1949 a whole new geopolitical order was constructed based on the values, myths, catchwords, and political-economic orientations of the two dominant states: the United States and the Soviet Union. The intellectual genealogy of political geography was ill-suited to this new world. For one thing, in their rhetoric both sides offered different conceptions of the political, on the American side liberal and on the Soviet side Marxist, from the statist one that had long dominated political geography. For another, the entire world was drawn into the bipolar conflict in a way that the world had never been divided previously. But this was seen by all sides as an ideological more than a territorial struggle, even if it had obvious geographical correlates (the 'Iron Curtain' running through Europe, the threefold division of the world into US and allies, the Soviet Union and allies, and a 'Third World' of mainly formerly-colonized countries in which the US and Soviet Union competed for influence, etc.). Of course, a more adaptive field in touch with intellectual currents in adjacent fields such as political science and diplomatic history might have had something of a more positive response. The personal danger of questioning the conventional wisdom needs emphasizing. In the United States, figures who did offer alternative perspectives were likely to receive subpoenas to appear before congressional committees investigating 'Un-American activities' or find difficulty in acquiring academic posts. As it was, in the 1950s nothing very new emerged in political geography in Western Europe and North America that was not based on the conventional wisdom established by Bowman and a small group of fellow-travelers, of whom Richard Hartshorne (1950) and Stephen Jones (1954) were perhaps the most influential.

Most importantly, however, the early Cold War years in the United States saw the explosion of the 'behavioral' view of politics and international relations. From this point of view, the United States provided a global 'norm' of individual and collective behavior against which other parts of the world were compared for the degree of 'abnormality' or deviation from the American norm. From studies of the 'appeals of Communism' (Them) to 'the civic culture' (Us) and 'the authoritarian personality' (Them, again), American social science was redefined in behavioral terms with little or no interest in, even contempt for, structural, historical, or institutional explanations of differences in political attitudes. This 'psychologizing' of politics had no room for the role of geography in any meaningful sense, except as the aggregation of psychological traits and their association with specific states.

As Ron Robin (2001) shows in meticulous detail, a 'military–intellectual complex' came to power in the United States during the Cold War in the most prestigious universities, Harvard, MIT, Stanford, and Yale in the lead, devoted to reducing international and comparative politics to comparative psychological pathology with the US as the healthy mental specimen against which the others were compared and found wanting.

By way of apocryphal example, the paranoid schizophrenia of the John Nash character in the 2001 film *A Beautiful Mind* is plausibly delusional because his paranoia involved the search for 'codes' planted by Soviet agents in the stories of US magazines and newspapers. One can imagine American social scientists of the 1950s doing content analysis of such sources in pursuit of psychological profiles of journalists ('Communist' versus 'free') without any suggestion of madness on their part.

The revitalization of Geography as a whole in the United States in the 1960s had knock-on effects in political geography. A new generation of geographers discovered an interest in the spacing of social forms, such as urban settlements, land uses, and migrant flows. They increasingly addressed these empirically, using the quantitative research methods popular in fields such as economics, demography, and urban sociology. The net effect was to improve the social status of Geography as a university subject, at least among adjacent fields in the social sciences. Though the initial revival was to become the subject of controversy, particularly over theoretical and methodological issues, it did set the scene for a revival of political geography.

The slow erosion of Cold War sensibilities was also very important to the revival. The Civil Rights struggle in the United States and the Vietnam War were key in opening up discussion about the assumptions upon which the Cold War had been based. They drew attention to the contradictions between what the United States stood for in Cold War discourse and the reality, as many people saw it, in the United States and in US government behavior around the world. How true to its self-confessed beliefs about human rights was the United States? Was not the Vietnam War the outcome of a civil war rather than an instance of the global conflict between 'democracy' and 'communism'? In a wide range of fields the Cold War had had intellectually stultifying effects. It had encouraged the idea of a permanently divided globe in which idealized ideological differences between the United States and the Soviet Union were all that mattered. This began to break down in the 1960s. In my opinion, it is no exaggeration to speak of a revival or even a reinvention of political geography as an older generation passed away and was replaced increasingly by a more diverse and intellectually adventurous group of academics coming to intellectual maturity at a time of great social and political change.

As a result, research in political geography began to revive, connecting the field both to other currents within Geography and to relevant work in other disciplines. I find it useful to think of the revival in terms of three intellectual 'waves' sweeping through the field between the 1960s and 1990s: from the spatial-analytic focus of the earlier years (and onwards, because each wave has continued to flow), followed by radical political-economic perspectives in the 1970s and 1980s, and then by postmodern perspectives from the late 1980s.

Overview

In this chapter I want to do several things. First of all, I want to provide some sense of the geopolitical context that political geography had to face after World War II and, with a few exceptions, the irony of having little or anything new to offer in the way of understanding it. I then want to account as best I can for the revival of political geography beginning in the 1960s. This was not a 'one-shot deal' but a cumulative series of influences from both inside and outside the world of universities over the period between the 1960s and the 1990s. Much of the chapter, however, is taken up with laying out and providing examples of the three intellectual 'waves' that I argue have swept through the field and still provide its basic intellectual structure today. I end with a discussion of how the 'edges' between the three sets of perspectives are starting to erode and new perspectives trying to draw from more than one are beginning to emerge. I suggest that the end of the Cold War and the emerging transnational geopolitical order is more than a simple backdrop to this intellectual transition, thus laying the groundwork for Chapter 5: 'The Horizon'.

The Cold War geopolitical context

The total victory of the American–British–Soviet alliance over Nazi Germany and imperial Japan and the deployment of forces it produced in 1945 had two immediate consequences. One was that Soviet influence now extended over Eastern Europe and into Germany. This stimulated both a direct confrontation between the US and the Soviet Union and a continuing US military presence in Europe to 'contain' possible Soviet expansion. The US, concerned about revitalizing world trade and American economic development, needed to protect and aid potential allies in order to meet its goals. The other consequence was that there was little major opposition in the US to a 'forward' US presence in Europe and, increasingly, elsewhere around the world. Unlike after World War I, when the United States turned its back on a major global role, this time there seemed little alternative. Europe and Japan were physically and psychologically devastated. What domestic opposition there was, on both left and right, rapidly disappeared after 1947 with the Soviet subversion of Czech democracy, the view that Greece, Italy, and France, in different ways, faced the prospect of possible Soviet-leaning governments, the 'loss' of China to Communist revolution in 1949, and the fear that economic chaos abroad would have extremely negative effects in the United States itself.

Such activities as the Marshall Plan for European economic recovery, the founding of NATO to coordinate military planning between Western Europe and North America, and the institution of such organizations as the General Agreement on Tariffs and Trade (GATT) and those emanating from the Bretton Woods Agreement of 1944 (in particular, the IMF and the World Bank) represent major American initiatives to construct a new world order beyond the territory controlled by the Soviet Union. The logic of this approach was that military expenditures would provide a protective shield for increased trade across international boundaries. This would, in turn, redound to American advantage. Making this possible, however, required establishing globally those institutions and practices that had already developed in the United States, such as: mass production/consumption in industrial organization; electoral democracy; limited state welfare policies; and government policies geared towards indirect stimulation of private economic activities. Taken as a whole, these features constitute an 'embedded liberalism' that it was believed by American leaders would provide both economic growth around the world and protect the United States from the political-economic threat posed by the Soviet Union.

Under the dictatorship of Stalin from 1943 to 1947 the Soviet Union constructed a formidable military economy that required as its premise the existence of a major external threat. The recent experience of invasion by Nazi Germany meant that the idea of external danger was not hard to sell to the Soviet population. Associated with this sense of external threat was a popular identification with regimes and revolutionary movements that were opposed to the reinstatement of capitalism-as-usual around the world. Within the Soviet bloc, the fear of the United States was used to justify an incredibly brutal repression of political dissent through a vast system of concentration camps (the so-called *gulag*). 'Enemies of the people' could be sent away on the flimsiest of grounds, condemned using biological-hygienic terms not dissimilar to those applied by the Nazis to Jews and other 'racial inferiors:' vermin, pollution, and 'poisonous weeds' requiring 'ongoing purification' through peremptory imprisonment for long terms. Thus, the Cold War had two sets of roots; one set in the United States in the fear of a repeat of the Great Depression of the 1930s if international commerce was not rapidly re-established, and the other set in the Soviet Union with the fear that the Soviet experiment in a planned territorial economy and society would fail if it did not rise to the challenge posed by American containment.

By European standards, both the United States and the Soviet Union were peculiar states. They both had origins in revolutions with explicit ideological agendas. They both claimed popular mandates that transcended particular ethnic, class, or even national interests. They offered themselves as uplifting examples of political-economic experimentation in a world mired in postwar poverty and gloom. Within the two countries, the lack of social and ethnic homogeneity meant that precisely what was either 'American' or 'Soviet' was unclear, so the threat of the 'un-American' and the 'anti-Soviet' became central to official definitions of national identity. In each case, the threat of external danger from an equivalent but mirror-image Superpower anchored national populations, and intellectuals, into a political consensus about the broad parameters of 'national security.'

The main consequence of this shared sense of vulnerability was an idealization of each by the other. Each became a super-potent adversary in the eyes of the other. As the United States came to personify capitalism to Soviet citizens, so did the Soviet Union represent Communism to Americans. Each became the geographical manifestation of a totally opposing political economy. Each was also seen by the other as uniquely powerful: a real threat without the human flaws and institutional drawbacks that each saw in itself. Definite domestic interests were served by this geopolitical reductionism. In the Soviet Union it disciplined potential dissidents into supporting a monolithic state apparatus. In the United States it produced a consensus around economic policies expanding mass consumption, a permanently enlarged military (with a budget to match), and opposition to any politics (usually of the left) that could be construed (through guilt by association with the Soviet Union) as subverting the United States from within. In short, it eroded American democracy. The very identity of being American became associated with a narrow political spectrum at home and a virulently anti-socialist/anti-Soviet position (they were usually not distinguished) abroad.

Crucially, however, and this clearly sets the United States apart from the Soviet Union, the process of political representation and judicial politics in the United States also offered the possibility of opening up American politics to those whom it had hitherto largely excluded from public life when they challenged the reality of the claims made on their behalf. Thus, the black civil rights movement and movements to expand the rights of a wide range of groups, from women to gays and lesbians, could point to the US Constitution and the Bill of Rights as mandating equal treatment throughout the United States if the United States was indeed the 'homeland of freedom' it claimed to be in US Cold War discourse.

In the geopolitical setting that arose from the late 1940s onwards the ideology of the Cold War developed the following major characteristics: a central systemic–ideological conflict over political and economic organization; 'three worlds' of development in which the American and Soviet spheres of influence (respectively, the First and Second Worlds) vied for expansion in the Third World of former colonies and non-aligned states; an homogenization of global space into 'friendly' and 'threatening' blocs in which idealized models of democratic capitalism and Communism reigned free of geographical contingency (over there is all like that); and the naturalization of the ideological conflict by such key geopolitical terms as containment, domino effects (linking distant events back home through the image of falling dominos), and hegemonic stability (each side needs a leader to enforce discipline on the others).

It is little exaggeration to claim that in the five decades after 1945 American influence was at the center of a remarkable explosion in what can be called 'inter-actional' capitalism, moving beyond the territorialized approach hitherto dominant in the world economy and as evidenced by the inter-imperial rivalry of the period 1875–1945. Based initially on expanding mass consumption in the industrialized countries of Europe, North America, and Japan, it later involved the reorganization of the world economy around a massive increase in trade in manufactured goods and foreign direct investment. Abandoning territorial imperialism, 'Western capitalism ... resolved the old problem of overproduction, thus removing what Lenin believed was the major incentive for imperialism and war' (Calleo, 1987: 147). The driving force was mass consumption in the industrialized world, particularly in the United States. The products of such industries as real estate, household and electrical goods, automobiles, food processing, and mass entertainment were all consumed by increasing numbers of people within (and, progressively, between) the producing countries. The welfare state helped sustain demand through the redistribution of incomes and purchasing power. If in the late nineteenth and early twentieth centuries the prosperity of the industrial countries depended on favorable terms of trade with the underdeveloped world of Asia, Africa, and Latin America, demand was now stimulated at home. Moreover, until the 1970s the income terms of trade of most raw materials and foodstuffs tended to decline. This meant that the prices for such goods went down even as the cost of manufactured imports increased. This had negative effects in general in the Third World, but it encouraged some countries to switch to export-based industrialization which later paid off as they found lucrative export markets for their manufactured goods (as in, for example, Taiwan, Mexico, South Korea, and China). The globalization of production that followed has slowly undermined the clear identity between products and the places they are manufactured as different phases in production are located in different countries depending on what mixtures of costs and benefits they offer to producers. It is not clear how sustainable a world economy can be that involves a fundamental split between the location of production, particularly of manufactured goods, on the one hand, and the location of consumption, on the other.

A vital factor in allowing the United States a commanding role in the world economy, even as its own economy often sputtered rather than totally out-produced others, was the persisting but historically episodic political–military conflict with the Soviet Union. This had two major peaks in intensity in the late 1940s and early 1980s when each side perceived the other to be increasingly hostile and dangerous and in the early 1960s when the US government worried about Soviet advantages in satellite and missile technologies. The mid-1970s was a period of maximum co-operation or détente when American goals of retreating from the military disaster of Vietnam and cutting military spending coincided with Soviet interest in stabilizing military expenditures. Each side blundered into major military misadventures that came to have major domestic consequences. For the US it was Vietnam where a political commitment to the government of South Vietnam in the late 1950s led to a massive build-up of troops by the late 1960s but with increasing opposition from within the population of the United States who were never clear what the war was about. Claims that the war was to prevent the spread of Communism seemed implausible to those, including not a few who had spent time fighting in Vietnam, who saw it as a civil war between competing factions rather than a local manifestation of the Great Global Struggle between Good (the US) and Evil (the Soviet Union). For the Soviet Union it was the intervention in Afghanistan in 1979 to prop up an allied government in the face of hostility from religious and ethnic opponents who received backing from the United States. In this case military failure was also compounded by popular distaste for the intervention in the Soviet Union as largely unrelated to either Soviet national security or to the support of noble ideals.

Even in periods of détente, such as the late 1970s, the overarching Cold War served to divide the world into two spheres of influence and to tie allies into this geopolitical structure. For a long time this imposed an overall stability on the world, since the US and the Soviet Union were the two major nuclear powers, even as it promoted numerous 'limited wars' in the Third World where each of the Superpowers intervened or armed surrogates to prevent the other from achieving a successful 'conversion.' For all their material weakness, however, Third World countries had considerable leverage. They had to be wooed and often they resisted. The world map was no longer a 'vacuum' to be filled by the Great Powers. The global military impasse between the Superpowers protected the territorial integrity of existing states. Any disturbance of the status quo threatened to bring down the entire structure on the heads of all concerned.

Few expected this system ever to change. It became a part of everyday life around the globe. In the end it was the collapse of the Soviet Union that brought about the demise of the Cold War. Undoubtedly, many factors precipitated the Soviet collapse between 1989 and 1992. Among these pride of place must be given to the following: the failure of the Soviet economic system to provide a rising standard of living to most of the population, an increasing technological lag behind the rest of the industrial world, the burden of a huge military budget, and the disappearance of almost any political idealism from the political elite. But the impact worldwide has been huge. Not only have the certainty and stability that the Cold War gave to world politics disappeared, this coincided with an increased global economic interdependence that introduced added uncertainty and a lack of global institutional means to deal with it. As the Soviet Union disintegrated, its people had to define themselves anew in largely ethnic–national terms, because there was little else upon which to rebuild political identity. The United States also lacked an external enemy against which to define national identity following the Soviet collapse, at least until the devastating terrorist attacks on targets in New York City and Washington DC on 11 September 2001. Whether shadowy networks of terrorists devoted to this or that cause but united in their hatred of the United States as a symbol of world capitalism/globalization/intellectual freedom/religious diversity (take your pick) can substitute for the former Soviet Union is open to doubt. The Soviet Union at least offered a plausible alternative to the 'American way' and was a competitive state with global aspirations. It also tied allies such as Germany and Japan closely to the United States. The essentially negative example offered by Islamic terrorists suggests that they will not easily substitute for what has been lost with the demise of the Soviet Union. They offer little that is attractive to most Americans (or people more generally). Satan, as the great English poet John Milton knew only too well, must be tempting as well as evil.

The dilemma of postwar political geography

The dilemma facing political geography after World War II was twofold. One was the need to move beyond the old frameworks in a time when an ideological dispute based on political–economic differences between the United States and its erstwhile ally the Soviet Union had largely displaced the fundamentally territorial inter-imperial rivalry of the period 1875–1945. Although attempts were made to fit the US–Soviet Cold War into a Mackinder-style geopolitical model, this never matched either the technological or the ideological conditions of the Cold War. The political geographers of the time had nothing else much to offer. The political geography textbooks of the period 1945 to 1960 in the United States and Britain (for example, Pearcy, Fifield *et al.*, 1948; Weigert, 1956; East and Moodie, 1956; Alexander, 1966) cover more or less the same ground using the same organizational frameworks as the texts from the 1930s. Political geographers defined themselves as teachers rather than researchers; an unfortunate trend when major universities, especially in the United States, were defining themselves as research universities. As political geographers failed to come to terms with new conditions their possible roles were usurped in the United States by figures in such fields as diplomatic history and international relations who rushed in to fill the intellectual gap in providing advice and geopolitical soothsaying to demanding governments. Area studies programs staffed by non-geographers arose to fulfill the traditional role of university Geography departments in teaching students about 'foreign areas.'

It would be wrong to focus simply on the deficiencies of the personalities involved, such as Bowman and others, or on the complacency and provincialism of many geographers. The intellectual genealogy of the field was a considerable burden. After all, the Nazi geopoliticians were part of the history of the field. To the extent that the field had intellectual forebears they were figures such as Ratzel and Mackinder whose ideas were not easily translated into the context of the Cold War as it was understood in the United States and Western Europe. The contemporary divorce of economic and political geography also hindered the possibility of reconstituting political geography around the workings of public sector investment or the workings of local governments in the absence of willingness to tackle international issues in other than traditional inventory terms. Above all, however, this was not a period of major theoretical innovation in any of the social sciences, except offering the blandest and most officially acceptable interpretations justified by application of the word 'scientific' to frequently descriptive and uncritical studies. In the period from the late 1940s until the late 1950s a political correctness stalked the United States in the form of 'McCarthyism.' This was the fear that academic research and writing would be labeled as 'subversive' and 'Un-American.' Political geographers had the example of one of their own to bear in mind every time they put pen to paper from 1950 onwards: the case of Owen Lattimore.

This case broke into public view in March 1950 when Senator Joseph McCarthy (Republican of Wisconsin) named Lattimore as the 'top Russian agent in this country [the United States].' At the time, McCarthy was at the height of his powers, naming former government advisors and officials, such as Lattimore, and a whole variety of others, such as Hollywood screen writers and directors, as Communist agents and 'dupes.' This witch hunt descended on Lattimore because of his writings on China and close association with the Institute for Pacific Relations (IPR), an organization founded in 1932 that funded and published research and writing on the Far East, and that McCarthy and his allies contended had become a 'Communist-front organization.' Lattimore had a long public track record of his views on the internal dynamics of Asian countries and the geopolitical consequences of Great-Power policies (e.g. Lattimore, 1945; 1949). His political 'mistake' lay in refusing to see the Soviet Union as a 'red menace' and in trying to understand the appeal of the Communism to the Chinese. But until 1948 he had encouraged the possibility of a rapprochement between Chiang Kai-Shek and the Communists in China. His attitudes made him an easy target for McCarthy and others, most significantly Senator Richard Nixon (Republican of California), who were looking for those in the United States who had 'lost China' to the Communists in 1949. In twelve days of grilling before the Senate Internal Security Subcommittee (over the period 26 February–21 March 1952), Lattimore attempted to rebut the charges and the evidence of previous antagonistic witnesses (including Karl Wittfogel). The Report of the Subcommittee, as David Harvey relates (Harvey, 1983: 7), 'relieved Mao and millions of Chinese of any responsibility for their revolution and concluded that "but for the machinations of the small group that controlled [the IPR], China would be free, a bulwark against the Red hordes." It also recommended the indictment of Lattimore for perjury, charging that he had been "a conscious articulate instrument of the Soviet conspiracy" since the 1930s.'

The charges against Lattimore were eventually dropped on 30 June 1955, but not until he had been subject to numerous court appearances and considerable legal costs. Meanwhile he had been on leave of absence with pay from the Johns Hopkins University in Baltimore. His position on campus proved difficult, however, and in 1963 Lattimore left the United States to lead a Chinese Studies Program at the University of Leeds in England. The Lattimore case illustrates a general point about the first part of the dilemma of postwar political geography in the United States: 'how dangerous it is to cultivate perspectives on geopolitical questions that deviate from certain narrow conceptions of national interest or offend some dominant political line. Hardly surprisingly, geopolitics dropped out of Geography and political geography became a dull backwater after the McCarthy years. Geographers felt safer behind the "positivist shield" of a supposedly neutral scientific method. All of which adds up to a decided abrogation of social responsibility, an understandable but ignoble currying of professional safety and security in a highly politicized world' (Harvey, 1983: 10).

The second part of political geography's postwar dilemma was the crisis of the naturalistic approach to knowing that had hitherto dominated the field. In particular, the attribution of causal powers to physical features had lived on in Geography, in general, and in political geography, in particular, long after other fields such as economics, cultural anthropology, and psychology had abandoned it. Yet, to many geographers, particularly in the United States, to abandon the essential grounding of human (and political) geography in the facts of nature was to abandon Geography as a subject. Of course, the essence of the Cold War was a denial of the importance of relative location or physical features as the determinant of conflict and the claim that ideological competition (and psychological attributes) had displaced the imperial rivalries of the previous epoch. Consequently, because they were intellectually out of touch with the new era, leading figures in political geography focused more on policing the boundaries of the field, declaring what was and was not Geography, rather than engaging in much innovative or novel research. The political geographer Richard Hartshorne is the exemplary case. He largely abandoned research on political boundaries to excavate Geography's past in German regional geography and defend the 'exceptionalism' of Geography as a field bridging physical and human phenomena using the idea of the 'region.' I say this as someone who has found Hartshorne's arguments about regions insightful and useful. Whether someone of such a conservative cast of mind as Hartshorne, however, could have ever challenged conventional Cold War thinking even if he had not buried himself in policing the boundaries of Geography and devoted himself to the cause of the political boundaries he had studied in his youth is open to question.

Further reinforcing the commitment to naturalism was the attempt to re-establish Geography's intellectual reputation after the politically disastrous association with Nazism and the administrative blow of the closure of Harvard University's department after World War II (where Derwent Whittlesey had given political geography a high profile) by showing the intellectual *bona fides* of the field by clarifying its 'nature' as defined by Germanic scholarship (in particular that of Hettner) and adopting the vocabulary of the 'hard sciences,' which, in contradistinction to 'soft' fields such as Geography, impressed grant-givers in Washington DC and in private business with arguments liberally laced with terminology such as the 'fact-value distinction,' 'objectivity,' 'disinterestedness,' and 'the scientific method.'

The American research universities of the post-war era, however, were singularly unreceptive to Geography's claim to scientific status, given its seeming lack of utility in providing the state with neutral research results on which pragmatic public policies could be based. Its focus was just too broad or 'generalist' and its methods just too different from those of the laboratory sciences that had the highest kudos. Louis Menand (2001: 45) makes the general point: 'scholarly tendencies that emphasized theoretical or empirical rigor were taken up and carried into the mainstream of academic practice; tendencies that reflected a generalist and "belletrist" approach were pushed to the professional margins, as were tendencies whose assumptions and aims seemed political.' James Bryant Conant, chemist and the president of Harvard who closed the Geography department there, was also one of the main designers of the system of federal funding of universities that oriented these institutions to providing knowledge judged relevant for fighting the Cold War (Geiger, 1993; Graham and Diamond, 1997). If, as Ambrose Bierce once wryly observed, 'war is God's way of teaching Americans geography,' then the Cold War was to prove the exception to the rule.

There were some who did offer relatively new departures in political geography, suggesting that the tenor of the times was not the only factor in relegating the field to the margins of academic enterprise. Their careers were outside the mainstream academic orientations of the times, even though they did have personal and intellectual connections to mainstream figures such as Hartshorne. What was more important is that they were much more broadly educated and mixed with scholars from a wider range of backgrounds than was typical of most American and European geographers. The people I have in mind are Jean Gottmann and Harold and Margaret Sprout.

As mentioned in Chapter 2, Jean Gottmann (1915–94) was an iconoclastic figure. An academic and linguistic nomad, he moved backwards and forwards across the Atlantic for over twenty years. A refugee twice over, from Kharkov in the Ukraine to France in the aftermath of the Russian Revolution and from France to the United States following the Nazi invasion of France, Gottmann was the veritable citizen of the world in his work as in his life. He was the first major political geographer for whom national allegiance was not a driving force in his thought.

Though he was more than sympathetic to the formation of the State of Israel, Gottmann's political geography is truly cosmopolitan. He came to speak to two audiences, largely outside the confines of academic Geography itself. One was that of specialists in international relations, the other that of urban planners and architects. Though Gottmann saw his work in political geography as closely related to that on cities, his impact was largely divided between the two communities. His lack of orientation to the world of academic Geography in either France or the United States possibly explains both the lack of attention given to him in disciplinary histories and his lack of concern to ingratiate himself with the conventional wisdom in political geography.

Gottmann's theory of political space found its full formation in the early 1950s but was expressed in a variety of forms down until the 1970s and 1980s (Muscarà, 1998). Gottmann displayed a communitarian rather than a statist or liberal conception of the political. His works see the world as partitioned politically as a product of both (1) interactions between forces of external change (circulation) that move people, goods, information, and ideas and (2) the symbols and beliefs of territorially defined social groups (iconographies) who stabilize their existence by a 'common mooring' in terrestrial space. The goal is to see the distribution of political power in terms of dynamic tendencies rather than permanent states (Gottmann, 1952; 1973; 1980). Gottmann connects the basic two elements in tension with an opposition that he learned from classical philosophy and ancient history – that between Plato's ideal city-state, on the one hand, a closed, protected, and largely self-sufficient territorial entity, and the Alexandrine network of cities, on the other hand, an open, accessible, system of connected nodes. If the former represents the total victory of iconography, for the latter circulation is the prevailing force. Consequently, the oscillation in human history between closed and open territorial systems is explained by Gottmann as the movement between the two 'ideal types,' as the need for 'safety' and 'rescue' competes with the need for 'resources' and 'opportunities.' The political geography of nation-states, therefore, is not a permanent state of affairs. Indeed, the American example of hyper-urbanization is used by Gottmann in his famous book *Megalopolis* (1961) to argue for a 'shift from the political geography of nation-states, typical of the Old World, to a political geography at the urban scale, typical of the New World: a geography of dots and lines, of flows, nodes and networks stemming from the interaction of the concrete needs of the communities. This fact explains why there is no substantial discontinuity between his writings in political and urban geography, but rather an evolution of the latter from the first' (Muscarà, 1998: 163).

If Gottmann represents a clean break with much of the political geography of the 1950s, Harold and Margaret Sprout seem at first sight as very much in the mainstream. Affiliated with the Center for International Relations at Princeton University, the husband and wife writing team often refer to the writings of Bowman, Hartshorne, and others, in their many works published between 1939 and 1978 (Sprout and Sprout, 1939; 1943; 1962; 1965; 1978). Perhaps their most important book, *The Ecological Perspective on Human Affairs* (1965), draws from a series of essays previously published in the 1950s. What is distinctive about the Sprouts' writing is their reworking of the physical–human divide in Geography in terms of an 'ecological' perspective that surveys the ways in which environmental factors are often seen by practitioners (and scholars) as driving the course of international politics and proposes a behavioral approach that incorporates such perceptions and the limitations that environmental factors exert on the accomplishment of policies prosecuted with perceptions of environmental effects in mind.

The distinction between (1) making decisions and (2) operational results and the different role of environmental factors – populations, resources, etc. – in each is fundamental. To the Sprouts this is where environmental determinism was particularly problematic. It presupposed that political outcomes could be predicted from environmental and locational conditions. They use their framework also to criticize the psychological and system ideas current among American scholars of international relations, arguing that the lack of attention paid to the geographical milieux in which policies are made by political leaders reduces the likelihood that decisions will yield desired results. A 'possibilism' similar to that advocated by Vidal de la Blache informs this perspective. But it is one in tune with the behavioral orientation of American social science in the 1950s and 1960s, determined to eschew statist understandings of the political in favor of a liberal one that gives political leaders and popular opinion a strong role and thus plays up 'the fruitlessness of deterministic predictions' (Sprout and Sprout, 1965: 199).

Gottmann and the Sprouts offered routes out of the impasse into which political geography had fallen. If Gottmann offered a political geography informed by wide reading in political theory and a personal history that saw political territoriality as always historically contingent, the Sprouts provided a way of 'keeping the physical in political geography' while placing it in the context of human perception and decision-making. In both cases, however, the lack of institutional connection to academic Geography and their orientation to other fields (such as international relations and urban planning) that did not necessarily have a theoretical commitment to the issues they identified reduced their impact and left the mainstream of political geography much as it had been since Bowman.

Why a revival?

Geography as a whole revived in the 1960s. Initially, political geography failed to attract much attention from the 'new' geographers. They were obsessed with modeling the impact of distance on settlement spacing, flows of migrants from place to place, and the location of industries and agricultural land uses. These topics lent themselves to both the quantitative methods that were seen as the measure of the 'science' the new geographers claimed as their mantle and the focus on spatial analysis that they saw as the future focus for the field as a whole. The subject-matter of political geography, with the notable exception of elections, did not seem to have much to offer in the search for 'spatial laws.' The almost exclusive focus on the state was out of step with the urban and within-state concerns of the new human geography. Political science did not offer the inspiration for locational models that economics and sociology supplied to other sub-areas of the field. Textbooks continued to survey the geography of bits of politics, such as boundaries, capital cities, administrative areas, electoral districting, geostrategies of the US, etc., but with little interest in how the parts related to the whole. In failing to come to terms with the loss of its physical–determinist base, political geography had lost its way. At first blush, neither Geography nor other fields had much to offer by way of salvation. Until the late 1960s the outlook was bleak. Yet, help was soon on its way.

In the first place, I want to stress the role of external social and political conditions more than the intellectual efforts of political geographers or other scholars. The events of the late 1960s in North America and Western Europe brought practical politics to the fore in the everyday lives of both ordinary people and academics. The race riots, civil rights marches, Vietnam War demonstrations, and student rebellions of the time had a deep impact on social science. In all fields they brought political questions to the center of concern in ways that they had never been before. In Geography this tendency was expressed in three ways. One was by bringing issues of the distribution of power into the analysis of economic and social phenomena such as residential segregation by race and class in American cities and the global distribution of economic development. These were no longer seen as purely market-driven or a matter of free choice but the outcome of systematic bias in political institutions, such as local governments and school districts, managing the distribution of public goods. From this point of view, all of Geography became political geography, at least of a kind. From the mantra of 'states are everything' that had long animated political geography, Geography as a whole confronted the claim that 'politics is everywhere.'

Another expression of the political quality of the period was the politicization of Geography through public analysis of the field itself: who runs it, for whom, with what ends in mind? In the 1960s higher education had expanded massively in the United States and elsewhere. An important consequence was the recruitment into student bodies and the ranks of university teachers of people from social backgrounds hitherto largely excluded from this world. They did not always accept the norms of personal conduct and political outlook that had evolved in academia during the postwar years. They also challenged the benign acceptance of statehood and international geopolitical hierarchy as 'facts of nature.' A significant example of this comes from France where Yves Lacoste crafted a new 'geopolitics' based on a critique of the old version as essentially Geography's contribution to war-making by powerful states and insisted on the irreducible spatiality of politics within as well as between states and the importance of using geographical scale (local, national, global, etc.) as a method of political-geographical analysis (see, for example, Lacoste, 2001). Lacoste's 'geopolitique' is one of the most obvious fruits of the explicit politicization of political geography to emerge in the early 1970s (Claval, 2000; Hepple, 2000).

In addition, there was a dramatic increase in academic mobility, particularly within the English-speaking world, which brought people with very different social and national backgrounds to those countries, such as the United States, Canada, and Australia, that were most active in recruiting new graduate students and staff. The politicization was not simply disinterested or idealistic, however, because power within the field over staff appointments, publication outlets, professional reputations, and external influence was also very much at stake. The expansion of universities had the effect of dramatically increasing the number of students and faculty, increasing the volume of research and publication, and encouraging new intellectual trends and 'niches' so as to find employment for graduate students and gain access to funds for research and graduate financial support.

Finally, political geography was discovered by a new generation without much background or interest in the older studies. They tended to view the sub-field naively as something they were inventing afresh rather than an old enterprise into which they should be inducted. Without the old obsession with defining disciplinary boundaries, they searched around in other fields for inspiration and found it in economics, radical sociology, anthropology, economic history, and, even, in political science. At the same time, they embarked on explicitly redefining the field as the geography of politics more than the geography of states. Whatever the geographical scale or context – urban, regional, national, world-regional or global – as long as power pooled up in some places, political organization privileged some in some places over others elsewhere, and territorial boundaries were used to exclude and include, political geography had research questions of interest.

Second, however propitious the time, nothing would have happened without the contributions of the specific people making the new political geography. Three types of contribution were crucial. The first, associated particularly with Kevin Cox, Roger Kasperson, Ron Johnston, Peter Taylor, and Richard Morrill, involved the revitalization of electoral geography. The focus here was on quantitative detection of the local dependence of election results in terms of local social indicators indicating patterns of social interaction and the ways in which electoral systems and districting methods affect the overall balance between political parties after elections. Elections provided good information upon which to postulate and measure the impact on social life of local and regional differences. Rather than just ends in themselves, therefore, when examined geographically elections provide an entree into understanding the social dynamics of politics without presupposing either the individualized voters or national homogeneity of much orthodox political science.

The second, also associated with Cox and emerging in the early 1970s, was a focus on urban conflicts. The main idea was that much urban politics is about who gets what with respect to public goods and public bads and that this is determined largely by where you live (Cox, 1973; Cox et al., 1974). This is because most public goods and services are delivered by municipal governments to local areas and public bads, such as air pollution and noxious land uses, are located closer to people who cannot afford to live elsewhere and do not have the power to intervene effectively in 'locational conflicts' to keep such public bads at bay. This was developed in the 1970s as a welfare approach to political geography moving out from the early urban emphasis to examination of the distribution of goods and bads at a range of geographical scales using the same logic for each (Cox, 1979).

Finally, the new human geography attracted the interest of scholars in other fields, such as political science, diplomatic history, and sociology, who began to contribute their own type of political geography to the academic literature. Stein Rokkan, a political sociologist, Immanuel Wallerstein, a historical sociologist, Alan Henrikson, a diplomatic historian, and political scientists such as Bruce Russett,

Richard Merritt, and Jean Laponce combined their own disciplinary expertise with certain geographic concepts – such as center-periphery, region, and distance–decay relationships – and methods – such as grouping procedures to show UN voting blocs (Russett), schematic maps showing the territorial structure of statehood in world regions such as Europe (Rokkan), and series of world maps to show historic shifts in the perception of global centrality (Henrikson). Geographers such as Jean Gottmann, Paul Claval, and Owen Lattimore actively encouraged the interdisciplinary rapprochement through their participation in the Permanent Research Committee on Political Geography of the International Political Science Association (IPSA). This organization played a much more important part in the initial revival of political geography than did the International Geographical Union (IGU) which remained mired in the talking-shop posturing of the Cold War. The term 'political geography' was proscribed by the IGU and still has not been rehabilitated. Interestingly, it is the non-geographers who helped most to re-establish the interest in geopolitics and international affairs that had been eclipsed in the postwar years. The geographers, for the most part, spent their energies until the 1980s on expanding the scope of political geography in new directions rather than attending to such issues as the rise and fall of dominant states, the geographical structure of empires, and the geographical origins and development of the European state system. Less hidebound by the heavy hand of political geography's past, the non-geographers were more capable of crafting political geography's re-engagement with both the spatiality of states and the geography of world politics.

By 1980 there had been a remarkable resurgence in political geography as a multidisciplinary enterprise after the long dormancy of the postwar period. This was to deepen in the course of the next decade both with respect to the amount of new research (manifested in the founding of new journals, particularly *Political Geography Quarterly*, later *Political Geography*, in 1982 by Peter Taylor) and the theoretical development of the field beyond spatial analysis in a number of directions especially those associated with political-economic perspectives and, more recently, postmodern approaches of various types. It is to the three theoretical frameworks and the various subjects of inquiry in contemporary political geography that I now turn.

Three 'waves' of theory

The 1960s was a time when Geography underwent a 'spatial turn.' Space or distance was defined as the field's 'variable' (like the 'economic' in economics). Older definitions, such as the regional and the environmental were (temporarily) eclipsed. Not surprisingly, the initial revival of political geography, coinciding with this development, also took on a spatial-analytic cast. The search was on for distance–decay effects in the influence of voters on one another in the choice of political party and externality-field effects from noxious facilities and 'undesirable' neighbors on decisions to participate in neighborhood political protests. There was also considerable interest in the impact of districting methods on election results, the modeling of distance–decay effects on the possibility of war breaking out between states, and the spatial organization of local and regional governments. These interests and the spatial-analytic approach they tend to share have persisted, and revived somewhat with the arrival of sophisticated spatial mapping methods associated with computerized geographical information systems (GIS). But they are nowhere near as prevalent as they once were.

A good example of the theoretical logic informing the spatial-analytic approach is provided by Kevin R. Cox and David R. Reynolds (1974). After a brief review of the neglect of geographical considerations in studies of power and conflict, the authors identify two factors that they see as leading to an increased concern for space in political studies: the increasing effect of externalities (effects on others who are not parties to a transaction) on people in industrial societies and the adoption of 'systems' perspectives in political science that tend to increase the attention given to outcomes of the political process (who wins where) rather than just the political process itself. So, even if politics in the past could be thought of as 'spaceless' this is no longer the case. The focus on urban settings and the spatial patterns produced by externalities (think of pollution plumes from factory chimneys and the benefits from living inside the catchment boundary of a high-quality high school) firmly distinguished the approach from previous ones. The logic, however, is not specific to either the urban scale or to such local external effects. It can be extended to interpret national and international relations in similar terms, as can be seen in Cox (1979).

During the 1970s Geography experienced something of a turning away from the dominance of the spatial-analytic perspective. In the context of an extended period of political and economic crisis in many Western countries, many turned towards theoretical perspectives that could encompass the current situation as well as offer fresh understandings of old topics. A revived political economy proved especially attractive. Drawing in particular from Marxist and neo-Marxist writing in political economy, scholars framed political-geographical phenomena in terms of global patterns of uneven development and the processes that they claimed produce them. One variety of this approach, that of the world-systems theory associated with Immanuel Wallerstein, proved particularly influential in political geography. It has been popularized in Peter J. Taylor's textbook (1989) and in numerous publications by Taylor and others. Theoretically eclectic, drawing its main tenets from such different thinkers as Fernand Braudel, Karl Marx, and Karl Polanyi, this perspective tends to explain most other phenomena with respect to where they are located within a global division of labor (core, periphery, semiperiphery) produced by the historical workings of the capitalist world economy. Under the political-economic rubric, however, can be found a range of perspectives, some adhering closely to an orthodox Marxism (e.g. Harvey, 1992) privileging processes of capital accumulation pure and simple and others exploring the autonomous powers of states (e.g. Mann, 1984; Skocpol, 1994). What joins them together is their view of space as a surface upon which political-economic processes (whatever the specifics) are inscribed and embedded but which is nevertheless essential to the outcome of the processes (e.g. providing the 'spatial fix' to the declining rate of profit by moving investment from one place to another, defining the spatial limits to state autonomy, etc.).

The 1980s did not relieve the sense of crisis, only this time the consequences were even more profound for political geography. Over the years many thinkers had questioned the pretensions of 'grand theories' and 'master narratives' in the social sciences, pointing how they 'over-reached' the empirical evidence used to support them. Others had suggested that knowledge was more a product of language and conventions of study than based on independent 'facts' about the world. As a result, one critique, associated particularly with feminism and postcolonialism, came to emphasize the partiality or 'situatedness' of knowing; knowledge is a function, at least in part, of the standpoint or subject-position at which a scholar is located, particularly the historical experience of power relative to others and, thus, the capability to tell your story and those of others like you (Krishna, 1993). Another critique came to play up the role of language and writing in offering meaning to readers. From this point of view, the world is written not discovered or explored (Barnes and Duncan, 1992). In other words, in this poststructuralist or deconstructionist view, writers recycle metaphors and tropes rather than discover new knowledge. Finally, some identified the tenuousness of all claims to tell 'stories' about other people and their places. Even 'emancipatory' narratives, stories told to benefit the interests and identities of others, involve a quest for transcendence that disciplines and limits the aspirations of presumed beneficiaries. In this postmodernist view respect for irony, ambiguity, and the paradoxes of existence remain as the only guarantees against imposing order on others. To the extent that it is possible, one looks for the stories that groups share to understand their self-constructions. At the extreme, however, one can never 'speak for others' (Alcoff, 1991–92).

These are distinctive critiques, however, and the use of the term 'postmodern' to cover all of them is problematic (Duncan, 1996). I use it to convey the sense common across all of them that knowledge is both political and deeply compromised by the language and social conventions of academic fields and historical-geographical contexts (Gregory, 1989). Some writers move uncertainly across the critiques in their work without much sense that these are philosophically distinctive. In moving beyond critique, the focus increasingly has been on the question of 'identity' – the relation of the self to larger social groups and the world at large – and how answers to it depend on cultural context (language, understandings, experience, etc.).

The three 'waves' I have identified above continue to flourish within contemporary political geography. At the same time that they have 'washed over' the field they have also helped to stimulate and refine a number of distinct areas of study within political geography. To the long-established themes of geopolitics and the spatiality (or geographical organization) of states and other polities three other themes have been added since the 1960s: geographies of social and political movements (including electoral geography); places and the politics of identities; and geographies of nationalism and ethnic conflict.

Perspectives and subject areas

Table 4.1 attempts a cross-tabulation of the three types of perspective with the five subject-areas of political geography. In each entry in the table is an example of an article or book that conforms to a particular combination of elements. In describing these in the following pages, the hope is that the structure of approaches and subject-matter in political geography will become apparent. Some of the examples are described relatively briefly, while three, those of Rokkan (spatial-analytic), Osei-Kwame and Taylor (political-economic), and Ó Tuathail (postmodern) are given somewhat greater attention. These three represent key examples of each of the three types of approach to political geography. All of the examples used here appear in a reader (Agnew, 1997a) that can be consulted to see them in their entirety or as substantial extracts of longer publications.

Table 4.1 Matrix of perspectives and subject areas

Subject areas	Perspectives		
	Spatial-Analytic	Political-Economic	Postmodern
1. Geopolitics	Henrikson	Corbridge	**Ó Tuathail**
2. Spatiality of states	**Rokkan**	Mann	Krishna
3. Movements	Bennett and Earle	**Osei-Kwame and Taylor**	Routledge
4. Places and identities	Murphy	Wacquant	Forest
5. Nationalism	Conversi	Williams	Johnson

Geopolitics

Until the 1980s there was little by way of a revival of interest in geopolitics. The explicit geopolitical language used during the years of the Nixon administration in the US (1969–74), however, did encourage a return to the topic (Hepple, 1986). One of the best pioneer attempts at re-engaging between US foreign-policy making and geopolitics is a study written by Alan K. Henrikson in 1980. The author uses a center–periphery model of global political centrality to argue for shifts in the perceived centrality of the US to world affairs on the part of Americans. In other words, the history of US foreign relations is the history of a shift from perceived peripherality to perceived centrality. Henrikson traces this history using a chronological series of maps in which the US moves with fits and starts from the edge to the center of the world. After commenting how ill at ease Americans can be in terms of their relative global status, and how little they know about anywhere else, he shows how a policy of global engagement emerged slowly out of continental and hemispheric renderings of America's place in the world. He identifies the Spanish-American War and World War II as particularly important in shifting the US to 'world leadership' and a sense of geographical centrality. He also notes the failed attempt by President Woodrow Wilson after World War I to engage forcefully with the rest of the world, suggesting that Wilson had run far ahead of the American population in this respect. A map that represents the decisive movement of the US to global centrality shows the US going from hemisphere defense to global offense following the Japanese attack on Pearl Harbor in 1941 (Figure 4.1).

Other writers, such as Saul Cohen (1973), Patrick O'Sullivan (1986), John O. Loughlin (1986), and Jan Nijman (1992), have also made important contributions to geopolitics using spatial-analytic perspectives, if with less emphasis on either the perception of national centrality or the use of maps and more on the 'objective'

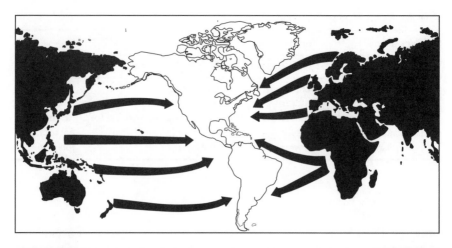

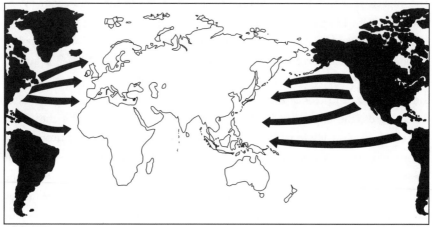

Figure 4.1 The future of the western hemisphere according to
Nicholas Spykman (1944): from western hemisphere defense to global offense.

global factors, resource access, contiguity of competing states, etc. conditioning
geopolitical relations.

One criticism of this approach would be its neglect of the world-economic context in which the geographical framing of foreign policies takes place. America's
rise to global prominence owes at least something to its economic position. Yet,
even as it has achieved global political centrality, the US has also changed the
nature of the competition upon which global competition has long rested. It
brought its home-based focus on economic expansion to bear beyond its boundaries (Agnew, 1999). As a result, it seems as if economic prowess is now as important in its own right as its translation into military might and political influence.

Interstate competition now often seems to be as much or more 'geoeconomic' than 'geopolitical.' But the change in global conditions may be more profound than this. Stuart Corbridge (1994), for example, claims that the global context has changed to the extent that states are no longer the singular actors of world politics. All manner of international regulatory organizations and private businesses are now important actors in world politics in their own right. The contemporary world 'geopolitical economy' has three centers – the United States, Japan, and the European Union – but these are themselves divided among a series of city hierarchies linked by flows of capital and by financial and trade connections to distant sites around the world. This world is not driven by zero-sum (winner-take-all) competition between states but by relative ability to insinuate localities and regions into the circuits of global capital. Many states in fact have little if any capacity to encourage or retard economic development. With such 'quasi-states', and uncertain sovereignties among the more powerful ones, there are both opportunities for a less militarized world but also for new political instabilities (such as those represented by international terrorist networks and religious-based political movements).

This sort of historical political economy, arguing for the role of changing historical conditions in world politics, is a relatively recent development. More deeply entrenched are perspectives that emphasize the permanent importance of the 'geopolitics of capitalism:' seeing the present day as only the latest in a series of reorganizations of business ('capital') at different geographical scales to resolve the long-term tendency of the rate of profit to fall without a constant search for a 'spatial fix' (Harvey, 1982). Others, such as world-systems theorists and advocates of cyclical models of history, stress the emergence of new hegemonic states out of the ruins of past epochs because of, respectively, clustering of technological advantages (Wallerstein, 1993; Taylor, 1989; Derluguian and Greer, 2000) or fewer military obligations relative to national economic capacity (Kennedy, 1986).

As Corbridge notes early in his article, the end of the Cold War has coincided not only with an upsurge in writing about geopolitics from a variety of perspectives but also with an explicit questioning of the geographical assumptions and language upon which the practices of foreign policy are based. A self-consciously 'critical geopolitics' has developed in which the ways in which politicians and the media represent places and their strategic significance take center-stage (Ó Tuathail and Agnew, 1992; Ó Tuathail, 1996). Informed by such post-structuralist writers as Foucault, Derrida, Virilio, and Baudrillard, emphasis is placed on deconstructing the discursive strategies used to make foreign-policy 'situations,' 'crises,' and 'wars' intelligible with respect to both a global 'big picture' and to past events seen as analogies to present ones (such as Munich/appeasement and Vietnam/quagmire in US foreign-policy discourse). Some writers have tended to stress the ways in which popular geopolitical representations serve to anchor national identities (Campbell, 1992; Sharp, 2000). Others have focused more on how the representations frame the conflicts that flare up to challenge the dominant actors in world politics. It is to one of these that I now turn.

Gearóid Ó Tuathail (1993) provides a detailed analysis of the Gulf Crisis and War of 1990–91 in terms of two main themes: (1) the placing of the Gulf 'situation' in the big picture of the end of the Cold War and the desire of American political leaders to 're-territorialize' the US as the sole Superpower, and (2) the war as an example of the 'dematerialization' of place through the use of new high-tech weapons and the immediate visibility of the war on television screens around the world as a type of 'war game' in which the place the war was happening was incidental to the demonstration of high-tech capability.

The two themes are developed in relation to the speeches and actions of American politicians, particularly President George Bush. Ó Tuathail (1993: 6) acknowledges that the Iraqi invasion of Kuwait in August 1990 'had complex regional origins' but that the 'subsequent narration of this event as the globally significant and threatening "Gulf Crisis" must be traced back to dilemmas created for the United States and Atlanticist security structure by the end of the Cold War.' The Cold War had given a structure to both world politics and American society, from dividing up the world, targeting military forces, and organizing military production to containing political dissent. The Gulf Crisis offered an opportunity to write a 'general threat narrative' to replace the one that had been lost and thus to make the 'United States' meaningful again as an enterprise in world politics. 'Recurring inscription strategies' were used to this end by American politicians and official commentators. Those of particular importance in offering 'reasons' for the US intervention related to (1) oil in general, the defense of Saudi Arabia, oil reserves and supplies, and the 'chokehold' that Iraq would have on the world oil supply if allowed to occupy Kuwait and (2) the pursuit of a 'New World Order' based on the rule of law and the defense of existing sovereignties (such as Kuwait's). Those of importance in situating this crisis and war in relation to past American experience included analogies with World War II (in particular, comparing Iraqi dictator Saddam Hussein to Hitler) and Vietnam – the 'syndrome' of popular American opposition to colonial-type wars having been overcome by the prospect of victory in the Gulf.

This discursive emphasis is supplemented with an account of the role of television and military technologies in making the Gulf War a spectacle in the way other wars had not been. Drawing from the French war theorist Paul Virilio, who sounds weirdly reminiscent of early twentieth-century Italian Futurists, the Gulf War is seen as offering 'provocative evidence of the eclipse of place by pace' (Ó Tuathail, 1993: 18). Rather than containment and strangulation, the American war strategy relied on using aerial assaults by missiles and other munitions to overcome the defensive advantage of the Iraqis. This approach was visible to observers in the dramatic news footage capturing the pinpoint bombing achieved by the American-led forces. Ó Tuathail cautions against accepting the idea that this is a totally new kind of war in which all of the old rules no longer apply. But he does claim that the net effect of both the discursive and technological strategies pursued during the War has been to 'efface place' in the sense, first, of dehumanizing and distancing from observers the truly horrific consequences of high-tech warfare and, second, understating the rich cultural variety of the places subjected to acts of war. Whether this is all that new, of course, is in fact open to question.

Ó Tuathail reminds us that despite recent changes in the workings of the world economy geopolitics remains closely attached to the conduct of wars. As guide and inspiration, the modern geopolitical imagination reduces places to points on a map that then cease to have inherent qualities and only count in a calculus driven by global desire. This vision is not new but has a long genealogy going back to the European encounter with the rest of the world from the sixteenth century onwards (Agnew, 1998). The content of this vision does change, however. The challenge to the student of geopolitics is to detect what is changing at any particular moment and what is not and whether these can be understood in purely representational terms or reflect interests and identities masked more than revealed by discursive constructions. Language is as much rhetorical and persuasive as it is representational. It is thus not always as revealing of motivations and desires as might seem at first glance. The theoretical richness of Ó Tuathail's attempt at connecting discursive with technological power is revealing of how limiting reliance on one to the exclusion of the other can be.

Spatiality of states

With geopolitics this is the most established area of study in political geography, if usually under a number of different labels such as territoriality, geography of state formation, and the geography of administrative areas (including federalism). The spatiality of states refers to both the external bounding and the internal territorial organization of states. Studying boundary claims, frontier disputes, and territorial organization have long been important research areas in political geography (Kasperson and Minghi, 1969; Sack, 1986). There is also a large body of writing on local governments as sub-state actors and the specific geographical features of federal systems (Paddison, 1983). This kind of work continues to flourish. But increased attention is now being given to the spatiality inherent in the modern state system of competitive state sovereignties claiming total jurisdiction over their populations in their territories and how this came about.

This emphasis is not simply an intellectual happening independent of the times. The modern territorial state is now in question in ways that would have been unthinkable even twenty years ago. A whole set of phenomena bear witness to this: the onset of globalization in finance and production, the explosion of migrant and refugee populations escaping the collapse of states (from Sierra Leone to Somalia and Afghanistan), the fiscal crisis of the Western welfare state, the collapse of the 'strong' states of the Soviet Union and Eastern Europe, the rise of supra-regional (as in the European Union) and global (as in the IMF and UN agencies) forms of governance, the rapid increase in ethnic and regionalist conflicts within and between states. The image of a 'fixed' territoriality to political organization can no longer be taken for granted. This has encouraged a search for the historical roots of the territorial state as a form of governance and speculation about the limitation or displacement of state sovereignty as a governing principle of international relations.

The increasing popularity of less state-centered and coercive conceptions of power has also contributed to questioning established conventions about states and their grip on people and territories. These reflect changes in territorial organization and in historical understandings of statehood. For one thing, the expansion of regional tiers of government within states has led to a decentralization of power from previous concentrations in central bureaucracies in capital cities. For another, the sense that the history of statehood has been more complicated than dominant accounts in the social sciences have made it, has inspired perspectives more sensitive to the limits than to the strengths of state power. The world contains a variety of state forms that cannot be reduced to a single model of statehood. More generally, states have never had the exclusive monopoly on the means of violence that much political theory might lead one to expect (Thomson, 1994).

The idea that there is a necessary link between political community and territory is an old one in Western political theory. But only with the rise of the modern territorial state in sixteenth-century Europe was there finally a close affiliation between the two. Only since then have citizenship and territory been conjoined.

This connection has become so taken for granted that much debate in political geography has assumed that territorial sovereignty is a realized ideal and turned to questions about the character of the state apparatus or political institutions associated with different kinds of state (capitalist–socialist, democratic–authoritarian, etc.). There is much to commend this approach, not least because questions about citizenship rights, access to institutions, and the role of states in legitimizing social divisions receive critical attention. This internal orientation, however, neglects the geographical underpinnings of statehood itself and the critical role of the internal/external distinction that is a vital attribute of modern statehood. The clear bounding of territories by states is one of the main differences between modern European-style political organization and the types of polity that prevailed in nomadic, clan, imperial, absolutist, and feudal societies around the world in the past.

Stein Rokkan (1980) spent many years investigating the historical roots of statehood in Europe. In this article he traces the process from the collapse of the Roman Empire down to the twentieth century. His purpose is to show the various spatial elements involved in state formation, particularly how core-areas of states emerged, and the role of urbanization and relative location in Europe (central versus seaward and landward fringes) for state development. The experience of specific states is thus placed within the experience of Europe as a whole. Not for Rokkan the dominant strategy in previous studies of taking an ideal-type case, typically France or England, and seeing all other states as imitators of the prototypes.

The main characteristic of Rokkan's approach is that it is typological. He attempts to draw up a geographical template or simplification for Europe as a whole with north/south and east/west bands designating the regional and local impact of Europe-wide historical events such as the collapse of the Roman Empire and subsequent ethnic patterning of Europe, the spread of feudalism and the emergence of a central urban belt from Flanders in the north to Italy in the south, the effects of the Protestant Reformation and the subsequent Catholic Reaction, and the imposition of unitary and federal models of government. Consequently, the political map of Europe is seen as the outcome of a series of determinative Europe-wide processes – economic, military-administrative, and cultural – but with distinctive local and regional effects on the types of states and their internal structures.

Though there is no single 'master map' on which all of the varied processes can be displayed, Rokkan does provide a spatial-analytic matrix for Europe in which the processes can be inferred from the outcomes as shown on the map (Figure 4.2 is a map of his matrix). This is a classic spatial-analytic maneuver: reasoning back from

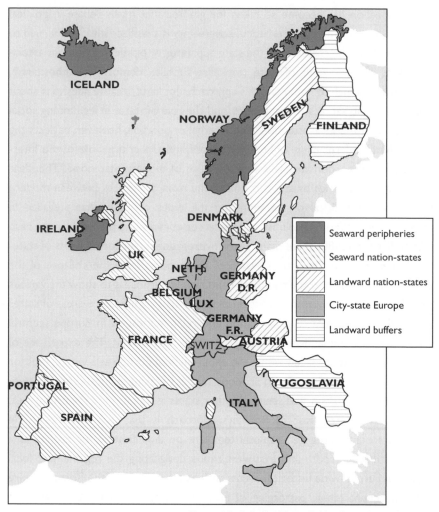

Figure 4.2 A map of Stein Rokkan's typology of political systems of twentieth-century Western Europe.
Source: mapped from Rokkan (1980: table 4.2)

present day spatial form (what the map looks like) to the mix of processes that produced it. What makes it different from other research in this genre is its historical emphasis; seeing the map as the cumulative outcome of centuries of continent-wide 'shocks' producing different effects in different places because of different prior accumulations of shocks. What is most notable on this mapping of European state formation is how it combines 'system characteristics' (physical size, city structure – one dominant city versus many cities, linguistic unity/division, nation-state development, seaward-landward location, and city-state history) with actual empirical examples of combinations of the system characteristics. It therefore provides a means for both looking at Europe as whole and for understanding the trajectories of its various parts but always in relation to the whole.

Recent research by Tilly (1990) and others (Tilly and Blockmans, 1994) suggests that Rokkan's spatial-analytic approach misses important causes of the rise of territorial states in Europe. Their political-economic approach draws attention to relative military capacities (based largely on tax systems) and the differential rise of merchant and industrial capitalism in various parts of Europe. But they see states as emergent actors in their own right rather than simply the 'instruments' of social classes such as merchants or industrial capitalists. While some, such as Wallerstein (1974) and Anderson (1974), have given more importance to the growth of trade and new social classes, if in different ways, others have emphasized the rise of state autonomy as one of the features of modern state development. Perhaps the best example of this perspective is provided by Michael Mann (1984).

Mann's (1984: 187) central point is that 'the state is merely and essentially an arena, a *place*, and yet *this* is the very source of its autonomy' (his emphasis). What he means by this is that the modern state's very territoriality is what gives states (as opposed to groups from within society such as social classes) a high degree of autonomy. It does so because through the control over territory the state deploys infrastructural power. This is the result of the state responding to demands from within society and the society responding to the provision of infrastructural goods and services by the state. Only the state can exercise authoritative power within a circumscribed territory. Other social groups are lacking in this capacity. In addition, therefore, to the despotic power that groups can exercise if they gain control over states, infrastructural power accrues to the state itself but only because it is a territorial enterprise. As a result: 'Where states are strong, societies are relatively territorialized and centralized' (Mann, 1984: 213).

Territoriality is a necessity for complex agrarian and industrial societies, therefore, because the state penetrates into the life of social groups as these groups give up powers to the state in return for various favors. In turn it is the very territoriality of the state that guarantees the state a degree of autonomy in relation to society. Its powers cannot be reduced to those of any one group. The state's capacity to do things for groups that they cannot do for themselves (infrastructural power) is the reason for this. This is distinctive from the despotic power exercised by state elites which derives from their social roles, is usually precarious, and cannot insinuate itself like infrastructural power into the routines of everyday social life.

Of course, the success of the state as an autonomous actor depends on the extent to which its powers are vested with legitimacy by its population. From a broadly postmodern perspective, an argument such as Mann's serves (even if inadvertently) such a purpose. It naturalizes and normalizes 'the state' as an actor in peoples' lives. A postcolonial perspective would add to this the violence that statehood brings in its train. The experience of political independence for the former colonies of European empires serves to bring attention to the arbitrary nature of the bounding process involved in statehood and the difficulties boundary-marking entails for those living at the borders. People must choose one side or the other; there is no recognized borderland identity, only competing state ones. Sankaran Krishna (1994) uses the metaphor of 'cartographic anxiety' to convey how discourses about an Indian 'nation' are used to define the borders of the Indian state. The 'body politic' of India is defined in terms of a physical map that tries to conjure up a 'historical original,' a 'homeland' that never existed prior to British colonial rule. So, not only those at the borders of India are caught up in an exercise in spatial self-definition that is the essence of nation-statehood: abstracting from history a set of stable, legitimate boundaries that fix the history of the state in place and guarantee it a place in future. The map, therefore, is an attempt at answering definitively the anxiety that comes from being 'suspended forever in the space between the "former colony" and the "not-yet-nation"' (Krishna, 1994: 508).

This returns us to the dilemma created by the fact that Western thinking about governance in general and democracy in particular is usually centered around the state. But state spatiality is based fundamentally on exclusion from concerns about what is external and with the penetration of the state into society. As Machiavelli taught in *The Prince*, politics is possible only within state boundaries, reason of state operates beyond them. The spatial attributes of modern statehood, therefore, have more than passing relevance to the great questions of political theory about citizenship and democracy. They are at the heart of debates about the possibilities of democratic governance in a world in which many decisions affecting us all on a daily basis now increasingly emanate from distant seats of power beyond the reach of territory-based authorities.

Geographies of social and political movements
Much of politics is about mobilizing groups of people to obtain either public goods (and remove public bads) or redress grievances from political and economic organizations, of which the most important is usually the state. Public goods are policies and the provision of regulations and resources that benefit specific groups

and places. Social movements often arise spontaneously around particular issues at specific locations. Sometimes they expand to encompass like-minded and similarly organized people elsewhere. They die out when a cycle of activity has passed or they become formal interest groups or political parties. Historically, and in the process of state formation, the 'repertoires' of collective action strategies used by movements tend to shift from the localized and sporadic to the national and systematic; from burning the hay ricks of landlords to mass demonstrations in capital cities, nationwide strikes and boycotts (Tilly, 1986).

But even when the issues they promote and the strategies they use are non-local, movements must still have roots somewhere. They cannot successfully mobilize unless they can attract recruits across a range of places. Of course, if local memberships opt for different goals and strategies then mass mobilization becomes problematic. This is more likely when states are less centralized and local autonomy provides alternative institutional outlets to a focus on the center (Tarrow, 1994: 62). The shared experiences and social interaction of living together in places provide a major stimulus to join movements. Absent such social incentives provided by living together in places, people are susceptible to leaving political action up to others. This is the so-called free-rider problem: that you can benefit from the exertions of others, so have no incentive to participate yourself. That so many people do engage in political action of various types is testimony to the role that the regular rounds of everyday life exert in socializing people into politics.

The period since the 1960s, particularly during the years 1965–84, has been one of intense social movement activity around the world. Like previous periods of intense activity, such as between 1880 and 1910, many people have chosen to act with others in pursuit of common goals that might in other historical conditions have appeared unrealizable. Increasingly, such goals are not national in scope, even as national organizations and institutions remain the main targets of political action. From environmental problems to human rights questions, new social movements have grown to address issues that do not admit of ready national-level solutions. Yet, the difficulties of organizing transnationally are such that states remain the major 'opportunity structures' within which social movements operate.

Many political parties, particularly progressive ones and ones on the extreme right, have begun life as social movements. So there is a continuum of movements running from localized, ephemeral social movements at one end to formal, institutionalized, and state-oriented political movements at the other. Political parties have received much more attention from political geographers than have the less formal social movements. This has largely methodological roots. Parties run in elections, so election results can be used to make inferences about the nature of support (which social groups support which parties) and the incidence of political ideologies among entire voting populations. There is now a large body of research in electoral geography showing the geographical co-variation between political parties, political ideologies, social groups, and specific places. An important thrust of this research has been to identify the ways in which places mediate between political choice and social groups. Distinctive geographies of political parties, therefore, are not simply the result of a coincidence between where certain social groups reside and votes for different parties but of the way places structure political ideologies and affiliations (Agnew, 1987; Miller, 2000).

The structuring role of place in politics is the focus of an article by Sari Bennett and Carville Earle (1983). This offers a geographical analysis of an important issue in American political history: the failure of a socialist party to take root at the turn of the twentieth century, the last great period of social movement activity in the United States before the present post-1960s one. Previous interpretations of this failure have isolated the role of ethnic divisions among American workers, the general prosperity of American workers or the faulty political tactics of socialist leaders (particularly their strident rhetoric and maximalist demands for total social transformation). Bennett and Earle prefer to emphasize the geography of the Socialist Party vote across the north-eastern United States in the presidential and congressional elections of 1912, tracing the basis of success to the sedimentation of trade union or 'labor power' in the years after the Civil War. In a statistical analysis amply illustrated by maps, they reason backwards from the spatial pattern of support for the Socialist Party to what might plausibly have brought about the failure of the Party to either expand nationally or build on its initial places of strength. They identify two factors operating differentially across the north-eastern United States that undermined the prospects of the Socialist Party in presidential and congressional elections: the increasing gap between skilled and unskilled wages in the larger cities, which divided the working class, and the industrial diversity of large cities, which reduced the relative numbers of unskilled workers in the heavy industries that stimulated political militancy. The Socialist Party had been successful largely in smaller cities with heavy industries. A base in the growing, larger cities eluded it and prevented its expansion onto the national scene.

This spatial-analytic reasoning is fairly typical of much research in electoral geography. The major criticism that can be directed at it is that it is reductive, searching for potential causes that operate differentially across space. In contrast, political-economic approaches frame spatial variation in political party or social movement activity in terms of an overarching theory of political economy. Party success or failure is seen in terms of the cycles of the economy and the balance of social forces at any point in time. A good example of this structural reasoning is provided in an article by Peter Osei-Kwame and Peter J. Taylor (1984).

The authors use a world-systems framework to argue that political parties in Ghana in the period 1954–79 were constrained by the country's location within the global division of labor to compete over which economic strategy best served the country (loosely, import substitution versus basic commodity-export orientation) while appealing to different ethnic clienteles with divergent interests in commodity-export production (i.e. production of cocoa beans for export). Osei-Kwame and Taylor use a quantitative analysis of election results to identify a number of different sub-periods in which different parties prevailed, largely through isolating in opposition the party most representative of the Akan (Ashanti) ethnic group – closely identified with cocoa growing and, hence, most opposed to the 'semi-periphery' economic strategy of import substitution pursued by the governing parties. The great political conflict throughout much of the period between Nkrumah of the Convention People's Party and Busia of the United Party was based around this division, with the former representing government centralization and protectionism and the latter decentralization, liberalization, and open trade. But it was also a politics of faction in that the centralizers had to 'shop around' to put together a coalition of places against the liberalizers whose base remained relatively stable over time. Osei-Kwame and Taylor interpret this as a pattern likely to be found in other 'peripheral' states and former colonies in which political parties must work with a limited number of economic policy alternatives in the presence of major ethnic divisions.

Using a common set of electoral districts to facilitate comparison of elections over time, the authors use the technique of factor analysis to show that, with the exception of the 1969 election when the Akan (including Ashanti) cocoa regions emerged victorious, the election results favored parties stronger in the other non-cocoa growing regions, with relative shifts among them over time. With military coups and governments replacing elected governments in 1966 and 1972, four electoral patterns are identified for 1954–55, 1960, 1969 and 1978–79 when elections did occur (Figure 4.3). There is no 'normal' or stable voting pattern in Ghana but a series of distinct mobilizations based on different coalitions across places in the country. In 1954–55 a 'national mobilization' for Nkrumah's party (positive factor scores) is scattered around the country, if with a clustering in his home area in the south-west, with opponents (negative factor scores) in the central Ashanti

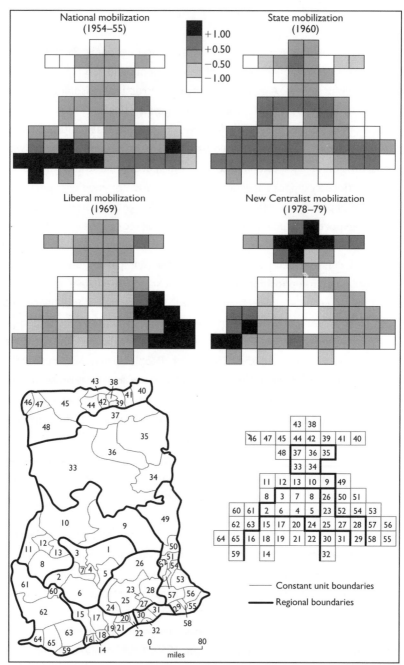

Figure 4.3 Osei-Kwame and Taylor's map of constant units of elections in Ghana, 1954–79, and cartograms showing the changing 'factor score' patterns for a T-mode factor analysis. Constant units are constructed by combining electoral districts to produce a common area data base for 1954–79. The cartogram locates each constant unit as close as possible to its real geographical location. Each district is reduced to the same size on the cartogram. The factor score cartograms use the constant areas to map the clustering of votes for different political parties/groupings across the elections. The titles of the cartograms each indicate the salient characteristic of each election or set of elections.
Source: redrawn from Osei-Kwame and Taylor (1984: 211, 213)

region (west-central) and in the north. In 1960 Nkrumah won a referendum on a new Republican constitution and election as president. This produced a pattern of 'state mobilization' similar to the earlier one but with opposition in the north, in Kumasi (Ashanti), and in urban areas in the south. In 1969 an Akan versus Ewe ethnic pattern emerged, with Nkrumah in exile and the Ewe party (from the south-east) representing the centralizers and the Akan, the liberalizers. This time, and this time only, the liberalizers won, only to be overthrown in 1972 military coup. Elections in 1978 and 1979 showed that a 'new centralist mobilization' had emerged, pitting the Akan region (negative factor scores) against centralizing factions now dominant in the south-west and the north (positive factor scores).

The possibility of multi-causal mobilization or spontaneous agency is excluded from a structural account of party politics such as this. The structural position of Ghana within the world economy and the correlation of production for the world market with ethnicity are seen as the driving forces behind political mobilization. Yet, other authors have noted that resource conflicts, governmental interventions, and resistance to established power structures can arise even when political resources and opportunity structures are not richly available (Pred, 1990: Staeheli, 1994). From this point of view, the relative success of political parties and social movements cannot be reduced to location within the global division of labor.

Authors operating with a 'postcolonial' strain of argument have been particularly prominent in questioning the singular importance of economic considerations in political mobilization. This sort of approach is represented in an article by Paul Routledge (1992) who provides a geographical account of one local social movement in India. He sees this movement as emanating from a 'terrain of resistance' (a whole set of local conditions) against the coercive, cooptive, and seductive powers of the state. The movement in question has devoted itself to opposing the Indian government's attempts at establishing a number of military facilities (in particular the National Testing Range for missiles) in the Balasore (Baliapal) District of Orissa, north-east India. Routledge traces both the activities of the movement in taking direct action against moves to set up the Testing Range and the sources of local activism. He sees the movement as a response to the perceived 'militarization' of Orissa by local groups most affected by this trend (Figure 4.4).

His argument, however, is that there is a geography to the origins of this social movement. He identifies a set of local and locational conditions that have contributed to the mobilization of local people against state plans. Key among these is a local 'sense of place' that cannot be reduced to either a set of local material interests or local externality fields, to adopt spatial-analytic terminology. The idiom

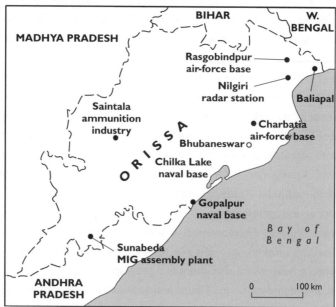

Figure 4.4 Location of Orissa in India and the location
of Baliapal and military sites in Orissa.
Source: redrawn from Routledge (1992: 226)

of the movement is strongly connected to this feeling for or identity with place through the songs and dramas used in political activities such as demonstrations and setting up barricades. The case strongly suggests that collective political action, at least in India, involves cultural codes that are very place specific. Routledge gives a similar interpretation to other social movements in India, linking their growth to the democratization of Indian society and popular opposition to the depredations of an overbearing state.

The claim of Alexis de Tocqueville in *Democracy in America* that there are greater political opportunities when society is stronger than the state and when there is considerable 'local patriotism' seems strongly supported by this Indian case study. Perhaps it is the withering of local opportunities and the decline in local identities that accounts for the recent erosion of political participation in many Western countries. At the same time, the geography of political organization (the ways in which structures of governance, political parties, and social movements are orga- nized over space) seems increasingly out of kilter with the cultural complexity and shifting economic geography of the time. Whether connecting in cyberspace or opening up institutional channels at local and supra-national levels will help to revive political participation remains to be seen. Of course, the decline in political participation may also be a cyclical downturn more than a structural trend. We have certainly seen that before. The trend of growth in social movements from the 1960s until 1984, particularly marked in Europe and the United States, may have been unsustainable.

Places and the politics of identities

Many of the 'new' social movements for racial civil rights, ecology, women's rights, gay rights, and religious purposes that sprang up in Europe and North America beginning in the 1960s are not simply about satisfying 'interests' but also, and more importantly, about 'identities.' They are about the struggle for public recognition of identities that have been either stigmatized or suppressed within the wider soci- ety. Much contemporary politics, therefore, is a politics of identity, involving strug- gles over the recognition and legitimacy of different social identities. The seemingly instrumental character of older social movements, such as labor unions, has obscured the degree to which they also involve struggles for recognition and self- respect. Nevertheless, the self-conscious concern for identity is distinctively modern if not entirely recent (Calhoun, 1994). When all-encompassing 'identity schemes,' such as kinship, prevail within a society there is little problem. Only when we live in a world in which social networks are diffuse and there is limited cultural consensus do individual persons face the difficulty of identifying who they are in relative isolation. Identity politics is about struggling to establish the recognition of collective differences in identity within a society where those differences are either not sanctioned or are unacknowledged.

Identities are created through the stories people tell themselves and others about their experiences. In this way people come to see themselves as part of larger collectivities with common histories. People present themselves to one another in terms of stories and tell stories about one another. These narratives are attempts at creating a unified self, one that makes the self intelligible. Lives and stories are intertwined to become identities. From this viewpoint, identity is about the connection drawn between a 'self' and a community of communicators or storytellers with whom one identifies (Mackenzie, 1976; Lovell, 1998).

The struggle for identities in an unstable world is a result of the breakdown of the relatively unreflexive and totalistic identity schemes in which everyone 'knows their place.' Increased communication across ever-widening distances and the collapse of custom-based communities disrupt conventional identifications. Yet, it is remarkable that even in this world one can say that 'Those who share a place share an identity' (Mackenzie, 1976: 130). This is so for a number of reasons. First, because even as people strive politically to establish identities that are not necessarily place-specific they do so within a 'geographical field' of shared relevance, such as the territory of a state (Calhoun, 1994: 25). Second, as they struggle for one identity people usually share other identities, of which the most important are usually those of the people among whom they live. People have multiple identities and loyalties that derive from the overlapping social worlds in which they live their lives (Calhoun, 1994: 26). Third, communication, social interaction, and reactions to distant events are all filtered through the routines and experiences of everyday life. For most people these are still geographically constrained. Even if not always strictly localized, 'shared social spaces' still define the limits for the social appropriateness of given identities (Mackenzie, 1976: 131). Finally, 'imagined geographies' are important within many identities, such as that of 'African-American' with its roots in African diaspora, slavery and the southern US, and contemporary expression in the 'black ghetto,' and migrant identities of diasporic groups caught between different social worlds (Mohanty, 1991; Davies, 1994; Morley and Robins, 1995). Places are thus shared, if only in the imagination.

The concept of identity is not without its problems. The term itself can seem to imply a solidity and permanence to 'identities' that the politics of identities is all about establishing. There would be no point to the politics if the identities were already secure and not subject to denigration by more powerful 'others.' The danger of 'essentializing' identities does not mean that identities are socially constructed 'out of thin air' without any meaningful relationship to 'natural differences.' Given that much racial discrimination is based on reactions to biological differences such as skin color, for example, it is not surprising that an 'African-American' identity would involve reference to skin color. This does not mean that there are the sorts of *real* racial differences of bundled traits that were the stock in trade of Friedrich Ratzel, only that biological differences are *seen* as defining social and cultural differences that feed into identities. In this case the history and expectation of discrimination is more important than anything else. Finally, the relationship between identities and interests is ambiguous. The theoretical problem lies in drawing too neat a line between the two, as if identities and interests must stand in opposition to one another. In fact, political mobilization and action in any particular case cannot usually be reduced to either one or the other.

Even given the generally postmodern tenor of the concept of identity, in particular its constitution out of stories rather than psychological traits or economic interests, the relationship of geography to the politics of identities has been addressed from within each of the three broad streams of political-geographic thinking. Each type of perspective, however, tends to pick up on a specific aspect of the relationship. From a spatial-analytic point of view the focus is on the *boundaries* (social and jurisdictional) that help to define political identities. Political-economic approaches are more interested in the processes of *spatial inclusion and exclusion* that help to create the circumstances in which groups can acquire identities. Postmodern perspectives, broadly construed, privilege the ways in which identities are expressed through attempts at *associating identities with places*.

Alexander B. Murphy (1993) provides an example of the approach that emphasizes the causal connection between boundary delimitation and identity maintenance/formation. Jurisdictional boundaries within states, in this case that between Dutch-speaking (Flemish) northern Belgium and the French-speaking south, are seen as boosting the identities of the groups who already inhabit the different regions. As the pursuit of 'ethnic identity,' particularly by the historically less powerful Flemish, has come to dominate Belgian politics, one solution has been to devolve government functions to the regional level thus reinforcing the differences between regions and the identities of the two groups. Regional boundaries within Belgium, therefore, have reinforced if not offered a new foundation for the social identities with which Belgian politics as a whole has become increasingly intertwined. From this perspective, boundaries can be read as signifying the mutual acceptance of different zones of interaction and practice for social groups within one country.

But from a political-economic viewpoint this approach remains agnostic about whose interests have been best served and what the logic behind the need to define such rigid boundaries has been. Rather than focus on the boundaries themselves, therefore, a more appropriate concern should be with the processes of spatial inclusion and exclusion that boundary delimitation represents. This is the approach taken by Löic J.D. Wacquant (1994) in his account of the contemporary black ghettos of large American cities. Though not politically divided from central cities, these are effectively separate social worlds in which quite different social and economic processes prevail from those in surrounding areas. Thirty years ago black ghettos, such as Harlem in New York, the Southside of Chicago, and South-Central in Los Angeles, were also separated. But the new 'hyperghettos' have lost the mixture of social classes and have different relationships with the wider society than was formerly the case. True to a political-economic perspective, Wacquant sees pressures from the wider society as crucial in this transformation with internal changes as having only indirect impacts. Using Chicago as his illustrative case, Wacquant shows that the 'new' ghetto has two distinctive features: (1) a decaying inner core with satellite working-class and middle-class neighborhoods; and (2) a massive amount of physical decay and social collapse in the ghetto core. The 'classic ghetto' gained its communal strength and identity from an organizational infrastructure (churches, lodges, the black press, etc.) that has withered away. Abandoned by government and industry, the hyperghetto is a wild zone beyond ordinary society, lacking in legal job opportunities, good schools, and much hope for the future.

This narrative of a 'spoiled identity' suggests the central dilemma for identity politics from a political-economic perspective: that perpetuating an identity, in this case that of the contemporary black ghetto and its people, may mean abandoning the possibility of pursuing constructive interests. These can only be pursued elsewhere; hence the emptying out of the core ghetto by its most upwardly mobile residents. David Harvey (1993: 64) clearly identifies the tension between identity and interests for the political-economic perspective when he writes:

> The identity of the homeless person (or the racially oppressed) is vital to their sense of selfhood. Perpetuation of that sense of self and of identity may depend on perpetuation of the processes which gave rise to it. ... [T]he mere pursuit of identity politics as an end in itself (rather than as a fundamental struggle to break with an identity which internalizes oppression) may serve to perpetuate rather than challenge the persistence of those processes which gave rise to those identities in the first place.

A seemingly happier coincidence between identity and interests is mapped by Benjamin Forest (1995) for a group of gay men who used the process of creating a new municipality in West Hollywood, California in 1984 as a strategy for destigmatizing and gaining popular acceptance for their identity. Forest surveys the coverage given by the gay press to the incorporation of a new local government jurisdiction and identifies from their accounts a set of themes that related 'gayness' to the place that was being incorporated. As a 'gay place,' West Hollywood became a concrete anchor for an abstract identity that was otherwise both intangible and threatening to the larger population. A gay identity was thus stabilized and advertised as non-threatening by associating it with the achievement of political independence for an hitherto unincorporated area of Los Angeles County, wedged between the City of Los Angeles and Beverly Hills.

The place was crucial to this campaign because it allowed a set of usually separate features of gayness to be brought together, both stereotypical (creativity, aesthetic sensitivity, etc.) and counter to stereotypes (maturity, commitment, etc.) A moral narrative was constructed that used the relatively high percentage of gay men in a place as a positive rather than a negative phenomenon. This case is taken as an illustration of the more general claim about how representations of places figure in the making and remaking of identities, a major theme of postmodern and postcolonial thinking in political geography (e.g. Duncan and Ley, 1993; Thrift and Pile, 1995; Nuttall et al., 1996).

Whether identity politics involves race, ethnicity, or sexual orientation, therefore, there are important links to the places in which the identities in question are defined and pursued. What one makes of identity politics and how one construes the role of geography in how it operates, however, will depend on the theoretical perspective that is adopted. Like the identities themselves, the meanings ascribed the role of geography in identity politics are highly contested.

Geographies of nationalism and ethnic conflict

The word 'nationalism' dates from the late eighteenth century although there is considerable dispute over whether it is a totally modern phenomenon or has older roots. The multiple forms that nationalism has taken make it hard to offer definitions that are all-encompassing. This has not discouraged attempts at doing so. Two approaches have dominated. The first views nationalism as a political ideology that exalts the 'nation' to a central value and in which 'national interests' supersede all others (Breuilly, 1982; Hobsbawm, 1990). The second sees nationalism as an autonomous social force or causal variable in history that, arising first in

England and/or Germany, spread through a dual process of elite imitation of existing 'models' and mass disaffection with existing identities first into the rest of Europe and then around the world. The element of attachment to a people or *volk* goes back to the German philosopher Hegel, but the emphasis on elite imitation is a more recent innovation (Greenfeld, 1992).

If the problem with the first approach is that it dissolves nationalism into 'its' particular manifestations and sees it as derivative of the rise of modernity, the problem with the second is that it reifies the 'people' as a primordial entity and regards nationalism as a natural inheritance from the past rather than as something that must be constantly recycled and reworked to keep it fresh. Each approach misses one or more key feature of nationalism that the other identifies. On the one hand, nationalism is a type of practical politics mobilizing groups by appealing to common identities and interests. But it is also, on the other hand, a set of ideas about the 'nation' as the singular reference for an identity that began as the vesting of sovereignty in the people (as in France and the United States) and then spread under the label of 'national self-determination' elsewhere largely on ethnic grounds. In other words, if the politics of nationalism concern the pursuit of presumed share interests and identity as a population occupying a common territory, the sense of communality that justifies this rests on the appeal to a mythic national past.

From this point of view nationalism is a type of politics that depends on claiming a non-political legitimacy to gain control over a state and pursue other goals, such as expanding the national territory or excluding those who are not thought to share the common past. The relationship to statehood is crucial. Only with the rise of the territorial state does the nation appear as the natural and unitary form to which the state must aspire. The idea of the 'nation-state' at the heart of nationalism presupposes the creation of either cultural uniformity (as in German-style ethnic nationalism) or a civic 'religion' based on a founding myth and a set of 'special' institutions (as in American-style civic nationalism).

In recent years, particularly with the end of the Cold War and the discipline this imposed on both international relations and the possible 'break-up' of existing states, nationalism has been strongly associated with the proliferation of ethnic conflicts, even though many of the conflicts to which the qualifier 'ethnic' is applied also have other roots (caste, class, and region, among others). Many states are multi-ethnic and thus subject to this pressure. The bureaucratization and corruption of existing states, regional economic disparities, and the unfreezing of Cold War boundaries have contributed to the upsurge in communal and ethnic conflicts. These are particularly intractable when they involve competing territorial claims, few alternative identities, and inter-ethnic economic competition. Violence is important for validating the seriousness of your claim and encouraging others to accept your inter-ethnic conflict as a zero-sum or winner-take-all game. Without the protection of your own state there are no guarantees against the violence directed at you by the other groups (Agnew, 1989; Kaufmann, 1998).

Yet, states have increasingly begun to accommodate to ethnic and regionalist movements preaching secession or regional autonomy. Often movements will settle for much less than outright separation, satisfied with regional devolution, language rights, and recognition of their 'difference.' As a result, the number of ethnic (and related) conflicts has been in decline (Gurr, 2000). Of course, a number of high profile, seemingly intractable conflicts, such as that between Israel and Palestine, and new ones, such as those in Indonesia between the central government and groups in Aceh (northern Sumatra) and West Irian (New Guinea) suggest that even if numerically in decline, ethnic conflicts are not soon likely to completely disappear. As long as there are multinational states and distinctive ethnic identities there will be tensions between the two. What is also clear, however, is that many ethnic groups manage to co-operate with one another without large-scale violence (Fearon and Laitin, 1996).

The question of how national (and ethnic) groups establish and maintain their territorial boundaries is a contentious one. It is usually addressed indirectly within the confines of the two broad approaches to nationalism outlined previously: instrumentalism and primordialism. Daniele Conversi (1995) provides a spatial-analytic alternative to these non-geographical approaches. He does so by drawing together three theories – the ethno-symbolist, transactionalist, and homeostatic – around the question of boundary definition. He sees nationalism as resting on a process of social categorization in which groups identify themselves in opposition to other groups with pre-existing ethnic markers serving to differentiate them one from the other. Internal 'ethnic' content and the spatial segmentation produced by territorial boundaries thus interact to provide the basis for a particular nationalism (good case studies broadly taking this approach are offered in Sahlins, 1989 and Kürti, 2001). One may rely more on content, another more on opposition or antagonism across boundaries. In either case: 'nationalism is a struggle over the definition of spatial boundaries, that is, over the control of a particular land or soil' (Conversi, 1995: 329).

Conversi is concerned with how boundaries fix nationalism. But he pays no attention to the material conditions under which nationalisms of various types emerge and flourish. Colin H. Williams (1989) uses a version of world-systems theory to frame discussion of the explosion of ethnic separatist movements around the world since the 1970s. He uses case studies of separatist nationalism from Spain, France, and Nigeria to make the claim that the resurgence of nationalism in its separatist guise is the 'playing out of minority aspirations unsatisfied during the critical period of state formation' (Williams, 1989: 340). Changes in the political economy of capitalism, particularly the renewed attractiveness of small areal size with globalization, now make it feasible for those groups ill-digested by existing states to strike out on their own. A range of local factors also figure in each case, for example the aftermath of the Civil War of 1936–40 in Spain for Basque nationalism, the hypercentralization of the French state for Corsican nationalism, suggesting that the material determinants cannot be solely responsible. Other political-economic perspectives would be likely to give greater emphasis to the degree of forced cultural assimilation, economic exploitation, and military suppression of subsidiary groups.

Many scholars have become disillusioned with the typologies (ethnic versus civic, separatist versus chauvinist, integral (fascist) versus unification, etc.) and lists of conditions that both spatial-analytic and political-economic perspectives tend to come down to. How the national or ethnic past from which the present identity draws is remembered has become increasingly important for these critics. How is the claim to primordiality reworked and reinvented to keep people in the fold? In this postmodern construction, the production and configuration of national images in film, literature, landscapes, and monuments are viewed as the ways in which national identities are forged and reshaped.

The sacrifices of war and the heroism of national political activists are the most frequent subjects of monumental commemoration. Nuala Johnson's (1995) article examines the role of such monuments in Irish national identity. She argues that landscape forms such as statues not only are constant reminders of a collective past but that they also help to 'spatialize' public memory by linking the history of the nation to specific, concrete sites within it. This serves to remind everyone, however remote from the actual battleground of nationhood, of communality with their fellow co-nationals. The nation itself can also be represented in statue form, frequently as a female: a heroic maiden or doting mother signifying the 'land' for which so much has been sacrificed. Johnson points out, however, that the meaning of statues is not straightforward, even when evidently celebratory or heavily gendered. They are subject to contending interpretations as to what they say about the past. Hence, there are always possible reinterpretations that can lead to new views of the past. What is clear is that, from this point of view, nationalism is never finally written in stone even if the statues themselves are.

Understandings of nationalism and ethnic conflicts differ considerably, therefore, across the three sets of perspectives. What is becoming obvious, however, is that rather than being totally antagonistic in their assumptions and approaches, the three offer possible complementarities, given their different orientations and distinctive voices. That they still remain separate perspectives speaks to the continuing impact of affiliations to different traditions of thought and the intellectual tribalism (training, journal policies, habits of mind, reading lists, etc.) that keeps the field divided more than engaged in common conversation.

Crossing theoretical divides

There are signs of theoretical rapprochement. This is particularly the case in some recent research and writing on geopolitics and the rise of deterritorialized forms of power, such as those associated with so-called global cities and world-city networks. For example, Agnew and Corbridge (1995) attempt to bridge the divide between political-economic and postmodern perspectives by showing how 'geopolitical order' – based on trends in the practical political economy of world politics – and 'geopolitical discourse' – the ways of seeing and thinking about world politics – interrelate to produce the everyday practices of world politics. They identify different historical periods in which order and discourse relate to one another in distinctive ways to resolve the difficulty that arises in ahistorical accounts of giving priority to one over the other. Their historical geopolitics represents an attempt at engaging with both political-economic and postmodern perspectives rather than privileging only one of them. Similar, if less formal, attempts at relating political-economic to cultural aspects of geopolitics also animate such feminist writing as that of Cynthia Enloe (1990), the writing on global cities of Saskia Sassen (1991), and the work of Denis Retaillé (2001) and Jacques Lévy (2001) on 'geopolitics in history.'

In a different vein, an interesting combination of political-economic and spatial-analytic perspectives is apparent in the Beaverstock et al. (2000) project on world-city networks. Criticizing the state-oriented understanding of the world that dominates both world politics and the social sciences, they propose instead a focus on the world of flows, linkages, and connections among the world's cities. They bring together the explosive growth of service industries, the increased importance of information technology, and the tremendous development of worldwide direct investment to propose a theoretical framework for mapping what they call 'the intercity global network.' Taking a roster of 55 world cities, they show how firms from some set up shop in the others (e.g. Figure 4.5). Empirical analysis of these linkages shows that there is a definite hierarchy to them, with some cities, such as London and New York, currently sitting on top. This pattern suggests that 'networks' are beginning to challenge 'territories,' if not for the first time (see Rokkan, 1980 on the central European city belt), as an organizing principle of global geopolitics. Importantly, however, the authors note that 'World cities are not eliminating the power of states, they are a part of a global restructuring which is "rescaling" power relations, in which states will change and adapt as they have done many times in previous restructurings' (Beaverstock et al., 2000: 132).

In the future we can expect to see more 'violation' of the theoretical boundaries that have subdivided political geography in the recent past, if only because the world to which political geography is applied is changing rapidly and in ways that make the previous 'intellectual division of labor' increasingly irrelevant. In particular, the emerging 'geopolitical order' is one that challenges the fixed spatial claims of spatial-analytic perspectives, the unchanging political-economic imperatives of many political-economic perspectives, and the focus on dominant discursive representations of postmodern approaches.

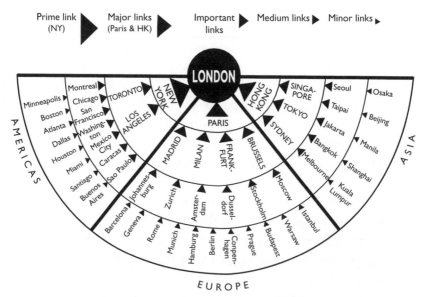

Figure 4.5 World city links to London.
Source: Beaverstock, Smith and Taylor (2000)

After the Cold War

The modern geopolitical imagination that arose to prominence in Europe beginning in the sixteenth century is in question in ways that would have been unheard
of only twenty years ago. Its state-based understanding of politics irrespective of
which geographical scale is under consideration seems increasingly limited and limiting. Its account of the spatiality (spatial organization) of world politics as totally
territorial has relied on three assumptions that are increasingly problematic:
(1) that states have exclusive sovereign power over discrete territories; (2) that
domestic and foreign are separate and distinct realms; and (3) that the boundaries
of the state define the boundaries of 'society' (Agnew, 1998). These assumptions
have always been contestable, but it is only recently that they have been seriously
undermined by changes in the practices of world politics. Globalization, the rise of
information technologies, the growing power of the world-city network, and the
end of the Cold War have come together to erode state sovereignty, blur boundaries between the 'inside' and the 'outside' of states, and produce a common global
society facing dangers that do not emanate from a single state or source but from
the risks of and opposition (in the form of atavistic religious and cultural movements) to the capitalist modernity of the post-Cold War years. Threats from global
warming, increased worldwide economic inequality, and global terrorism are all
symptomatic of the geopolitical order after the Cold War (Ó Tuathail, 2000b).

Since the 1970s, but at an increasing pace, the world has been marked by a
decentering and deterritorialization of the means of production, destruction, and
communication. Two related trends have been particularly important in bringing
this about. The first has been the collapse of the world system first mapped out at
international conferences at Bretton Woods and Yalta in 1944–45. These two
agreements imposed geopolitical order, respectively, on world monetary and territorial affairs. Bretton Woods created a fairly stable system of fixed currency
exchange rates and Yalta froze the boundaries of post-war Europe and established
the spheres of influence of the Cold War. The Bretton Woods Agreement ended
in 1971 with the US abrogation of the use of the dollar as the world's reserve currency and of the US government as the lender of last resort. Yalta came to a close
in 1989 with the downing of the Berlin Wall.

Following the collapse of Bretton Woods the world has seen a vast expansion of
a volatile financial system based in major global cities (making possible the research
about world cities alluded to earlier) and the breakdown of many national barriers
to the flow of capital. One important consequence has been the globalization of
production by transnational companies, investing directly in locations around the

world to take advantage of local and national cost differentials so as to lower costs and increase the rate of profit. Since the downing of the Berlin Wall in 1989 and the collapse of the Soviet Union in 1992 the world has seen an explosion of ethnic, religious, and 'civilizational' conflicts on a scale previously unknown. Some of these reflect the lack of a basis to politics after Communism other than national or ethnic differences (as in the former Yugoslavia). Some are the result of the lack of fit between ethnic and state boundaries (as in Kashmir, Spain, Ireland, and Sri Lanka). Others have their roots in resentment at the spread of consumer values and American popular culture or American support for countries unpopular with their neighbors (such as Israel). Even though the number of ethnic conflicts diminished by 2000–01, the other conflicts, particularly that between the West and elements in the Islamic World, have increased unabated. One way of describing the dual impact of the collapse of the Cold War system as a whole is to characterize it as 'Jihad vs McWorld,' the first term representing religious-cultural reaction to the spread of western consumerism and kitsch (as in many Hollywood films and American TV shows) represented by the second (Barber, 1994).

The second trend has been the emergence of a 'world of flows' challenging the dominance of the world of territories that characterized the Cold War geopolitical order. Rapid movements of capital, goods, and people around the world now openly challenge the ability of states to channel and limit transactions across and within their borders. This explosion of movement has been made possible by a host of new technologies, particularly in the areas of communications – the Internet, satellite television, and wireless telephones, transportation – particularly mass jet travel, and information processing and analysis – business software, e-commerce, web pages, etc. In this new technological world, space is constructed much more in terms of nodes and networks than in territorial blocs. As a result, the geopolitical nostrums of the Cold War, from military containment strategies to the imagining of fixed territorial opponents and command-and-control systems, become moot. Instead, as populations of different ethnic, national, and religious origin become intermingled in the developed, industrial parts of the world, they bring with them the hopes, fears, and hatreds of the places they came from and remain in contact with some of those they left behind. Identities, therefore, are increasingly diasporic (scattered around the world) and multiple; creating cultural circumstances in which it is more and more difficult to identify clear territorial threats and dangers.

This is not to say that territoriality as such has been eclipsed. It is more that the territorial state, itself a creation of Europeans since the sixteenth century, provides less and less of the monopoly over the means of violence, control over economic transactions, and basis to political identities that it once did, at least in many parts of the world. Theorists of speed and cyberspace miss the fact that events still unfold somewhere and in a world still divided politically into territorial units of one sort or another. Rather than write in terms of flows *versus* territories and speed *overcoming* space, it is better to say that the territorial regime of stable territorial sovereignties and relatively fixed spheres of influence associated with the Cold War has begun to shift in an as yet unpredictable direction towards a mixed territorial regime of flows between nodes in networks and territorial regulation and identity construction at and between a range of geographical scales – national, local, regional, and world-regional. We must remember that even as the terrorist attacks on the United States in 2001 indicate the appearance of political networks operating beyond the confines of the state system, the attacks also helped to reinforce the American sense of a security territory associated with the American 'homeland' and the terrorists themselves seem to have a profoundly territorialized view of present world politics (a 'pure' Islamic world contaminated by a 'corrupt' America) and a future utopia (an Islamic/Arab world liberated from Western influences).

This is the geopolitical context in which political geography will be made in the foreseeable future. It is very different from the contexts in which political geography was first 'invented' and later remade. But it is not all new, either. Even as 'borderless risks' seem to proliferate, many features of politics remain relatively unchanged. The next chapter suggests some of the topics that are of emerging significance for political geography. How these are dealt with is the likely task for making political geography over again in the early part of its second century. Of course, the process of making a field is an inherently uncertain one. As the geopolitical context changes, so will what we do and how we do it. As previous chapters emphasize, this is how things went in the subject's first century.

chapter 5
THE HORIZON

Trying to identify what is on the 'horizon' of political geography requires divining from recent trends ones likely to emerge into prominence because of their fit with the emerging geopolitical context. This is highly speculative and subject to rapid obsolescence, so why do it? The purpose is certainly not to exclude other topics from any future political geography or to offer an encyclopedic inventory of all contemporary trends in subject matter. Rather, I want to draw attention to the current 'making' of political geography to show how active the redefinition and reworking of the field actually is. This is not to simply endorse what I consider the *avant garde* and disregard what has been emphasized in the past. The purpose is to illustrate the flow of influence between the contemporary geopolitical context, on the one hand, and the making of political geography, on the other.

By and large, the new 'themes' are not simply additions to the list identified in Chapter 4 – geopolitics, places and the politics of identities, etc. – but also raise metatheoretical and methodological issues (what concepts to use, how to conduct research, etc.) for established themes as well. This is particularly the case with two of the three new themes explored in this chapter – geographical scale and normative political geography. But it is also the case with the third – the political geography of the environment – if only, for example, because environmentalist movements raise important questions for such established themes as geopolitics and the geographies of social and political movements.

Two background conditions are important in understanding much of what follows. First, a conversation rather than a dialogue of the deaf has begun to emerge between advocates of the three major theoretical 'waves.' Some examples are given towards the end of Chapter 4. This perhaps reflects the deradicalization and routinization of what were once seen as totally opposing perspectives as their proponents achieve professional recognition and higher intellectual status. But it is also possibly the result of changing times in which geopolitical instability and uncertainty makes the theoretical certainty (even if about the certainty of uncertainty in some varieties of postmodernism) of the different positions increasingly untenable. Possibly, some new Great Idea is awaiting realization in the new times after the Cold War. What seems more likely to me is an increasing theoretical eclecticism, as students educated more broadly than past generations emerge into prominence to deal with an increasingly volatile and geographically complex world.

Second, this world to which political geography directly addresses itself seems riven by religious, civilizational, and economic divisions that take very different geographical forms from the state-based colonial and worldwide ideological systems that characterized the periods of inter-imperial rivalry (1875–1945) and the Cold War (1945–89) during which political geography was previously made and remade. On the one hand, the world economy and many political movements (including religious ones) are organized in terms of spatial networks more than territorial blocs, as noted at the end of Chapter 4. On the other hand, claims are made by leaders of dominant states and political movements on behalf of the welfare of huge geographical areas and their populations (such as the West, the Islamic World, etc.) as if these were homogeneous entities. These claims are often informed by a tremendous nostalgia for a period in the past (such as medieval Islam or a Golden Age of state-based capitalism or the European welfare state) and for the 'purity' of territories from 'foreign' contamination but which now must confront a world in which people of diverse cultural origins increasingly live intermingled and interdependent with one another on a practical everyday basis.

In this context, three trends in political geography appear particularly significant. The first represents the continuing drift away from state-centrism towards according a central role to 'geographical scale' in understanding the geography of power. The second is a return to the old physical–human nexus of political geography, but now in relation to how human threats to the natural 'environment' are mediated by political institutions and political movements. The third is the question of the nature of politics and its connection to the diversity of human experience. Political geography is finally addressing normative political issues concerning citizenship, democracy, group rights, and the role of intellectuals. For each of the trends, a general introduction is followed by a number of examples to illustrate how political geography is presently being made by its practitioners, often with clear reference to the current geopolitical context.

Geographical scale

In political geography, geographical scale is usually thought of in terms of either the fixed or the emerging dominance of one level over others in political organization and behavior. In particular, the national and the global have achieved a privileged status as the geographical scales at which politics is said to be determined. In the former case, this is because a spatial ontology based on states rules out autonomous sources of political agency at other scales. In the latter case, a spatial ontology emphasizing global relationships, either geopolitical or economic, rules out much if any autonomy at other scales, except that resulting from a state's or a region's relative location in global geopolitics or within the global division of labor. Each is also seen in either/or terms. Each excludes the other as causally significant in its own right, except as a moment in the workings of the other. Needless to say, other geographical scales receive short shrift indeed.

These orthodox understandings of geographical scale have been called into question by recent trends in the workings of world politics and the world economy, particularly the emergence of newly powerful global city networks (e.g. Beaverstock *et al.*, 2000), global political networks (of transnational companies, international migrants, drug dealers, terrorist groups, etc.) (e.g. Held, 2000), cross-border regional compacts (e.g. Blatter, 2001), and political movements concerned with large-scale and global issues relating to the physical environment, human rights, and arms control (e.g. Princen and Finger, 1994; Price, 1999). All of these enterprises and networks operate across scales rather than restricting their activities to only one. With the value of hindsight, the past also now seems less singularly national or global than it once appeared (for a brilliant account to this effect, see Wolf, 1982) . Until recently political geographers remained intellectual prisoners of the first age of geopolitics in the 1890s, but now seem to have begun to see the past in terms of the workings of processes across scales. In my view this seems likely to become an important feature of a non-state obsessed but equally non-globe entranced political geography (see Marston, 2000).

One important preliminary, before providing some examples of what is at stake in taking geographical scale more seriously, is to define what I mean by geographical scale. If cartographic scale refers to the scale of information or density of information on a map, geographical scale refers to the level of geographical resolution at which a given phenomenon is thought about, acted on, or studied. Conventionally, terms such as 'local,' 'national,' 'regional,' and 'global' are used to convey this meaning of scale. It is not the amount of information on a map, therefore, but the scale at which a particular phenomenon is framed geographically that matters. There is nothing very determinative about the terminology used to convey geographical scale of reference. The 'local,' for example, can be used to refer to areas of vastly different sizes. Even the 'global' may not mean worldwide but, rather, a geographical scope simply beyond the 'continental.' There is a certain arbitrariness to the terms except that each only makes sense in relation to the others. So, within this constraint, geographical scale is imposed on the world and not inherent to it. Given that the terms are very much universal, however, it seems that today people pretty much everywhere tend to think about and organize themselves politically in reference to similar understandings of geographical scale.

The idea of geographical scale is analogous to the idea of 'levels of analysis' in which one scale or another is regarded as key to explaining a given phenomenon. The doctrine of 'reduction' presupposes that the lowest level is always the best, whereas 'holism' presupposes that the whole is always greater than the sum of the parts, and hence that the most encompassing geographical scale is the best one. Reduction looks to isolated individuals, atoms, or neurological nets to explain human behavior. Holism looks to Capitalism, Culture, or the World-System. The idea of 'emergence,' however, suggests that many phenomena of interest in a field such as political geography cannot be adequately understood in terms of either reductionism or holism. Rather, phenomena are brought about across levels. In this view, only rarely is there a single scale at which total explanation can be found. From voting decisions to military strategy the influences on what is done emanate across scales from the localized to the globalized, with a change in the 'balance' of influences as nearby and distant influences fluctuate in their relative impacts.

Three examples can serve to illustrate the importance of considerations of geographical scale in contemporary political geography. The first is the role of territorially embedded networks of power in world politics. The particular case explored here is that of the so-called al-Qaeda network of militant Islamists associated with the 11 September 2001 attacks in the United States. The second is the changing 'balance' of geographical scales in electoral politics, explored here with reference to Italy between 1948 and 2001. The third example is of the emerging global system of finance linking major global cities and offshore banking centers in loosening the bonds of national financial regulation and currency markets and, consequently, undermining the close match between financial flows and national territories. In each case, however, it is the intersection of processes across scales rather the singular dominance of one scale (i.e. global networks *versus* states or the local) that is at work.

Geographical scale and terrorism

Terrorism, the targeting of civilians and military personnel for death and dismemberment by militant non-state groups, is a political strategy originating in nineteenth-century anarchist attempts to unseat governments by assassination and social mayhem. Later it was adopted by groups involved in colonial struggles for national independence. Indeed, until the 1980s terrorism was almost always directed towards specific national governments and their territories by groups seeking to unseat those governments or break off part of the national territory for a new state. Classic examples would include the Stern Gang during Israel's war of independence, the IRA and ETA trying to force the British and Spanish governments, respectively, to unite Northern Ireland with the Irish Republic and break the Basque provinces away from central rule, Palestinian terrorists engaged in struggle against Israel, and various terrorist groups in Italy and Germany during the 1970s and 1980s. Some of these groups, of course, relied on financial support from sympathizers elsewhere. The IRA, for example, depended on funds collected among Irish Americans. The IRA and Palestinian groups received military support from various pariah states, such as Libya. But the goals were essentially nationalist and the networks of support were usually national and, at most, international. Until 11 September 2001 many of the world's most deadly terrorist attacks still involved nationalist groups rather than transnationalist networks (Table 5.1).

Many terrorist groups are still largely national in orientation. The Palestinian Islamic movement Hamas, for example, is largely oriented towards suicide bombing of Israeli civilian and military targets. The Zapatista movement in the Mexican state of Chiapas, frequently portrayed as a movement critical of globalization as represented by the NAFTA agreement between the US, Canada, and Mexico, is in fact largely oriented to Mexican national politics and the demand for land reform in the Mexican South. Its use of Internet web sites to attract worldwide attention is not enough to make it a global network. For that you also need both goals that extend beyond the boundaries of a single state and targets with global significance. The Zapatistas have shown evidence of neither. But new groups, taking their strategic cue from older Islamic groups with nationalist goals such as Hamas (in Palestine), Islamic Jihad (in Egypt and Palestine), and Hezbollah (in Lebanon) that specialized in suicide bombings have gone transnational. The *al-Qaeda* group, for example, headed by the Saudi millionaire, Osama bin Laden, is charged with a long list of terrorist attacks (including the plane attacks on the World Trade Center in New York and the Pentagon in Washington DC on 11 September 2001) directed towards the United States but largely oriented towards undermining the governments of a number of states in the Moslem world, particularly Egypt and Saudi Arabia, and establishing a modern version of the Caliphate that prevailed throughout the Islamic world in the years following the death of the Prophet Muhammad. Originating in the US-government's sponsorship of groups in Afghanistan following

Table 5.1 Terrorist attacks 1983–2001, by death toll and whether nationalist or not

Date	Place	Death toll	Nationalist or not
April 1983	Air India flight (Irish coast)	329	YES (Sikh)
April 1983	US Embassy, Beirut	63	YES (Hezbollah)
October 1983	US Marine barracks, Beirut	241	YES (Hezbollah)
October 1983	Bus station Sri Lanka	150	YES (Tamil)
December 1988	UTA flight, Chad	170	YES (separatists)
December 1988	PAN AM flight, Scotland	270	YES (pro-Palestinian)
February 1993	NY World Trade Center	6	NO (Islamic Jihad)
February 1993	Jewish Center, Argentina	96	YES (Hezbollah)
April 1995	Bus in Tel Aviv	22	YES (Hamas)
April 1995	Federal Building, Oklahoma City	168	YES (US right-wing)
June 1996	US barracks, Saudi Arabia	19	NO (al-Qaeda?)
June 1996	Tourists in Egypt	62	NO (Islamic Jihad)
August 1998	US embassies, Kenya & Tanzania	147	NO (al-Qaeda)
August 1998	Omagh, N. Ireland	29	YES (Real IRA)
October 2000	USS Cole, Yemen	17	NO (al-Qaeda)
October 2000	Apartments, Moscow	118	YES (Chechen)
September 2001	World Trade Center and Pentagon (incl. those on 4 hijacked planes)	c.3120	NO (al-Qaeda)

the Soviet invasion of that country in 1979, the al-Qaeda network turned its attention to the US once the Soviet Union had withdrawn in 1989. Based in the Sudan through the early 1990s, Osama bin Laden, moved to Afghanistan with the establishment of the extreme Islamist Taliban government there in the mid-1990s (Rashid, 2000; Mishra, 2002). This is where his agents came for training. Recruited across the Arab diaspora in Western Europe and among disaffected young men in Saudi Arabia, Egypt, and elsewhere, and funded by bin Laden's family fortune, other Saudi money, and contributions from Moslem groups in the United States and elsewhere, al-Qaeda consists of cells of activists taking advantage of the geographical mobility and social openness of western societies and the new technologies of globalization (the cell phone, the fax, international money wiring, etc.) to plan and carry out terrorist attacks in the hope of stimulating an anti-Moslem backlash in the United States, reprisals in the Islamic world that encourage recruitment of activists, and the withdrawal of American forces from the Arab world (Saikal, 2000).

Al-Qaeda is undoubtedly a new type of political actor engaged in a new type of terrorism. Some 'thirdworldists' – commentators in Europe and the United States who see any movement emanating from the Third World as progressive and revolutionary simply because of where it is from – might compare Osama bin Laden to Che Guevara, the hero of the Cuban revolution and believer in spreading peasant revolution, but Che operated country by country and never advocated terrorist acts against civilians. Radical chic in the 1960s did set great store by Che's internationalism, he certainly had wealthy European backers, but his was a bottom-up rather than a top-down political strategy. He was also, we should remember, a socialist egalitarian, not a proponent of religious hierarchy and essentialist gender and religious distinctions. *Al-Qaeda* is worldwide in operation, bringing together operatives of diverse national origins in a loose global network, motivated to challenge the hegemony of western capitalism and replace it with a puritanical version of political Islam throughout the Arab world (and elsewhere). Its terrorism is geared towards highly symbolic targets with no distinction drawn between civilian and military casualties. Such targets are chosen to encourage recruitment of activists by creating a backlash when reprisals follow the spectacular acts of aggression. To a degree it also represents 'blowback' on the United States of the policy of the Reagan administration in the 1980s of supporting radical Islamists against Soviet interests in Afghanistan and elsewhere (Johnson, 2000).

But *al-Qaeda* is not some sort of deterritorialized entity without connections to particular places. Its utopia rests on an imaginative geography of a restored Caliphate. It had to have a hiding place in the mountains of Afghanistan, protected by a friendly regime. Flushed out of there it must find shelter somewhere else. It recruits its agents among the dissatisfied middle-classes of certain states in the Arab world. Its targets are military, diplomatic, and financial institutions associated with the United States. The United States is a geopolitical abstraction seen as an earthly Satan. The religious inspiration is fundamental to its goals and to its language. These are a mirror image of the idea of the 'clash of civilizations' proposed by the American political scientist Samuel Huntington in 1993 (O'Hagan, 2000). In this case an Islamic world is seen as in a death struggle with an infidel civilization represented by the United States, captain of the materialist West. The corruption and failure of states in the Islamic (particularly the Arab) world are put down entirely to cultural pollution emanating from the West. Only by expelling the West can the pollution be swept away. Yet, this civilizational focus may be its weakness. For many potential recruits the question of whether to support *al-Qaeda* or an allied regime, such as the Taliban in Afghanistan, comes down to ethnic and kinship ties more than religious beliefs or attitudes to 'the West.' If *al-Qaeda* cannot win locally, it will not succeed globally.

There is a geographical embeddedness to *al-Qaeda*, therefore (Halliday, 2001). It is not simply a disembodied network loose in a post-territorial world. What is difficult to grasp is that it is a cross-scale phenomenon: it operates across national boundaries and has transnational goals and appeal. It is a product of a globalized world, in that its operations would not be possible but for the ease of communication and movement at a world scale that has emerged over the past thirty years. Its geographical imagination is of a Pan-Islamic world in which *sharia* or Islamic law will prevail and will be enforced by religious police such as those of Saudi Arabia and the Taliban in Afghanistan. Its short-term goal, however, is the overthrow of a number of Arab governments by stimulating civil war. To do this, it must recruit local adherents who are more interested in local issues than in the 'clash of civilizations.' The attacks of 11 September 2001 were a provocation intended to stimulate a backlash from the United States government that, in turn, would radicalize large sections of Arab public opinion against their current governments. The goals and operations of *al-Qaeda*, therefore, can be adequately understood only if placed in a multiscalar context.

One of the effects of the terrorist attacks of 11 September 2001 has been to revive the discourse of territorial danger and vulnerability in the United States that the end of the Cold War had seemingly undermined. Guarding the borders – Homeland Security – has once more become the leitmotif of American politics, with moves towards a heavy remilitarization of the country, a reinscription of the federal government as a centralized seat of power, a questioning of the traditional openness to foreign immigration, and a revived attachment to national symbols such as the flag and the pledge of allegiance. Yet the United States economy has become incredibly intertwined with that of the world at large and particularly with its closest neighbors, Canada and Mexico. Huge quantities of freight must cross US borders every day for important sectors of the US economy to function at all (Flynn, 2002). The US automobile industry, for example, depends heavily on parts shipped backwards and forwards across the two land borders. At the same time, the move towards 'lean,' 'just-in-time' production, making items with parts shipped in shortly before use, puts a premium on minimizing delays at border crossings. The economic imperative thus comes up against the demand to improve border security, at all points of entry, notwithstanding the fact that the perpetrators of the attacks of 11 September 2001 entered the US legally at major airports. The increased sense of territorial vulnerability mandates that the entire external boundary of the US be reinscribed in national political consciousness. Initiatives to treat borderland regions as distinctive zones with respect to economic development and citizenship policies, because of cross-border labor flows and political cross-allegiances, come under intense criticism. If symbolic of the emergence of a new type of global political actor such as *al-Qaeda*, therefore, 11 September 2001 also represents the reinstatement of the national boundaries as a fundamental element in American politics. Consequently, analysis at a single scale is not adequate to understand what is going on. This is one reason why geographical scale must be taken more seriously in political geography.

Geographical scale and electoral politics

Another reason is that the theoretical lens offered by geographical scale offers a useful perspective on more conventional empirical topics in political geography, such as the geographies of political movements, the politics of economic development, and electoral geography (see, for example, Silvern, 1999; MacLeod and Goodwin, 1999; Agnew, 1997b). This has become increasingly apparent as established political affiliations that had 'nationalized' politics in many countries have eroded. For example, in the United States presidential elections seem to have become increasingly regionalized compared to the 1970s and 1980s, with Democratic candidates doing best in the north-east and on the west coast and Republicans dominating in the continental interior. Of course, American national elections have always had a powerful regional or sectional cast to them. But this aspect seemed to be diminishing until recently. Likewise, in Britain, Canada, Italy, and France, established geographical patterns of support for political parties have been significantly disrupted by voter realignments.

In the final analysis, these are shifts in the votes of individuals from one or party to another or none or the result of new individuals entering the stock of voters and others leaving, either through migration or death. But voting does not take place in a social-geographical vacuum. People are subject to all sorts of influences from the state of their economic surroundings, the social groups to which they belong, and the cultural match between their lives and the appeals of politicians. These influences tend to co-vary across places. Parties also vary considerably in how well they are organized from place-to-place and, hence, how well they can communicate their messages to potential supporters. How all of these influences come together affects the geographical pattern of votes, with a localized pattern resulting from the highest degree of fragmentation of the electorate, a regionalized pattern occurring when the electorate takes on a greater degree of homogeneity across a contiguous area, and a nationalized pattern reflecting a widely shared set of preferences across all electoral districts (Agnew, 2002).

Italian electoral politics since World War II can be interpreted in terms of three political-geographical 'regimes' in which the places out of which Italy is made have had different degrees of electoral similarity and difference that have dominated in different periods. The first regime, dominant from 1947 until 1963, involved a regional pattern of support for the major political parties based upon place similarities that clustered regionally. The second, in effect from 1963 until 1976, witnessed the expansion of the Communist Party (PCI) out of its regional strongholds into a nationally competitive position with the Christian Democratic Party (DC). This had different causes in different places but the net effect was to suggest a nationalization of the two major parties. The third, characteristic of the period since 1976, has seen increased support for minor parties, including regional parties such as the Northern League (Lega Nord), the geographical 'retreat' and political disintegration of the PCI and DC and a more localized pattern of political expression in general, reflecting the increased 'patchiness' of Italian economic growth and social change and the crisis of the system of existing parties after 1992.

The period 1947–63 is that of the classical electoral geography of Italy established most definitively by Galli and his colleagues (Galli and Prandi, 1970; Figure 5.1). They divided the country into six zones on the basis of levels of support for the three major parties, the PCI, DC and the Socialists (PSI), and the strength of the major political subcultures, the Socialist and the Catholic (Figure 5.1).

Zone I, the industrial triangle, covered north-west Italy and included Piemonte, Liguria and Lombardia. This was the region in which industrial production was concentrated in the 1950s. Socialists, Christian Democrats, and Communists were all competitive in this region.

Zone II, *la zona bianca*, covered north-east Italy and included the provinces of Bergamo and Brescia in Lombardia, the province of Trento, the province of Udine, and all of the Veneto except the province of Rovigo. The Christian Democrats were most strongly entrenched in this region and opposition was divided among a number of parties.

Zone III, *la zona rossa*, covered central Italy and included the provinces of Mantova, Rovigo and Viterbo; the whole of Emilia-Romagna except for the province of Piacenza; Toscana except for Lucca (an 'isola bianca'); Umbria; and the Marche, except for the province of Ascoli Piceno. In this region the PCI was most strongly established, especially in the countryside but increasingly in the cities.

Figure 5.1 The electoral regions of Italy, c.1963.
Source: *redrawn from Galli and Prandi (1970)*

Zone IV, the south, included the provinces of Ascoli Piceno, Lazio (except Viterbo), Campania, Abruzzo e Molise, Puglia, Basilicata, and Calabria. This zone was historically the poorest and most marked by clientelistic politics. In the 1950s, the Christian Democrats and the right-wing parties dominated the zone but were faced with increasingly strong challenges from PCI and PSI.

Zones V and VI, Sicily and Sardinia, had more complex political alignments than the peninsular south. For example, the PCI was well established in the southern

147

provinces of Sicily (especially the sulphur-mining areas), while Sardinia had a strong regionalist party.

There were strongly rooted cultural 'hegemonies' (party-based consensus building) in only two of these zones, *la zona bianca* and *la zona rossa*. However, in electoral terms, support for specific political parties was remarkably clustered regionally in 1953: the PCI in the center, the PNM (monarchists) and MSI (neofascists) in the south and Sicily, DC in the north-east and the south. In the 1950s, Italian politics followed a regional regime reflecting a similarity at the regional scale of place-based social, economic and political relationships.

The second period, 1963–76, marks a break with the regional pattern characteristic of the 1950s. Two electoral shifts were especially clear: the expansion of support for the PCI outside *la zona rossa* (along with its consolidation inside), particularly in the industrial north-west and parts of the south, and the breakdown of *la zona bianca* as a number of small parties made inroads in the previously hegemonic support for DC in parts of the north-east. The net effect of these changes was a seeming nationalization of the major parties, even though they still maintained traditional areas of strength.

These political changes were the fruit of the major economic and social changes Italy underwent in the late 1950s and early 1960s. A major expansion occurred in manufacturing and industrial employment, especially in the north-west, as a phenomenal boom or 'economic miracle' drew the Italian economy away from its predominantly agrarian base. At the same time that the industrial centers of the north-west were experiencing such dramatic economic and social change as a result of the economic boom and massive immigration, the rest of the country was experiencing shock waves emanating from the north-west. The extreme south (Puglia, Basilicata and Calabria) was a major zone of emigration to the north-west and, with the exception of Taranto, without much industry. Where industry was established it created pockets of new social and economic relationships in the midst of a rapidly depopulating rural society. In all these places and among immigrants from the south in the north, the PCI expanded its support in the late 1960s and early 1970s.

The other major feature of the period 1963–76 was the so-called breakdown of the Catholic subculture or dominant position in *la zona bianca*, or north-east, and subsequent loss of DC voters. The argument is that DC, being largely an electoral rather than a mass party with a large membership, had relied heavily on affiliated organizations, many of a religious nature, to mobilize its support. However, in the late 1960s as a result of heavy out-migration from rural areas in the Veneto, Trento and Friuli, the constituent subregions of *la zona bianca*, and the growing industrialization of some areas, such as Venice, Treviso, Trento and Pordenone, the traditional social networks and communal institutions upon which DC hegemony was based began to collapse.

The nationalizing political-geographical regime peaked in 1976 when DC and PCI together accounted for 73 percent of the national vote. Although this trend had distinctive causes relating to the geographically differentiated social and economic impacts of the economic miracle and their interplay with political and organizational traditions, it was widely interpreted as a permanent nationalization of political life. DC and the PCI were now national political parties.

The 1979 election indicated a much more complex geography of political strength and variation than had been characteristic previously. Since then, all parties have been less regionalized or nationalized than in the past. The 1983 and 1987 elections suggested a trend towards a localization or increased differentiation of political expression that has continued through the great political and electoral changes of the early 1990s. In 1983, DC lost 5.4 percent nationally , but PCI was not the beneficiary. Rather, it was smaller parties such as the PSI and the Republicans (PRI) in the north and the MSI in the south that gained the most. In 1987, DC recovered somewhat from 1983 but without a major geographical expansion. The major loser this time was the PCI, which lost ground in the northeast, the north-west and some provinces of *la zona rossa* to the PSI and a variety of smaller parties, including the Radicals (PR), the Greens, and Democrazia Proletaria (DP).

One cause of localization was the increasingly differentiated pattern of economic change after a previous era of concentration. While the economic boom of the early 1960s concentrated economic growth increasingly in the north-west, by the late 1960s there was considerable decentralization of industrial activity out of the north-west and into the north-east and the center. This new pattern of differentiated economic growth led some commentators to write of the 'three Italies' – a north-west with a concentration of older heavy industries and large factory-scale production facilities, a north-east–center of small, family-based, export-orientated and component-producing firms, and a still largely underdeveloped south, reliant on government employment but with some of the small-scale development (for example, in the vicinity of Bari or Caserta) characteristic of the 'third Italy' (north-east–center). This terminology, though useful as a general characterization of a new economic geography, masks both a much more uneven and differentiated pattern at a local scale and the linkages between localized development and the big firms of the north-west. High concentrations of employment in major growth industries have, in fact, been widely scattered.

Other causes have also contributed to the localizing political-geographical trend from the late 1970s to the present. One was the failure of the parties to successfully adapt to social and economic change. In Trento and Udine (in the north-east), for example, DC had problems adapting to the new economy. In large parts of the south and the north-west, the PCI was unable to capitalize on earlier successes mainly because, in the south, it had neither control over the state resources that lubricate the politics of many parts of that region, nor was it able to build a permanent following. In the north-west, its major vanguard of unionized workers was much reduced in economic importance at the same time that the other parties had become better organized and the particular problems of the southern immigrants, whom the PCI had previously recruited as voters, had largely receded from the political agenda.

The emergence of effective regional-level governments in Italy as whole since 1970 also reinforced the localization of interests and sense of place. Where parties have achieved some strength and legitimacy through control over regional governments, they have been able to build local coalitions for national politics based upon the pursuit of local interests. The PCI, for example, benefited from its control of or participation in the regional governments of Emilia-Romagna, Toscana and Umbria, but it suffered elsewhere, and other parties such as DC or the PSI benefited, because of its lack of control over patronage jobs and inability to write regional political agendas.

The former successes of DC and the PCI in, respectively, *la zona bianca* and *la zona rossa* rested to a degree on the social institutions with which they were affiliated (unions, co-operatives, clubs, etc.), as well as social isolation. However, the shifting orientations of these institutions and the rise of the consumer society opened up possibilities for smaller parties. There is some evidence that, after the late 1960s, ties between DC and the PCI and their supportive organizations, especially the unions for the PCI, had weakened. The parties themselves were responsible for some of this. In order to expand nationally, they often had to abandon or at least limit the ideological appeal that served so well in areas of traditional strength. They also had to respond in some areas to 'new' movements, such as the Greens, which opened them up for both factionalism and essentially localized forms of organization and ideology. More generally, parties do not always travel well. Thus, in comparing north-east with central Italy, the question of compatibility between 'party style' and 'local style' arises. As Stern (1975: 223) has noted in a comparison of the two regions in which DC and the PCI exerted their greatest influence in the 1950s and 1960s, *la zona bianca* in the north-east and *la zona rossa* in the center:

> The evolution of two very different forms of political hegemony, each with distinct characteristics that necessitate sharply contrasting forms of maintenance. The Christian Democratic variety that flourishes in north-eastern Italy is fueled efficiently by stable social organization that de-emphasizes the place of politics in community life. In comparison the Communist variant thriving in central Italy accents the urgent attention that political matters should command among the local citizenry and thereby constantly reaffirms the relatively recent sense of legitimacy that underlies PCI control.

Of course, these hegemonies always had local roots and in some localities their power has been quite visible and persistent, as studies of Bologna and Vicenza suggest. Although, as Tesini (1986) suggests for Bologna, things *could* have turned out quite differently.

Finally, in 1992 the system of parties in place since the end of World War II came to an end. As a result of the end of the Cold War and disputes over the meaning and appropriateness of the term Communist the PCI had already regrouped as two new parties, the larger PDS (Partito Democratico della Sinistra) and the smaller hard line Rifondazione Comunista (RC). As a result of investigation of systematic corruption in their operations, the PSI collapsed and DC disintegrated into three separate parties, the Partito Popolare to the center-left and two smaller factions to the right. The fascist MSI was reborn as a new 'post-fascist' conservative party, Alleanza Nazionale, and in 1994 a new party organized by the media tycoon Silvio Berlusconi, Forza Italia, attempted to replace DC on the center-right. The proliferation of smaller parties continued. But a new electoral system, in effect for the first time in 1994, forced parties to look for coalition partners before elections so as to run more effectively for the 75 percent of seats decided by majority votes in single-member districts. The other 25 percent of seats remain under the previously dominant system of proportional representation for candidates from party lists in multi-member districts. With the federalist/separatist Lega Nord a potent electoral force in many parts of northern Italy, all parties save Forza Italia and PDS (now known as DS for Democratici Sinistra) are now largely local or regional in strength. Even these two parties must coalesce with some of the others to achieve national-government office. As a result of the local strength of different parties support for all parties in 2001 is more obviously localized than it was in 1976 or in the 1950s.

Geographical scale and the new global finance

The 'new economy' that helped bring about the localizing regime in Italian electoral politics after 1976 was itself a response to two major economic changes throughout the industrialized world in the 1970s: the shift in manufacturing production from large factories to small-scale production across a wider range of locations and the collapse of the Bretton Woods system of managed currency exchange rates in 1972 (Piore and Sabel, 1984; Harvey, 1989; Agnew and Corbridge, 1995). If the former has underpinned to some degree the globalization of production across national boundaries, then the latter is partly responsible for the incredible expansion of a global financial system based on rapid interconnections between money markets and stock exchanges in major world cities and the explosion of monetary flows between those cities and offshore banking centers devoted to easing the movement of capital from place to place.

At first sight, this process would seem to augur a global economy based on flows in which place or territory and, hence, geographical scale 'below' the global, matters for very little. Surely this is potent evidence for the emergence of a purely global phenomenon: the global financial network? A case in point is that of so-called e-cash, covering electronic debit and credit cards, various forms of smart cards, and true digital money. Many financial transactions still require mediation by banks and other institutions. But, increasingly, direct buyer-to-seller relationships cut out all intermediaries, as people communicate over the Internet and avoid banks, wholesalers, and retailers. In this world, new communication technologies seem to have eliminated national borders and dissolved the link between income-producing activities and specific locations. Digitalization of finance is cutting money loose from its geographic moorings. Yet, monetary regulation presumes that customers and institutions share a common space. The very idea of controlling the money supply, for example, assumes that national territory defines the scope of the market. In this context, therefore, many speak of the 'increasing irrelevance of geographic jurisdiction in a digital world economy' (Kobrin, 1997: 75). Not only does this increase the possibilities of fraud, money laundering, and financial scams, it also represents the diminished efficacy of governance rooted in mutually exclusive territorial jurisdictions.

This understanding of global finance, and globalization more broadly, has become widely accepted. But it is deeply problematic. In the first place, its effects have hardly been global. They are by and large restricted to certain clearly demarcated regions of the world, largely consisting of certain centers in North America, Western Europe, and East Asia, with outliers elsewhere. The world after the Cold

War has taken on a radically different geographical structure but not one in which any location is interchangeable with any other (Figure 5.2). In fact, the opposite has been the case. During the Cold War both sides had incentives to stimulate at least a veneer of economic development within their respective spheres of influence and in countries that they were courting for support in their struggle against the Other. Absent this political interference, market processes tend to reward regions and localities that have crucial advantages (in skilled labor, access to technology, and capital) over other ones. Richard Gordon (quoted in Castells, 1996: 393) puts the matter succinctly:

> in this new global context, localized agglomeration, far from constituting an alter-
> native to spatial dispersion, becomes the principal basis for participation in a global
> network of regional economies … Regions and networks in fact constitute inter-
> dependent poles within the new spatial mosaic of global innovation. Globalization in
> this context involves not the leavening impact of universal processes but, on the
> contrary, the calculated synthesis of cultural diversity in the form of differentiated
> regional innovation logics and capabilities.

In the second place, globalization is not without its own geopolitical roots. The globalization of financial markets is not the product of irresistible technological and market forces. In fact, states have been major sponsors of it for a whole vari-ety of reasons: encouraging global financial centers as a strategy of economic growth (notably in the US and British cases), satisfying financial and banking lob-bies, facing difficulties in administering capital controls, and reacting to competitive pressures from other countries lowering barriers to capital mobility. The Bretton Woods Agreement had strongly endorsed the use of capital controls but its abro-gation by the United States in 1971 opened up the world economy to the possi-bility of an internationally competitive financial system, redolent of the period before the Great Depression of the 1930s. States reintroduced private global finance by giving freedom to market actors through liberalization of capital con-trols, coordinating with other states through collaboration between central banks, and choosing to limit controls on financial flows (Helleiner, 1995).

But a third factor has also been important. States have hardly abandoned finan-cial regulation to markets (Quinn, 1997). Far from it. But the variety of ways in which states engage in regulation has allowed for increased 'shopping around' between jurisdictions for the most auspicious fiscal and monetary conditions. It is the very division of the world into territorial jurisdictions, therefore, that has been a major stimulus to financial globalization. Indeed, 'new places' have come into

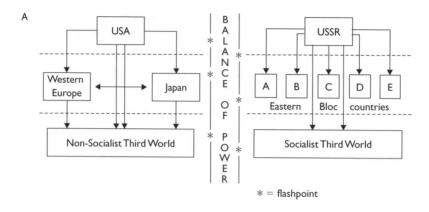

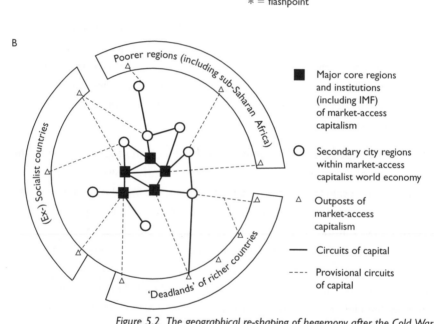

Figure 5.2 The geographical re-shaping of hegemony after the Cold War.
A. Hegemony of the Cold War geopolitical order
B. Hegemony of the post-Cold War geographical order
Source: Agnew and Corbridge (1995: 206)

existence as centers of global finance precisely because they offer regulatory conditions that facilitate the movement of capital. Offshore financial centers have grown up to host banking, insurance, and other financial activities away from onshore regulatory authorities. Examples of such centers include the Bahamas and the Cayman Islands in the Caribbean, Gibraltar and Jersey in Europe, Bahrein in the Middle East, Singapore and Hong Kong in the Far East, and Vanuatu in the

Pacific (Hudson, 1998). Beginning as tax havens for wealthy retirees or as poor areas with no alternative source of income, these places have become important nodes in global finance because they offer a haven from more rigorous onshore regulation but also because they are geared to the needs of the industries they serve without the political cross-pressures larger states must deal with. The different regulatory frameworks provided by different states, therefore, have had a powerfully formative influence on how global financial networks have developed.

Differences in interests between states also set limits to the expansion of global networks. This is a fourth important caveat to the image of global finance running rampant over national boundaries. By way of example, the US government and major financial interests have a particularly strong commitment to freeing financial markets that is not shared by most European and Asian states. One root of this lies in the greater reliance of European and Asian banks on interest income as opposed to US banks which receive far more of their profits from trading income, such as dealing in currency swaps and derivatives. European and Asian governments also have less faith in untrammeled markets, given the less positive economic growth profiles of Europe and Asia in the 1990s compared to the US and the devastating impact of loosened capital controls on Asian economies in 1997–98 (Wade, 1998–99).

Finally, the image of an untrammeled global world formed by cyber-networks rests not so much on empirical evidence as an enthusiasm for the world-without-boundaries prophesied since the beginning of human time. It is a kind of secular eschatology. It rests on the belief that connectedness with others and knowing them will automatically generate understanding and undermine conflict. Yet, the globalizing world is an incredibly uneven and unequal one, as argued previously. It is also an inherently fragile one, waxing and waning with global liquidity as inflated US stock prices (as in the late 1990s) or the infusion of new bank deposits (as with the 'petrodollars' deposited by the OPEC oil producers in the 1970s gave major banks cash to invest) lead to increased risk-taking in investments in 'emerging markets' and generally beyond the safe haven of 'home' markets (Soros, 1998–99; Pettis 2001). What connectedness does do is to make people in poorer places who have access to the new means of global communication increasingly aware of how different their lives are from those they come across on satellite TV or the Internet. At the same time, the absence of simple overarching conflicts (such as that of the Cold War) seems to have encouraged a turning away from the global or distant towards the local and national when it comes to news reporting in the US and Europe (Moisy, 1997). The opening up of global financial networks,

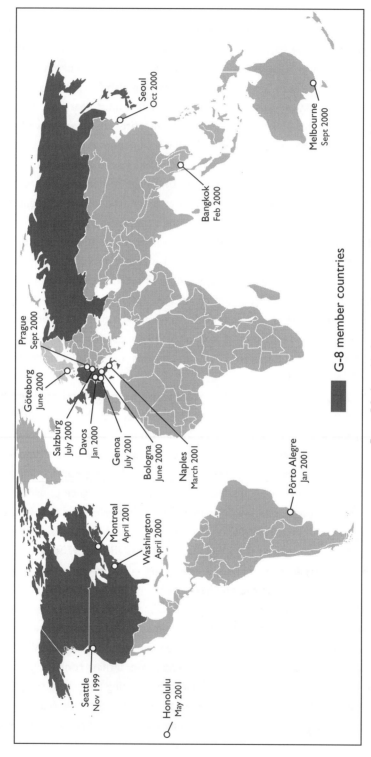

Figure 5.3 A world of protests. Sites of major anti-globalization demonstrations, 1999–2001.
Source: *author*

G-8 member countries

Seoul
Oct 2000

Melbourne
Sept 2000

Bangkok
Feb 2000

Prague
Sept 2000

Göteborg
June 2000

Salzburg
July 2000

Davos
Jan 2000

Genoa
July 2001

Bologna
June 2000

Naples
March 2001

Pórto Alegre
Jan 2001

Montreal
April 2001

Washington
April 2000

Seattle
Nov 1999

Honolulu
May 2001

therefore, is not paralleled by a surge in popular interest in the global. Ironically, for many people the local has become more important socially at exactly the time when the world as a whole has been compressed by the new communication technologies. Finding out about distant others, then, often can encourage a turn homewards. Yet, globalization is also mobilizing some people to fight against what they perceive as its depredations by organizing politically in transnational coalitions and disrupting the international meetings that symbolize its workings (the G-8 Summits, IMF and World Bank Meetings, etc.; Figure 5.3). They are acting globally in defense of the local and national (see pp. 171–73, 'Caring for distant strangers'). Consequently, geographical scales must always be thought of relationally: no one scale exists separate from the others.

Politics of the environment

Geography in its 1890s incarnation has become popular again, but now with people profoundly ignorant of the disputes and resolutions that have led from environmental determinism to the present pluralistic state of understanding of 'geography' detailed in Chapter 4. On one side are those, such as the economic historian David Landes (1998) and the economist Jeffrey Sachs (2000), both affiliated with that haven from geographical thinking, Harvard University, extolling warmed-over versions of environmental determinism in which physical conditions cause differences in economic and political development. On the other are those, such as the ecologists at the Worldwatch Institute (Brown, 1981; 1999), preaching global environmental sustainability in the face of a plethora of environmental dangers. In this view, a direct causal connection is drawn between global 'consumerism,' on the one hand, and a vast range of environmental disasters such as habitat destruction, global warming, and water pollution, on the other. In neither case are the roles of political economy, cultural invention, or institutional arrangements accorded much more than marginal status in accounting for contemporary global development and environmental problems. It is as if the past one-hundred years of political geography – and all the debates over environmental determinism and the mediating roles of discourse and institutions – had never taken place.

Needless to say, a priority for political geography should lie in helping to correct this ignorance. Yet, political geography has remained largely unconnected to 'nature–culture' debates in contemporary Geography as a whole and without much presence in the environmental studies curricula that constitute such an important part of Geography's presence within higher education in a number of countries, particularly the United States. There are a number of environmental themes that connect closely with the concerns of political geography.

One obvious theme is that of resource questions and the degree to which they have or might figure in conflicts. Non-renewable resources in great demand, such as oil, are clear candidates for bringing about conflict. Possible 'flash points' for resource conflict, particularly in the Middle East and Central Asia, have become the major focus of US government defense planning (Klare, 2001). But whether food and water shortages can directly precipitate conflict is subject to greater doubt than is possible conflict over world oil supplies (Rogers, 2000; Lowi and Shaw, 2000). Wolf and Hamner (2000: 123), for example, note that 'countries seem not to go to war over water.' Nevertheless, the links among environment, population, and military conflict are well worth investigating, not least to see how institutions mediate between physical-geographical conditions and inter-group and inter-state conflicts (Homer-Dixon and Blitt, 1998; Lowi and Shaw, 2000). In an increasingly globalized world 'risks' of all sorts, other than traditional military ones, are coming to dominate thinking about security and conflict (Albert, 2000; Ó Tuathail, 2000b).

A second theme is that of the geography of environmental movements: where they arise, how they organize geographically, and how they construct their goals (Bryner, 2000; Rubin, 1998). The idea of an 'endangered planet' has become a powerful metaphor in mobilizing people into support for a range of environmental organizations, from the 'managerialist' Worldwatch Institute to the direct action Greenpeace. Images of environmental insecurity often verge on the apocalyptic, suggesting that current levels of global consumption threaten 'humanity's' survival (Sprout and Sprout, 1978; Sutherland, 2000). Indeed, a case can be made that a 'green geopolitics' is under construction by environmentalist movements that challenges and, to a degree, displaces the older state-based geopolitics (Luke, 2000a; Dalby, 2002). Of course, even though there are *bona fide* differences over the extent of 'environmental dangers,' these are not simply inventions of over-active imaginations. In particular, erosion of variety of biological characteristics and functions among more complex organisms as a result of human pressures on those zones in which a large percentage of the world's plant and animal species are concentrated (so-called ecological hotspots) may well be a serious long-term problem for both global genetic variety and the quality of human life on earth (e.g. Myers *et al.*, 2000; Levin and Levin, 2002; Wilson, 2002).

Finally, a third theme is the way in which state policies in relation to agriculture, industrial development, urban growth, etc. produce political and legal dilemmas over the geographical distribution of environmental costs and benefits, environmental degradation, and other problems (such as food quality issues, negative effects of food aid on agriculture in poor countries, declining rural populations, impacts of urban development and highways on wild animals, maintenance of species diversity, etc.). In other words, how do states support agriculture, fund nature reserves, and encourage more profligate forms of urban development? From this point of view, states (and allied agents) are not so much the managers as the creators of environmental problems (Blaikie, 1985; McMichael, 1993; Peet and Watts, 1996; O'Hagan, 2001). Their actions deserve closer attention than they typically receive from environmental geographers who tend to see environmental problems as invariably natural rather than often political in origin.

I want to provide one case study for each of the three themes. The first is that of environmental risk and security in the work of Phyllis Mofson (1999), Simon Dalby (2002), Gearóid Ó Tuathail (2000b), Matthias Albert (2000) and others. The second is that of green geopolitics as explored by Timothy Luke (2000a) in his analysis of the Worldwatch Institute. The third is Andrew O'Hagan's (2001) discussion of agricultural degradation in Britain as a result of government policies.

Environmental security

Modern geopolitical thinking is dominated by a view of security that is essentially territorial: friendly and enemy blocs of space are posed against one another as spheres to be protected or contained against military and economic threats. Increasingly, however, the security situation faced by states and the world's population is both more global and more diffuse (Ó Tuathail, 2000b). Much of this has to do with the rise of consciousness about environmental problems said to threaten human existence. On the one hand, a whole set of problems are planetary in scope (global warming, the spread of nuclear and biochemical weapons, leaky nuclear reactors, over-fishing, etc.) yet must be addressed by the existing territorial system of government. On the other hand, many environmental problems afflict specific communities in particular places (technological and environmental hazards, air and water pollution, etc.) that pit social groups and political movements against one another in the struggle to avoid and displace environmental dangers.

In each case, however, threats can no longer be spatialized in national terms, as if state boundaries neatly matched the negative externalities of environmental danger. From this point of view, security is increasingly globalized and localized. A number of scholars have proposed studying environmental security in terms of the 'blowback' and 'boomerang' effects that arise in a modern global society in which the traditional calculus of 'risk' has changed dramatically (Ó Tuathail, 2000b;

Albert, 2000; Dalby, 2002). In this understanding, people are increasingly conscious of the side effects of economic growth and weapons production and thus begin to call the traditional 'rationality' of cause and effect into question. Consequently, the environmental side-effects of other human actions have become more important politically. The German sociologist Ulrich Beck (1992) has coined the phrase 'risk society' to describe this new 'modernity' in which the unintended consequences of industrialization and consumption are acknowledged and confronted.

This emphasis has led in two directions. In the first place, it has encouraged a rethinking of conventional views about security threats and political responses to them. One radical conclusion is that insecurity always may have been more characteristic of human societies than is often acknowledged, particularly by those in the defense–industrial complexes of the Great Powers who have proposed the idea of a singular 'national security'. Industrialization and the insulation of large numbers of people in developed countries from visible dependence on the natural world may have encouraged a certain hubris about the security of the human condition. With the rise of 'risk society,' the sense of human vulnerability has returned. In particular, the long-term tendency of human groups to move and disrupt political boundaries may be returning after a period of relative stability of populations in place (Dalby, 2000, drawing on Diamond, 1997); environmental consciousness has coincided with the moral critique of high mass consumption in some places when many people are destitute elsewhere, suggesting a link between environmental degradation and social justice; military security has increasingly produced environmental insecurity (witness the possible role of US weapons labs in the 2001 anthrax scare, worries about disposing of nuclear and biochemical weapons stocks, and the health side-effects of fighting in the Gulf War); and global pollution, pressure from farmers, and commercial lumbering are creating serious ecological 'hot spots' around the world where the survival of many plant and animal species is in serious question.

In the second place, the idea of 'risk society' has encouraged greater attention to the complex geography of environmental hazards produced by human actions. Phyllis Mofson (1999), for example, uses the notion of 'ecopolitical hierarchy' to represent the scales and attributes of environmental problems (Figure 5.4). If ecosystem complexity increases as one moves up the geographical hierarchy, so do the number of actors, political jurisdictions, and barriers to resolving any particular problem. As a problem is associated with higher levels in the hierarchy the possibility of resolution becomes more difficult. So, global climate change is much more difficult to manage than would be some local pollution problem.

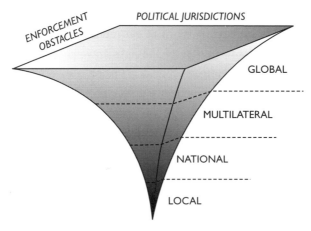

Figure 5.4 The ecopolitical hierarchy.
Source: *Mofson (1999: 247)*

This is undoubtedly true. But it does not mean that local or regional environmental problems are not also exceedingly complex and difficult to manage (Williams, 1999). Laura Pulido (2000), for example, has shown in some detail how environmental hazards in the Los Angeles region of southern California correlate very highly with areas in which racial minorities are heavily concentrated. Though in one respect this is easy to explain: whites are advantaged by the political system and are able to keep hazards at bay or move away from them relatively easily, the devil is in the details. The history of settlement, the class structure of the region, and the character of suburbanization in Los Angeles are all parts of a more complete explanation. The very high level of residential segregation by race in Los Angeles is one feature of the city that deserves particular mention. Another is that whites are now a small minority of the population of the city proper and a minority of the population of the region as a whole. That they are mainly middle-class and the bulk of the black and Latino populations is not is also important.

The overall point of Pulido's argument, however, is that the intentions of individual white people are not really the issue. What is significant is that politics in Los Angeles has historically depended on maintaining white social, political, and environmental privilege. The environmental burdens borne by different groups, therefore, reflect the largely hidden prerogatives of a racially stratified society. This means that the 'environmental security' of different populations at the local scale are also part-and-parcel of the 'risk society' and its boomerang effects. Environmental security is not simply a new set of demands on national security, therefore.

It applies to new sources of risk at geographical scales from the global to the local that cannot be simply managed in terms of old 'rational' (and national) models of security. In turn, this consciousness of the links between who lives where and the geographical impacts of environmental degradation is generating a new type of environmentalism geared to 'environmental justice' (e.g. Novotny, 2000).

Green geopolitics

How are environmental threats constructed and disseminated? Environmentalism has emerged as one of the most important sites of contestation of the largely corporate capitalist world economy that has come to dominate the world since the collapse of Communism and the break-up of the former Soviet Union. In order to garner support and build political coalitions, however, some environmental organizations have come to construct their messages in terms that mirror features of the corporate model they might be expected to criticize and the 'old' geopolitics that might seem to be redundant in a world in which conflicts between Great Powers are no longer the driving force of world politics.

Timothy Luke (2000a) focuses attention on the Worldwatch Institute, a Washington DC-based global environmental monitoring and lobbying organization as an example of what he terms a new 'popular geopolitics' in which 'the environment' is a challenge to be managed 'bioeconomically' so as to avoid global ecological collapse. Consequently,

> Human beings must check their increasing levels of population, reorganize their wasteful resource-intensive modes of production, and limit their rising rates of excessive material consumption. All of these ends, in turn, require a measure of geographical surveillance and degree of political administration perhaps beyond the powers of modern nation-states, but not beyond those exercised by some transnational inter-governmental organization following a new globalized green geopolitics.
> (Luke, 2000a: 362)

To Luke, this managerial model shares much in common with both corporate capitalism and classical geopolitics. From the former it gains its focus on expert auditing and from the latter it receives its emphasis on relative efficiency under conditions of scarcity in a closed world system. In this construction, the buzzword 'sustainability' becomes yet another expert discourse about exerting power over people and things. Likewise, the phrase 'spaceship earth,' associated with the photographs of the earth from outer space first seen in the late 1960s, represents the object that now must be managed as a whole. In this way 'ecology becomes a science of statist administration ... giving us a geopolitics written in the World-watchers' green political codes' (Luke, 2000a: 369).

The end of British farming?

The final case study concerns the environmental sustainability and survival of farming in Britain. Governments in both Britain and France, and elsewhere, have tried to maintain national agricultural production and a rural way of life, associated powerfully in both Britain and France with national identity, through massive direct subsidies and, where possible, import restrictions. The difference between them, however, is that a rich peasant culture has survived in France and helped to maintain a relationship between farming and the land and farm animals that has been all but lost in Britain. As an industrial, increasingly a post-industrial society, Britain has industrialized its agriculture to a degree largely unmatched anywhere in the world. This is the source of the scourges that have afflicted British farming over the past ten years: the massive outbreaks of BSE (mad cow disease) and foot-and-mouth disease. The fear is that British commercial farming might now go the way of the British coal industry unless it is reformed on a totally different basis.

What is so bad about 'industrialized' farming? Surely, it raises yields and keeps people in business who otherwise would have to quit? Well, if only the situation was so straightforward. What happened? Andrew O'Hagan (2001: 12) traces the problem back to the years after World War II when new government subsidies encouraged a new style of farming with dreadful long-term consequences:

> We [Britain] did the thing that peasant nations such as France did not do: we turned the landscape into a prairie, trounced our own ecosystem, and with public money too, and turned some of the biggest farms in Europe into giant, fertilizer gobbling, pesticide-spraying, manufactured-seed-using monocultures geared only to massive profits and the accrual of EU [European Union] subsidies. A Civil Service source reminded me that even the BSE crisis has a connection to intensive agribusiness: 'feeding animals with the crushed fat and spinal cord of other animals is a form of cheap, industrial, cost-effective management,' he said, 'and it would never have happened on a traditional British farm. It is part of the newer, EU-driven, ultra-profiteering way of farming. And look at the results,

Whether the EU is entirely to blame is doubtful. Only Britain seems to have the severely compromised food chain that could produce the devastating BSE epidemic; the wartime experience of agricultural intensification is a more likely culprit.

Whatever the origins, however, the crisis in British farming signifies a long-term problem that may come to afflict many other parts of the world as they adopt the industrialized farming methods pioneered in Britain. 'The way ahead is ominous,' writes O'Hagan (2001: 12), referring to the decline in biodiversity and increase in food safety problems in British agriculture. Genetically modified (GM) crops are the next specter likely to haunt British farming. At the same time, agriculture in Britain is increasingly at the mercy of several large supermarket chains and for many farmers, particularly those in highland areas who do not specialize, there is little future in farming. Soon, British bread may no longer be baked with British ingredients. O'Hagan (2001: 13) quotes one small farmer's lament about the impact of big agriculture and the subsidies that fuel it:

> In the early 1950s there were about 454,000 farms in the UK. Now there are half that number, and of these just 23,000 produce half of all the food we grow. In a period of unprecedented public support for agriculture almost a quarter of a million farms have gone out of business ... It is the manufacturers [food processors] and City investors who now dictate the UK diet.

Such farmers not only joke about moving to France.

Normative political geography

Political geography long avoided much concern about its presuppositions, such as the determining role of physical-environmental conditions in political organization, the historical-geographical origins of statehood, the 'necessity' for empire, the 'obviousness' of territorial expansion, etc. and their consequences for humanity. Two reasons for this lack of interest in the normative basis to political thought spring to mind. The first is the coincidence between the 'rise' of political geography in both its classic and spatial-analytic manifestations and powerful pressures towards naturalized, empiricist–descriptive, and positivist–predictive modes of analysis. 'Science' in a peculiarly narrow sense of the term tended to rule understanding. Concern for the normative – the implicit judgments about what is 'right' and 'proper' in political arrangements – was viewed as subjective, ideological, and speculative in counterpoint to scientific analysis that hewed closely to the 'facts' and saw theory as arising from observation rather than prior to it and hence conditioning of what constituted the 'facts' at hand. From this point of view, the normative is purely a question of personal political preferences and without standing in what is presumed to be 'objective' scholarship. This is how political geography was shut off intellectually from critical analysis of its concepts and presuppositions.

The second reason for the absence of a normative political geography has been the close connection between the field and *raison d'état* or service to the state. Career prospects, such as memberships in prestigious national organizations and clubs and appointment at important universities, funding of research, and successful political influence, have been based on accepting the political status quo rather than opening it up for questioning. Thus, and unlike mainstream political theory's rigorous focus on concepts such as interest, power, and sovereignty, little or no attention has been paid to critical analysis of the concepts that the field has been based on: territory and territoriality, space and place, nation-states and statehood, nationalism, sovereignty and national identity, power and hegemony, etc.

This theoretical aphasia finally began to dissipate in the 1970s with critiques of spatial analysis from broadly analytic-philosophical (e.g. Sack, 1986) and Marxist (e.g. Harvey, 1973) perspectives. But only in the 1990s did a critical attitude towards normative assumptions begin to permeate the field as a whole, extending from analysis of conventional views of state territoriality (e.g. Agnew, 1994; Agnew, 1999; Taylor, 1994) to the language of foreign policy (e.g. Ó Tuathail and Agnew, 1992), understandings of power (e.g. Allen, 1999), the violence of national boundaries (Paasi, 1995; Conversi, 1999; Newman, 2001), and place and political identity in democratic practice (Entrikin, 1999). Whatever else one might think about it, the so-called postmodern wave has had the effect of encouraging a much more critical outlook on the field and its practitioners, even though the postmodern attitude is itself cynical about the possibility of improving the human (or planetary) condition. Currently, four areas seem particularly important for the further development of a normative political geography, engaging with debates about actual changes in the world of politics and with important assumptions of political geography as a field as yet without the attention they deserve: transnational democracy, weapons and warfare, caring for distant strangers, and democratic states and intellectual freedom.

Transnational democracy

The first area concerns arguments about 'transnational democracy.' In modern political thought, political space has been almost invariably associated with the idea of state-territoriality; politics is about modes of government within and patterns of conflict and co-operation between the territories or tightly bounded spaces of modern states. Much thinking about democracy has been 'trapped' by its orientation towards states and their presumed monopoly over political life.

Plausibly, however, this rendition of the association between politics and place is both historically and geographically problematic. Not only is the state–territory relationship a relatively recent one, it is one that has never completely vanquished other types of political geography (such as network-based kinship, and city-state or core–periphery imperial political systems) around the world (Agnew, 1994). Writing about 'failed' or 'quasi' states in locations as diverse as East Africa, Central Asia, or Southern Europe, for example, often misses the fact that the absence of a working state bureaucracy throughout a given state's territory does not signify the absence of either politics or of alternative governance arrangements working locally or non-territorially through networks of some sort or another.

From this point of view, 'political space,' cannot be reduced to state-territoriality for two reasons. One is that states are always and everywhere challenged by forms of politics that do not conform to the boundaries of the state in question. For example, some localities have kinship or patronage politics, others have ethnic or irredentist politics oriented to either autonomy or secession, and others support political movements opposed to current constitutional arrangements including the distribution of governmental powers between different tiers of government within the state. The second is that state boundaries are permeable, and increasingly so, to a wide range of flows of ideas, investments, goods, and people that open up territories to influences that are beyond the geographical reach of current governmental powers.

To an increasingly vocal band of thinkers state–territory, society, and popular sovereignty are no longer congruent and this undermines the quest for democracy at the national-state scale. To David Held (1999: 102), for example, one of the foremost advocates of cosmopolitan democracy, as the presumed autonomy of the territorial nation-state is undermined so is the very basis to democracy:

> If democracy means 'rule by the people,' the determination of public decision-making by equally free members of the political community, then the basis of its justification lies in the promotion and enhancement of autonomy, both for individuals as citizens and for the collectivity.

The only response must be to create new institutions beyond the state that match the increased geographical scope of the forces that are no longer effectively controlled by national governments.

The form that such institutions might take ranges from 'scaled up' versions of American federalism (see Agnew, 2001b) and enlarged 'life worlds' (Habermas, 1998) to the democratization of 'global city-regions' (Scott, 1998). Before accepting the logic of globalization as a new approach to democracy, however, a number of objections need to be investigated. The first one is that the deliberative nature of democracy requires a 'common ground' or sense of place upon which to base a project of political equality and an allied commitment to common purpose. Territoriality has long served this vital purpose in democratic theory, providing a public space on which to anchor the abstract goals of democracy (Thaa, 2001). Trying to nurture political participation that strengthens collective deliberation is difficult enough within state boundaries that have well developed political institutions and some history of democratic practice; even a vibrant 'civil society' does not necessarily guarantee democratic outcomes (Chambers and Kopstein, 2001). Second, in democracy the public good necessarily remains contestable and subject to conflicting claims and arguments (Dahl, 1999). For argumentation about the public good, however, a shared public sphere with effective communication is needed which, in turn, requires a high degree of mutual understanding (e.g. Manin, 1987). This is much more likely to occur within a contiguous population rather than across a diffuse network.

Third, it is not clear that globalization has as yet undermined popular sovereignty within a defined territory as the ruling assumption underpinning most democratic forms of governance. Democracy and nationalism have developed side by side. Nationalism rests firmly on the modern doctrine of popular sovereignty (Yack, 2001). The great landmarks in the history of popular sovereignty – from the English Glorious Revolution of 1688, the North and South American wars of independence, the French Revolution of 1789, the 'springtime of the peoples' all over Europe in 1848 to the decay of the European colonial empires after World War II and the Soviet collapse of 1989–92 – are also the major events in the history of democracy. This symbolism will not be easily displaced. Political identities are still significantly national ones and democratic politics still rests significantly on national territories (e.g. Cerny, 1999; Brown, 2001).

Fourth, and finally, the networks that advocates of transnational democracy point to as a possible basis for transcending the territorial parameters of conventional democratic theory have serious 'legitimacy' problems. Non-governmental organizations (NGOs), in particular, often claim to represent the interests of this or that group and in return channel funds, expertise, and information from donors to target groups (Hudson, 2001). But to what degree can they legitimately make such a claim? To whom are the NGOs accountable? Whose views do they actually represent? What role should they play in the politics of the countries in which their operations are located? As yet, the ability of transnational networks to offer an alternative to conventional territorial forms of representation is open to more than reasonable doubt.

Weapons and war

Political power beyond state boundaries has often been seen as the projection of force by one state against another or others. Two ideas have long expressed this sentiment. One is the idea of anarchy in the space beyond the confines of one's ordered and domestic space that could only be managed by vigilant preparation for warfare. Without a substantial war machine prepared to strike at adversaries before they strike at you, a state is vulnerable to conquest and subjugation. The second is the very commonly held view that states are in competition with one another for scarce resources and go to war with one another to wrest control of these from other states. That these ideas rest on longstanding features of human society, such as male fantasies of control and domination of others and the need to demonstrate individual prowess in warfare, are now widely recognized and thus subject to challenge and resistance (Enloe, 1990; Goldstein, 2001; Sharp, 2002).

Beginning with the Cold War, however, the most militarily powerful states began showing reservations about using force against one another and, to a lesser extent, against weaker states. A reasonable inference to draw from this is that the orthodox assumptions no longer hold empirically as well as normatively (Deudney, 1995; Kaldor, 1999). This opens up the possibility of creating a world in which disputes between the most powerful states are less likely to lead to massive violence. The old moral question about the rightness of force as a solution to human conflicts take on new meaning in a historical context in which the efficacy of war is itself profoundly in question. Parenthetically, it is important to note that this trend does not necessarily portend a decline in total political violence. Indeed, there is a contemporaneous trend towards an increase in the prevalence of internal wars as state authority collapses in many states (from Colombia by way of Sierra Leone and Somalia to Afghanistan). This rather makes the point that state monopoly over the use of force is as increasingly problematic within state boundaries as it is beyond them.

From one point of view, therefore, the use of military force by powerful states against one another seems to be of declining utility. Three changes in military technology and two changes in the world economy seem crucial to this shift, notwithstanding inertial interests still committed to the production of weapons and the invention of threats to justify them in the United States and other major powers. The first military change is the impact of nuclear weapons. These have had the effect of not only introducing mutual deterrence but also of imprinting on potential combatants the likely escalation of all organized inter-state violence into nuclear exchange. The unprecedented destructiveness of nuclear weapons and the likely negative impact (through delayed radiation) on victors as well as the van-quished mean that their possessors paradoxically limit their military options by possessing them and discipline allies and adversaries alike by introducing the prospect of rapid escalation. Nuclear weapons also seem to favor defensive over aggrandizing military actions by raising the stakes for potential aggressors.

Even before the advent of nuclear weapons, however, a second feature of mod-ern warfare had begun to erode the rational basis for its use. The economic and political costs of war between reasonably well-matched adversaries now exceed any conceivable collective benefit to national populations that can derive from it. There are of course domestic interests that are still served by war and prepara-tion for it (weapons makers, military officers, etc.), only war now requires very costly investments that do not guarantee favorable results. The civil wars involving the intervention of the US in Vietnam and the former Soviet Union in Afghanistan and the terrorist attacks on the United States in 2001 are reminders that even in apparently asymmetric conflicts the best armed need not prevail. Indeed a case can be made, following the initially successful US military intervention in Afghanistan in 2001–02, that a combination of precision bombing and lightly armed special forces offer a better military capability for many asymmetric conflicts than large numbers of troops with heavy armor and artillery (see O'Hanlon, 1998–99).

Third, with respect to military factors, there is increasing revulsion among the world's most affluent populations with the human costs of modern large-scale war and the seemingly feeble benefits it generates. The use of military force faces a legitimation crisis. The loss of even a single pilot or soldier on the US side now causes a total rethinking of American force commitments. This is perhaps a reflec-tion of the increased visibility of the conduct of warfare in a visual age. Though televised war often takes a spectacular or entertainment form, it also introduces an immediate sense of the deadliness of war that civilians in previous epochs of modern technological warfare never experienced. At the same time there is disil-lusionment with the 'fruits' of war. Gains often seem incommensurate with sacri-fices. The political inconclusiveness of many recent wars (such as that against Iraq in the Gulf in 1991 and the NATO 'intervention' in Kosovo in 1999) adds to skep-ticism. The democratization of foreign policy-making in many countries has prob-ably added to the questioning (Gelpi and Griesdorf, 2001). Once reserved for small elites, foreign policy is now increasingly subject to public challenge and debate in ways unheard of thirty years ago. The significance of public opinion and, hence, publicity in foreign and domestic policy arenas has increased worldwide. In this context, the pursuit of political change through non-violent means has become increasingly possible and socially acceptable. In particular, successful non-violent struggles (from Mahatma Gandhi's strategy of passive resistance in India in the 1920s and 1930s to Martin Luther King Jr's freedom marches for equal civil rights in the US in the 1950s and 1960s, non-violent opposition to the Vietnam War, the 'velvet revolutions' in Eastern Europe in 1989, and numerous movements for social and environmental change in contemporary India) have made the case for sustainable political gains as a result of deliberately *not* resorting to violence (see, for example, Bondurant, 1958; Fairclough, 1987; Tollefson, 1993; Brinton and Rinzler, 1990; Routledge, 1994).

Finally, warfare has been far from a constant of modern human history. Recent studies suggest that if the twentieth century had the two most devastating wars, then earlier periods, particularly the eighteenth century, seem to have been relatively pacific. The lesson this historical record suggests is that wars between major powers are the ones to be avoided – at all costs (e.g. Hayes, 2002). With little or no correlation with a whole series of putative 'determinants' (arms spending, economic downturns, etc.), research on the global cycle of violence suggests that political agency is of prime importance in producing damaging wars, further implying that the devastating weapons that produce such outcomes can also be rejected. Witness the little-known Japanese decision to 'give up the gun' in 1637 (Perrin, 1979). Although particular features of early-modern Japanese society obviously played a role in abandoning a technology already in wide use after its introduction from Europe in 1543 – the size and domination of the warrior *samurai* class whose chivalric code and swordsmanship were threatened by the musket, lack of danger from foreign invaders with guns because of geographical isolation, attachment to swords as cultural artifacts, and general rejection of foreign ideas, such as Christianity and Western business practices, along with guns – the example does suggest that choices can be made that do not accept the inevitability of escalation in the adoption and use of military technology.

Paralleling these weapon- and military-related trends have been two trends related to the world economy. Interstate competition is now largely about capturing the benefits of global economic growth for one's territory more than about conquering another state's territory to capture its resources. Insertion into global corporate and financial networks now seems crucial to the course of national economic development. Exceptions help to show what is now largely the rule. Iraq's invasion of Kuwait in 1989–90 was designed to capture that country's assets. What it revealed was the extent to which Kuwait's assets, other than its oil reserves, were mobile beyond the boundaries of the state. Indeed, the Kuwaiti government-in-exile contributed handsomely to the liberation of Kuwait from Iraqi occupation by a UN-sanctioned force through its continuing access to a large number of significant foreign investments from which it could pay for US forces. At the same time, the main threats that increasingly face the world's most developed countries, such as the United States, are seen by significant commentators as flows of migrants that challenge national cultural homogeneity and hide potential terrorists rather than the traditional weapons threat from this or that state (except, perhaps, so-called 'rogue states,' such as North Korea and Iraq) (see Shapiro, 1999; Ó Tuathail, 2000b).

Second, technological change has opened the possibility of escaping from the dilemma of competitive states chasing the same resources that might previously have led states into war with one another. In the present era of informational capitalism, the most productive and profitable activities are no longer resource-intensive ones, such as heavy industries and extensive agriculture, but technologically-intensive manufacturing, such as electronics and biotechnology, and service industries, such as tourism, finance, and personal services. These are best achieved by either generating external economies in local clusters of firms (as in California's Silicon Valley) or by tapping into global networks of specialized labor and customized production (e.g. Scott, 1998). This is no longer a world in which territorially bigger is automatically economically or politically better. Hence, it is a world in which military force to achieve such rational goals as increased resources or to cope with the anarchy threatened by other states no longer seems to make as much sense as it once might have. In a world of rapid economic circulation the rational link between territorial states and military force has become frayed, if not yet cut. In this context the ethics of weapons and warfare can begin to take on a more central role than heretofore.

Caring for distant strangers

The Scottish philosopher David Hume once observed that ordinarily human empathy for others tends to diminish with distance, as people consider first their nuclear and extended families, then the local community followed by city or rural district, nation, geographical region, and, finally, the world beyond. In clan and intensely localized societies this may still be largely the case. As noted previously, the end of the Cold War has produced an increased parochialism in news-gathering in North America and Western Europe even as the world has opened up to increased communication. But thanks to television, films, and the Internet, the world can now often seem as close or even closer than our immediate neighbors. These technologies bring images of far-off suffering into our homes. They raise in a fundamentally new context the question raised by the Christian Gospels: Am I my brother's/ sister's keeper? Only now the question has the corollary: If I am I my brother's/sister's keeper who is my brother/sister? Or, in other words, if charity no longer just starts at home where does it stop? (see, for example, Miller and Hashmi, 2001)

Political geography has conventionally accepted Hume's common-sense view, with an added emphasis on the nation as the fundamental unit of 'caring.' What might be some of the implications of adopting a less distance–decay-based understanding of the ethics of caring? The first implication is to extend the notion of caring from the 'domestic' realm out into the world. If some feminist writers have associated an ethic of care with the familial and household realms and duties assigned to women in many societies, then extending the possible geographical scope of caring extends the political scope of caring as well (Robinson, 1999).

In the context of a so-called shrinking world, in which places are no longer adequately thought of as isolated spatial zones, two ethical responses have predominated. One has been to resurrect Immanuel Kant's idea of a single 'humanity' as a reaction to a world both seemingly more united but also more threatening (environmentally, socially, etc.) and a cosmopolitan ethics (focusing on common rights and impartial justice) appropriate to it. A foundation of this perspective is the idea that life chances are fundamentally a product of where you are born and, hence, a matter of fate or chance rather than worth or merit. As Stuart Corbridge (1998: 37) puts it:

> To the extent that these Other people could have been Us (the affluent), and to the extent that their lives are inextricably linked to our own, there are good reasons for attending to their needs and rights as fellow human beings in a manner that will make calls on our 'own' resources and entitlements.

A second ethical response has been to argue that this vision of a common humanity is largely illusory. Rather, the contemporary situation is one in which interconnection coexists with deep differences. The globalizing world economy is one that is highly unequal; indeed more unequal in many respects than that it has replaced. This means that caring cannot be simply about encouraging the powerful to 'care about' the individual rights and humane treatment of others they do not know on a 'face-to-face' basis, although it does not exclude these. It must be, rather that responding morally to others is a capacity that is learned. This involves a recognition that moral response is not a rational act of will, but an ability to focus attention on another and to recognize the other as real. Such recognition is neither natural nor presocial, but rather something that emerges out of connections and attachments. In the context of [global] North–South relations, then, strategies would require sustained and continued attention to the lives, relations, and communities of people in developing countries, rather than to their individual rights, or to the scope and nature of our obligations to them (Robinson, 1999: 46–47).

A second implication of putting Hume's geography of care into question is the need to understand that others may have different moral discourses and practices than the ones 'we' have. In other words, our caring must be aware of what matters to others. This does not necessarily mean endorsing moral relativism – I'm OK, You're OK – about, say, widow burning, clitorectomies, or child labor, but it does entail accepting the reality of a world of diverse moral belief and practice. David Smith (1999: 122–3) gives a number of nice examples of specific moral discourses, pointing out how in some languages there are no words equivalent to the ethics of recognition and responsibility that dominate Western understandings of morality, and how there exist very different orientations to self and the wider society. For example, in Mongolia moral discourse relies heavily on the use of heroic historical figures, rather than abstract rules, as guides to behavior, and is orientated towards what is good for me (the self) rather than towards the sympathy for others found in other moralities (Humphrey, 1997). Among the Fulani people of northern Nigeria, Smith – quoting Jacobson-Widding (1997) – explains:

> The three sins of lying, farting and stealing ... exemplify lack of self-control. The association is with shame rather than guilt: they are sins of commission, rather than omission in the sense of failing to meet obligations or duties. To show self-mastery is a way of recognizing the relative position of people who interact, how the Fulani define themselves in relation to others, rather than their respective individual identities. It expresses collective social personhood. (Smith, 1999: 123)

Moral cosmopolitanism can become moral imperialism if not sensitive to the myriad local moralities that are still alive and well around the world.

Democratic states and intellectual freedom

As political geographers have abandoned the cause of this or that state for self-consciously critical perspectives they have not shown much interest in the social and political conditions that make this possible. If in the past political geography was simply the servant of states, what has changed to make the field both less state-oriented and less beholden to state sponsorship? This transformation in the intellectual orientation of the field has coincided with the rising power of the United States and its academia, yet political geographers tend, in general, to be critical of the activities of its governments within and beyond American shores.

They often seem to take the side, if only through their one-sided critique of US actions, of various despots and authoritarian regimes with whom US governments have gone to war.

The contemporary making of political geography, therefore, has two seemingly contradictory features. On the one hand, the 'new' political geography relies on a high degree of toleration and relative freedom of inquiry in the United States, France, Britain, India, Israel, Finland and several other countries in which political geography has prospered, that cannot be found much elsewhere in the world. What these countries have in common is a commitment, however fragile and intermittent it has been historically (witness the shameful treatment of Owen Lattimore in the United States during the 'Red scare' of the early 1950s, described in Chapter 4) to freedom of thought. In China and Saudi Arabia, to choose two other countries at random, state control over intellectual life is almost complete. Political dissent that is typical of many widely published academics in the contemporary United States or Britain would lead to prison or death in many other countries. That this is not simply a West versus East phenomenon is apparent when the crimes of German Nazism, Italian Fascism, Soviet Communism and Maoist Communism in China are brought to mind. Political oppression is and has been widely dispersed geographically.

On the other hand, however, we political geographers tend to be hypercritical of US governments and their allies as agents of 'empire' or 'hegemony,' while often silently or openly endorsing various forms of tyranny elsewhere in the world. This is definitely not to say that a critical attitude towards the actions of US governments should be abandoned. It is to say that this attitude should be extended to other actors and places as well (for exemplary cases that do precisely this, see, for example, Slater, 1999; Watts, 1999). There is a tendency to presume that the only political agency in the world is that of the United States and its allies, thus diminishing a priori the political agency of others. For example, discussions of the Gulf War of 1990–91 that focus singularly on United States involvement without paying significant attention to Saddam Hussein and the government of Iraq could be at least guilty of implicitly endorsing Iraq's invasion of Kuwait and, perhaps, Saddam's other crimes, such as the chemical gassing of the Kurds in northern Iraq or his long and destructive war against Iran in the 1980s. Silence about one or other party matters enormously in accounts such as these. After 11 September 2001 who can doubt that the *idea* of the 'clash of civilizations' or a fundamental cultural opposition between East and West, not necessarily geographical territories so much as clusters of ideas and images about reason, cities, social mobility, and the roles of women (Buruma and Margalit, 2002), is a two-way street to war rather than simply one emanating from the West? Phony as it might be in terms of the actual character of different societies, it seems to provide a simple-minded template for zealots on both 'sides.' Bad ideas are not an American or Western monopoly.

From one point of view, *intellectual freedom* is a simple product of wealth sufficient to employ a group of people full-time as academics and intellectuals and of popular indifference to what they do as long as it does not undermine the wealth and power of the state providing the setting in which the intellectual freedom operates. This is a rather classic left-wing view of the 'critical intellectual' in contemporary US society. But not all wealthy countries produce critical intellectuals or invest much in higher education. So, it is not simply a combination of wealth and indifference that provides the basis for the growth of critical or dissenting thought. I would argue that it is rather a product of toleration and cosmopolitanism in the institutional settings in which such thought flourishes. Toleration is important because it allows for alternative conceptions of understanding and thinking *and for their propagation*. There must be a public space in which intellectuals can engage with one another. Importantly, therefore, toleration provides the crucial social requirement for arguing your case against alternative ones. Absent this possibility, conventional understanding is never put to the test. Cosmopolitanism is important because it presupposes a world larger than the one people typically inhabit on a daily basis and an associated sense of the need to positively accept and, indeed, value in some way or another the culturally heterogeneous form that this world takes. Even while being 'products' of their settings, critical intellectuals must be able to think beyond the 'common sense' of the worlds in which they were raised. Absent this, they cannot legitimately claim the appellation 'critical.'

But neither toleration nor cosmopolitanism can be simply embraced independent of social–political context. There is a historical geography to both. Over the course of human history toleration and cosmopolitanism as prerequisites for intellectual freedom have 'moved around.' For example, while at one time the Arab world was characterized by both, at least among dominant groups, this has long ceased to be the case. Today some sort of liberal democracy is a necessary, if insufficient, condition for both. Often, democracy as such gives an effective voice only to those in the majority. Resources, the valuing of liberal education, and safeguards against persecution are also necessary to its prosperity. The importance of liberal democracy to legitimizing and solidifying toleration is an uncomfortable fact for those of us who still find much to criticize in its practice. To accept toleration as a virtue, however, requires more than a set of material and institutional conditions conducive to it, including democracy. Richard Dees (1999) argues that groups must experience something akin to a 'conversion' to accept toleration as a virtue. Comparing early modern France and England, he sees this conversion as incontrovertibly contextual or geographical. For it to happen, he claims, groups with different beliefs must have the possibility to mingle with one another (not the least in the marketplaces of commerce), a common enemy helps to reduce the vitriol between them by creating an external foe (toleration rests to a degree on intolerance), wide diversity between contending groups reduces the threat to each posed by any other, and increased individual autonomy loosens group ties and creates the possibility for alternative intellectual and political bonds. Without these contextually specific conditions toleration will not take root.

Obviously, cosmopolitanism bears some relationship to toleration. But it is not the same thing, even though some discussions seem to suggest as much (e.g. Walzer, 1997). One can tolerate all manner of local groups and their ideas without accepting the main tenet of cosmopolitanism: the need to look outside of one's own experience or identity in order to understand it. Exile groups, expatriates, migrants, and transients can be the most effective instigators of cosmopolitanism. They make a positive ethic out of cultural borrowing. But if openness to other worlds and their ideas is one feature of the doctrine, another is the positive valuation of the settings in which the ideas are shared and reworked. The most important settings are large cosmopolitan cities (Ignatieff, 1993). These have long been and remain the sites in which alternative world-views engage and clash. It is out of this engagement and conflict that cosmopolitanism emerges. Around the world, however, cosmopolitanism seems a privilege reserved to those who live within the relatively secure boundaries of wealthy developed states and who value the vibrancy of cultural diversity. Elsewhere, particularly among those enamored of religious fundamentalisms geared to this or that apocalypse, it excites fear and hatred. To them cosmopolitanism, and toleration, are despicable; symbols of hubris and idolatry. Such sentiments are alive and on the march around the world today. Ian Buruma and Avishai Margalit (2002: 4) provide an illustrative anecdote:

> There is a recurring theme in movies from poor countries in which a young person from a remote village goes to the big city, forced by circumstances to seek a new life in the wider, more affluent world. Things quickly go wrong. The young man or woman is lonely, adrift, and falls into poverty, crime, or prostitution. Usually, the story ends in a gesture of terrible violence, a vengeful attempt to bring down the pillars of the arrogant, indifferent, alien city. There are echoes in this story of Hitler's life in Vienna, Pol Pot's in Paris, Mao's in Beijing, or indeed of many a Moslem youth in Cairo, Haifa, Manchester, or Hamburg.

Ironically, critical intellectuals (though rarely very cosmopolitan ones) have often been complicit in the rejection of the values of toleration and cosmopolitanism, finding much to praise in various forms of despotism and tyranny. Why should this be so? Having rejected *raison d'état*, they look for an inspiring alternative to the dull, mediocre, and psychologically oppressive regimes under which they live. This can be purely passive, refusing to identify sources of conflict in the world other than those they are immediately familiar with: those around them. But it can also be more active: what Mark Lilla has called the 'the lure of Syracuse' (Lilla, 2001: 193–216). By this he means the temptation of the intellectual to follow the path of the philosopher Plato to the ancient Greek city of Syracuse (in Sicily) in the instruction of the tyrant Dionysius.

Although Lilla tends to give precedence to the 'inner life' of intellectuals and their attraction to sponsorship by the powers-that-might-be, many of his case studies, from the Nazi celebrant Carl Schmitt and the Nazi sympathizer Martin Heidegger to the Communist sympathizers Walter Benjamin and Alexandre Kojève and, finally, to the Nietzschean Michel Foucault and the 'spiritual Marxist' Jacques Derrida, reveal three common features: an attraction to totalistic explanations putting faith in the explanatory power of a single force of factor – divine order, class struggle, authority or the *volk*, discourse, language *tout court*; an urge to impose this on everyone else, notwithstanding their own critiques of other intellectuals as dupes of the powerful; and the delusion that individual and collective identities are self-constructed in geographical isolation rather than constituted out of mutual contact and subsequent distanciation. The sad fact is that none of these avowedly *critical* intellectuals understood that their freedom to think and publicize their views depended on the very social–political conditions they criticized as abhorrent and in need of destruction. As Lilla (2001: xi) aptly makes the point:

> Fascist and Communist regimes were welcomed with open arms by many West European intellectuals throughout the twentieth century, as were countless 'national liberation' movements that instantly became traditional tyrannies, bringing misery to unfortunate peoples across the globe. Throughout the century Western liberal democracy was portrayed in diabolical terms as the real home of tyranny – the tyranny of capital, of imperialism, of bourgeois conformity, of 'metaphysics,' of 'power,' even of 'language.'

It is past time for intellectuals to acknowledge and examine the social–political conditions that make their work possible and to guard against the 'lure of Syracuse' by openly examining the roles of all of the actors they need to consider, not simply those nearby and well known whose crimes and misdemeanors may be more obvious but also perhaps less venal than those more distant and less familiar. Critically examining the political contexts of toleration and cosmopolitanism is a vital task for political geography in maintaining the field's own escape from the territorial trap of national parochialism in which it was long ensconced.

Conclusion

In this chapter I have endeavored to identify and describe three areas in which political geography is currently being 'made.' From the articulation of ideas about the mediating role in politics of geographical scale through the politics of the environment to the vigorous interest in the geographical aspects of normative political questions, political geography is currently under reconstruction. But this is not a new phenomenon. As this book tries to show, political geography has been remade numerous times in order to match the changing times and geographies it is hoping to map.

This is not to say that all is changing. Far from it. Many of the older topics retain considerable interest, even as they are placed in new perspective. History dealt a bad hand to political geography. The rejection of its classic environmental determinism after World War II meant that the field went into a long hibernation. During the Cold War the descriptive knowledge it could provide was not much in demand because the ideological nature of that conflict seemed to make places nothing more than chess pieces on a global game board. With the end of the Cold War the questions that political geography is concerned with have once more come center stage. Though the horizon beckons, the need is to have more people moving towards it, addressing the themes (and other, older ones) laid out here. The enterprise is open-ended as long as the world remains the complicated, dangerous place it is today.

chapter 6
CONCLUSION

If political geography once stood for attempts at explaining politics – understood largely as the geographical formation of statehood and interstate conflicts – by the 'facts of nature,' today it stands increasingly for efforts at understanding the distribution of political power across geographical scales through the geographical imaginations, group and institutional affiliations, and agency of people engaged in everyday struggles and conflicts. Easily the most important change in the 'making of political geography,' this reorientation of focus has been paralleled by a number of related changes. By way of conclusion, these are worth brief restatement, though all are raised in the course of previous chapters. Before going over the four features of the field as whole that exhibit the most change, however, I want to say something about the general approach to the 'making' of political geography taken in this book.

The approach

Though covering many of the main authors and figures in the history of political geography as well as the concepts upon which the field has been based, this book does not focus on the 'interior lives' of authors or see the field as made by entirely intellectual influences, such as characterize, respectively, the Great Men and history of ideas approaches to how fields of study develop and change. Rather, I have chosen to emphasize the importance of 'geopolitical context' in the long-term evolution of the field. Partly because the subject-matter of the field has always been strongly related to 'real-world events,' unlike say chemistry or physics, it has always had to find justification in its relevance to public and international affairs. At the same time, it has always been connected to the practice of politics, both actual and by aspiration, so it makes sense to think of the making of political geography in terms of the 'times' in which research and writing have taken place.

I have also made an effort to show that where and by whom it has been undertaken has also had important consequences for the nature of what has been made.

The movement in the intellectual center-of-gravity of the field, so to speak, from pre-World War I Germany to the contemporary Britain and the United States has undoubtedly affected the shift away from an exclusive focus on the geography of statehood. The increased recruitment of people into the field from a wide range of social, national, gender, sexual, and ethnic backgrounds has also undoubtedly widened the empirical scope and theoretical range of the field.

But this 'external' emphasis on historical-geographical context has limits. For one thing, there have always been 'exceptional' individuals or schools of thought that have gone 'against the grain' of the times, suggesting that authorship does indeed count for something. The examples of Reclus and Vidal in the early years and Jean Gottmann later serve as cases in point. There is agency in intellectual life as there is in politics, even if it is always subject to strong social influence. Finally, all is not change. 'Waves' of theory or differing political perspectives do not simply wash out previous ones. Once established, theoretical viewpoints put down strong roots that can continue to bear fruit even as they are eclipsed by newer ones. Struggling to account for new conditions they often appear anachronistic, as does environmental determinism today, but they remain as reminders of what were once widely accepted positions that could under certain circumstances come back to intellectual life.

The making of political geography

So, in addition to the less exclusive focus on statehood, what else has changed most in the making of political geography over the past one-hundred years of a university-based field of political geography? Four major changes seem to emerge out of the survey provided in previous chapters that flow across the field as a whole. Of course, many theoretical differences remain and will undoubtedly resist incorporation into some single disciplinary standard.

The first of these changes is a slow and hesitant shift from the objectivist 'view from nowhere,' masking as it does definite social identities and political interests, to a more nuanced appreciation of the 'situatedness' of knowledge. This is the idea that knowledge is always partial and biased, even as the aspiration remains that of convincing others of a 'truthful' explanation. This recognition has been important in allowing a more *critical* appreciation of the various phenomena studied in the field. The early years of political geography were less than intellectually stellar largely because the main practitioners hid their partisan objectives behind the veil of complete objectivity, using the 'facts of nature' to conceal the social, racial, and political agendas to which they were committed.

The second change has been a trend from naturalistic explanation in terms of environmental or social causes to an emphasis on political agency in historical-geographical contexts. In this respect, political geography evidences a return to pre-Enlightenment conceptions of the political as inherently related to the powers of association and commitment demonstrated in political discourse and action rather than the coercive effects of 'structures' pushing people to behave in this or that way. This behavioral understanding of power, common to statist, communitarian, and some liberal conceptions of the political, is under increasing challenge from views that emphasize human capability and performance more than human limits and deficiencies in the face of overriding 'forces' of one sort or another, be they cultural or economic.

The concepts of the field once received short shrift compared to descriptive empirical accounts of different 'problems' associated with boundaries, ethnic conflicts, global dispositions of military capacity, etc. Recently, however, the nature of the central concepts of the field – territory, boundary, place, state, nation, nation-state, sovereignty, and geopolitics – has become the focus of considerable analytical attention. Not only do these concepts form the core of the field, such as it is, most of them have also been neglected within the mainstream of political theory.

Finally, the field is increasingly characterized by an interest in historical contingency rather than deterministic explanation. By this I mean that historical periodization is seen as setting the limits to putative generalizations. Thus, what might count as a 'successful' account of ethnic conflict during the Cold War years may not in the very different context of the years since the end of the Cold War. During the Cold War, the colonial past and current prospects for exciting the interest of one another of the superpowers were probably more important than they would be today. As times change, therefore, so should our explanations.

The paradox of political geography

There is still something of a paradox to the making of political geography from the 1890s to the twenty-first century. Even as the field as such has suffered from the vagaries of its reputation within the academy and the wider world, the subjects it studies have persisted in significance, even if in periods like the years of the Cold War this was not always obvious. Now the subject-matter is challenged by the idea of a new world in the making that 'knows no boundaries.' With the world on the way to becoming a giant pinhead in which where you are counts for nothing, connectivity, interdependence, global culture, and cyberspace are displacing the bounded territorial spaces and grounded places that are the leitmotif of political geography. I hope that you see after reading this book that the pinhead world is a fantasy one. The world is still packed with political dramas that can only be adequately understood if placed in their geographic context. This is likely to be the case until the world becomes a smooth sphere with no resistance to human movement or without all of its current territorial divisions and inequalities.

Satire is a good antidote to abstract bombast. I return at the end, therefore to the view from the future in California according to the artist Sandow Birk, alluded to in the Preface. There is more than a resemblance to worlds past and present, notwithstanding the seemingly peculiar setting for a dreadful war: a war between two California cities and their hinterlands, Los Angeles versus San Francisco. Who would have thought? In Birk's (2000: 34–5) satire of 'The Great War of the Californias,' between Los Angeles and San Francisco, the last phase of the war sees the forces of Los Angeles in desperate straits.

> After extensive but fruitless negotiations, Orange County and San Diego had both decided to remain neutral. Arrogantly overconfident, the kingdom of suburban tract houses and theme parks tuned a blind eye to the sufferings of its more cosmopolitan neighbor. Busy with shopping and tennis, residents failed to perceive the threat looming behind the clouds of war. Similarly, the San Diego population was too preoccupied with maniacal fence-building on the Mexican border to comprehend the threat of an invasion from the north.
>
> Of all the territories with which the Angelenos pleaded for assistance, only Tijuana offered its support. On the eve of 24 August, she rose brilliantly to the challenge. Long-suffering Baja California sent wave upon wave of skilled guerrilla fighters whose bravery and intimate knowledge of the terrain turned the tide of the war. In the final draft of the peace accord, politicians voted resoundingly (119 to 56) to abolish the southern border of the Californias.
>
> But victory brought scarcity in its wake. Water, when it could be found, cost $14 a gallon. The price of *carne asada* rocketed to $22 a pound, and three-day rentals at Blockbuster were as much as $36 for new releases.
>
> During the celebrations attending the peace agreements, the crowd called out to Gomez [one of the LA Generals] to speak. Too exhausted to approach the podium, he refused. Instead, he asked the band to play a solemn rendition of 'I Left My Heart in San Francisco.' The Angelenos, many of whom were already planning bed-and-breakfast vacations in Fog City or plotting joint ventures with Silicon Valley dot-com

start-ups, roared with delight. Whereupon Park [an LA officer] rose and called for more somber celebrations.

'We are all Californians,' he said, 'And no one is the victor.'

In many respects, therefore, even as things do change, aspects of the past live on. So, even if it is California and not the United States that is at war, the war itself would not be totally unlike others have been. And this is doubly true of the aftermath: why did they go to war at all?

REFERENCES

Agnew, J. A. (1987) *Place and Politics.* London: Allen & Unwin.

Agnew, J. A. (1989) Beyond reason: spatial and temporal sources of intractability in ethnic conflicts, in **L. Kriesberg** *et al.* (eds), *Intractable Conflicts and their Transformation.* Syracuse, NY: Syracuse University Press.

Agnew, J. A. (1994) The territorial trap: the geographical assumptions of international relations theory. *Review of International Political Economy,* **1**: 53–80.

Agnew, J. A. (1997a) *Political Geography: A Reader.* London: Arnold.

Agnew, J. A. (1997b) The dramaturgy of horizons: geographical scale in the 'reconstruction of Italy' by the new Italian political parties, 1992–95. *Political Geography,* **16**: 99–121.

Agnew, J. A. (1998) *Geopolitics: Re-Visioning World Politics.* London: Routledge.

Agnew, J. A. (1999) The new geopolitics of power, in **D. Massey** *et al.* (eds), *Human Geography Today.* Cambridge: Polity Press.

Agnew, J. A. (2001a) The 'View from Nowhere' and the Modern Geopolitical Imagination, in **M. Antonsich** *et al.* (eds), *On the Centenary of Ratzel's* Politische Geographie*: Europe between Political Geography and Geopolitics.* Rome: Memorie della Società Geografica Italiana.

Agnew, J. A. (2001b) The limits of federalism in transnational democracy: beyond the hegemony of the US model, in **J. Anderson** (ed.), *Transnational Democracy.* London: Routledge.

Agnew, J. A. (2002) *Place and Politics in Modern Italy.* Chicago: University of Chicago Press.

Agnew, J. A. and S. Corbridge (1995) *Mastering Space: Hegemony, Territory, and International Political Economy.* London: Routledge.

Albert, M. (2000) From defending borders towards managing risks? Security in a globalized world. *Geopolitics,* **5**: 57–80.

Alcoff, L. (1991–92) The problem of speaking for others. *Cultural Critique,* **20**: 5–32.

Alexander, L. M. (1966) *World Political Patterns.* Chicago: Rand McNally.

Allen, J. (1999) Spatial assemblages of power: from domination to empowerment, in **D.Massey** *et al.* (eds), *Human Geography Today.* Cambridge: Polity Press.

Ancel, J. (1936) *Géopolitique.* Paris: Delagrave.

Anderson, P. (1974) *Lineages of the Absolutist State.* London: New Left Books.

Archer, K. (1993) Regions as social organisms: the Lamarckian characteristics of Vidal de la Blache's Regional Geography. *Annals of the Association of American Geographers,* **83**: 498–514.

Barber, B. (1994) *Jihad versus McWorld.* New York: Ballantine.

Barnes, T. J. and J. S. Duncan (eds) (1992) *Writing Worlds: Text and Metaphor in the Representation of Landscape.* London: Routledge.

Bassett, K. (1999) Is there progress in human geography? The problem of progress in the light of recent work in the philosophy and sociology of science. *Progress in Human Geography,* **23**: 27–47.

Beaverstock, J. V., R. G. Smith and P. J. Taylor (2000) World-city network: a new metageography? *Annals of the Association of American Geographers,* **90**: 123–34.

Beck, U. (1992) *Risk Society.* London: Sage.

Bennett, S. and C. Earle (1983) Socialism in America: a geographical interpretation of its failure. *Political Geography Quarterly,* **2**: 31–55.

Bentley, M. (1996) 'Boundaries' in theoretical language about the British State, in **S. J. D. Green and R. C. Whiting** (eds), *The Boundaries of the State in Modern Britain.* Cambridge: Cambridge University Press.

Birk, S. (2000) An introduction to the Great War of the Californias, in *Sandow Birk's 'In Smog and Thunder.' Historical Works from the Great War of the Californias.* Laguna Beach, CA: Laguna Art Museum.

Blaikie, P. (1985) *The Political Economy of Soil Erosion in Developing Countries.* New York: Longman.

Blatter, J.K. (2001) Debordering the world of states: towards a multi-level system in Europe and a multi-polity system in North America? Insights from border regions. *European Journal of International Relations,* **7**: 175–209.

Blouet, B. W. (1987) *Halford Mackinder: A Biography.* College Station, TX: Texas A & M University Press.

Boggs, S. W. (1940) *International Boundaries: A Study of Boundary Functions and Problems.* New York: Columbia University Press.

Bondurant, J. V. (1958) *Conquest of Violence: The Gandhian Philosophy of Conflict.* Princeton: Princeton University Press.

Bowman, I. (1921) *The New World: Problems in Political Geography.* Yonkers, NY: World Book Company.

Bowman, I. (1942) Political geography vs geopolitics. *Geographical Review,* **32**: 646–58.

Breuilly, J. (1982) *Nationalism and the State.* Manchester: Manchester University Press.

Brinton, W. M. and A. Rinzler (eds) (1990) *Without Force or Lies: Voices from the Revolution of Central Europe in 1989–90.* San Francisco: Mercury House.

Brown, C. (2001) Borders and identity in international political theory, in **M. Albert** et al.(eds), *Identities, Borders, Orders: Rethinking International Relations Theory.* Minneapolis: University of Minnesota Press.

Brown, L. (1981) *Building a Sustainable Society.* New York: Norton.

Brown, L. (1999) *State of the World.* New York: Norton.

Bryner, G.C. (2000) *Environmental Movements in the Twentieth Century.* Lanham, MD: Rowman & Littlefield.

Buruma, I. and A. Margalit (2002) Occidentalism. *New York Review of Books,* 17 January, 4–7.

Butler, J. (1992) Contingent foundations: feminism and the question of 'postmodernism,' in **J. Butler and J. W. Scott** (eds), *Feminists Theorize the Political.* New York: Routledge.

Calhoun, C. (1994) Social theory and the politics of identity, in **C. Calhoun** (ed.), *Social Theory and the Politics of Identity.* Oxford: Blackwell.

Calleo, D. P. (1987) *Beyond American Hegemony: The Future of the Western Alliance.* New York: Basic Books.

Campbell, D. (1992) *Writing Security: United States Foreign Policy and the Politics of Identity.* Baltimore: Johns Hopkins University Press.

Castells, M. (1996) *The Rise of the Network Society.* Oxford: Blackwell.

Cerny, P. G. (1999) Globalization and the Erosion of Democracy. *European Journal of Political Research,* **36** (August): 1–26.

Chambers, S. and J. Kopstein (2001) Bad civil society. *Political Theory,* **29**: 837–65.

Christison, K. (1999) *Perceptions of Palestine: Their Influence on US Middle East Policy.* Berkeley and Los Angeles: University of California Press.

Claval, P. (1994) From Michelet to Braudel: personality, identity and organization in France, in **D. Hooson** (ed.), *Geography and National Identity.* Oxford: Blackwell.

Claval, P. (2000) *Hérodote* and the French Left, in **K. Dodds and D. Atkinson** (eds), *Geopolitical Traditions: A Century of Geopolitical Thought.* London: Routledge.

Cohen, S. B. (1973) *Geography and Politics in a World Divided,* 2nd edn. New York: Oxford University Press.

Conversi, D. (1995) Reassessing current theories of nationalism: nationalism as boundary maintenance and creation. *Nationalism and Ethnic Politics,* **1**: 73–85.

Conversi, D. (1999) Nationalism, boundaries, and violence. *Millennium,* **28**: 553–84.

Corbridge, S. (1994) Maximizing entropy? New geopolitical orders and the internationalization of business, in **G. J. Demko and W. B. Wood** (eds), *Reordering the World: Geopolitical Perspectives on the Twenty-first Century.* Boulder, CO: Westview Press.

Corbridge, S. (1998) Development ethics: distance, difference, plausibility. *Ethics, Place and Environment,* **1**: 35–53.

Cox, K. R. (1973) *Conflict, Power and Politics in the City: A Geographic View.* New York: McGraw-Hill.

Cox, K. R. (1979) *Location and Public Problems.* Chicago: Maaroufa Press.

Cox, K. R. and D. R. Reynolds (eds) (1974) *Locational Approaches to Power and Conflict.* New York: Halsted Press.

Dahl, R. A. (1999) Can international organizations be democratic? A skeptic's view, in **I. Shapiro and C. Hacker-Cordón** (eds), *Democracy's Edges.* Cambridge: Cambridge University Press.

Dalby, S. (2000) Geopolitics and ecology: rethinking the contexts of environmental security, in **M. R. Lowi and B. R. Shaw** (eds), *Environment and Security: Discourses and Practices.* London: Macmillan.

Dalby, S. (2002) Environmental geopolitics, in **K. Anderson** *et al.* (eds), *Handbook of Cultural Geography.* London: Sage.

Davies, C. B. (1994) *Black Women, Writing and Identity: Migrations of the Subject*. London: Routledge.

Dees, R. H. (1999) Establishing toleration. *Political Theory*, **27**: 667–93.

Demangeon, A. and L. Febvre (1935) *Le Rhin: Problèmes d'histoire et d'économie*. Paris: Armand Colin.

Derluguian, G. M. and S. L. Greer (eds) (2000) *Questioning Geopolitics: Political Projects in a Changing World-System*. Westport, CT: Greenwood Press.

de Seversky, A. P. (1950) *Air Power: Key to Survival*. New York: Simon & Schuster.

Deudney, D. (1995) Nuclear weapons and the waning of the real-state. *Daedalus*, **124**: 209–51.

Diamond, J. (1997) *Guns, Germs, and Steel: The Fates of Human Societies*. New York: Norton.

Dijkink, G. (2001) Ratzel's *Politische Geographie* and nineteenth-century German discourse, in **M. Antonsich** et al. (eds), *On the Centenary of Ratzel's* Politische Geographie: *Europe between Political Geography and Geopolitics*. Rome: Memorie della Società Geografica Italiana.

Dumont, L. (1983) *Essais sur l'individualisme*. Paris: Seuil.

Duncan, J. S. and D. Ley (eds) (1993) *Place/Culture/Representation*. London: Routledge.

Duncan, N. (1996) Postmodernism in human geography, in **C. Earle** et al. (eds), *Concepts in Human Geography*. Lanham, MD: Rowman & Littlefield.

East, W. G. and A. E. Moodie (eds) (1956) *The Changing World: Studies in Political Geography*. Yonkers, NY: World Book Company.

Elon, A. (2001) The Deadlocked City. *New York Review of Books*, 18 October: 6–12.

Enloe, C. (1990) *Bananas, Beaches and Bases: Making Feminist Sense of International Politics*. Berkeley and Los Angeles: University of California Press.

Entrikin, J. N. (1999) Political Community, Identity and Cosmopolitan Place. *International Sociology*, **14**: 269–82.

Fairclough, A. (1987) *To Redeem the Soul of America: The Southern Christian Leadership Conference and Martin Luther King Jr*. Athens, GA: University of Georgia Press.

Farinelli, F. (2001) Friedrich Ratzel and the nature of (political) geography, in **M. Antonsich** et al. (eds), *On the Centenary of Ratzel's* Politische Geographie: *Europe Between Political Geography and Geopolitics*. Rome: Memorie della Società Geografica Italiana. Also as **Farinelli, F.** (2000) Friedrich Ratzel and the nature of (political) geography. *Political Geography*, **19**: 943–55.

Fearon, J. D. and D. D. Laitin (1996) Explaining inter-ethnic cooperation. *American Political Science Review*, **90**: 715–35.

Flynn, S. E. (2002) America the vulnerable. *Foreign Affairs*, **81**(1): 60–74.

Forest, B. (1995) West Hollywood as symbol: the significance of place in the construction of a gay identity. *Environment and Planning D: Society and Space*, **13**: 133–57.

Foucault, M. (1980) *Power/Knowledge*. Brighton: Harvester.

Gallagher, L. (1962) *Edmund Walsh S.J.: A Biography*. New York: Benziger.

Galli, G. and A. Prandi (1970) *Patterns of Political Participation in Italy*. New Haven, CT: Yale University Press.

Gambi, L. (1994) Geography and imperialism in Italy: from the unity of the nation to the 'new' Roman empire, in **A. Godlewska and N. Smith** (eds), *Geography and Empire*. Oxford: Blackwell.

Garton Ash, T. (1999) Hail Ruthenia! *New York Review of Books*, 22 April: 54–5.

Geiger, R. L. (1993) *Research and Relevant Knowledge: American Research Universities since World War II*. New York: Oxford University Press.

Gelpi, C. F. and M. Griesdorf (2001) Winners or losers? Democracies in international crisis, 1918–94. *American Political Science Review*, **95**: 633–47.

Gilman, S. L. (1992) Plague in Germany, 1939/1989: cultural images of race, space, and disease, in **A. Parker** *et al.* (eds), *Nationalisms and Sexualities*. London: Routledge.

Goblet, Y.-M. (1934) *Le crépuscule des traités*. Paris: Berger Levrault.

Godlewska, A. and N. Smith (eds) (1994) *Geography and Empire*. Oxford: Blackwell.

Goldstein, J. (2001) *War and Gender*. Cambridge: Cambridge University Press.

Gottmann, J. (1952) *La politique des états et leur géographie*. Paris: Armand Colin.

Gottmann, J. (1961) *Megalopolis*. New York: Twentieth Century Fund.

Gottmann, J. (1973) *The Significance of Territory*. Charlottesville: University Press of Virginia.

Gottmann, J. (1980) (ed.) *Centre and Periphery: Spatial Variation in Politics*. London: Sage.

Graham, H. D. and N. Diamond (1997) *The Rise of the American Research Universities: Elites and Challengers in the Postwar Era*. Baltimore: Johns Hopkins University Press.

Gray, C. (1989) *The Geopolitics of Superpower*. Lexington, KT: University Press of Kentucky.

Greenfeld, L. (1992) *Nationalism: Five Roads to Modernity*. Cambridge, MA: Harvard University Press.

Gregory, D. (1989) Areal differentiation and post-modern human geography, in **D. Gregory and R. Walford** (eds), *Horizons in Human Geography*. London: Macmillan.

Gurr, T. R. (2000) Ethnic warfare on the wane. *Foreign Affairs*, **79**(3): 52–64.

Habermas, J. (1998) Jenseits des Nationalstaats? Bemerkungen zu Folgeproblemen der wirtschaftlichen Globalisierung, in **U. Beck** (ed.), *Politik der Globalisierung*. Frankfurt: Suhrkamp.

Halliday, F. (2001) *Two Hours That Shook the World: September 11, 2001: Causes and Consequences*. London: Saqi Books.

Halper, J. (2000) The 94 per cent solution: a matrix of control. *Middle East Report*, Fall.

Hartshorne, R. (1950) The functional approach in political geography. *Annals of the Association of American Geographers*, **40**: 95–130.

Harvey, D. (1973) *Social Justice and the City*. Oxford: Blackwell.

Harvey, D. (1982) *The Limits to Capital*. Chicago: University of Chicago Press.

Harvey, D. (1983) Owen Lattimore: A memoir. *Antipode*, **15**: 3–11.

Harvey, D. (1989) *The Condition of Postmodernity*. Oxford: Blackwell.

Harvey, D. (1993) Class relations, social justice and the politics of difference, in **M. Keith and S. Pile** (eds), *Place and the Politics of Identity*. London: Routledge.

Hayes, B. (2002) Statistics of deadly quarrels. *American Scientist*, **90**(1) 10–15.

Heffernan, M. J. (1994) The science of empire: the French geographical movement and the forms of French imperialism, 1970–1920, in **A. Godlewska and N. Smith** (eds), *Geography and Empire*. Oxford: Blackwell.

Heffernan, M. J. (1998) *The Meaning of Europe: Geography and Geopolitics.* London: Arnold.

Heidegger, M. (1959) *An Introduction to Metaphysics.* New Haven, CT: Yale University Press.

Held, D. (1999) Democracy and globalization, in **I. Shapiro and C. Hacker-Cordón** (eds), *Democracy's Edges*. Cambridge: Cambridge University Press.

Held, D. (ed.) (2000) *A Globalizing World? Culture, Economics, Politics.* London: Routledge.

Helleiner, E. (1995) Explaining the globalization of financial markets: bringing the state back in. *Review of International Political Economy*, **2**: 315–41.

Henrikson, A. K. (1980) America's changing place in the world: from 'periphery' to 'Centre'? in **J. Gottmann** (ed.), *Centre and Periphery: Spatial Variation in Politics.* London: Sage.

Hepple, L. W. (1986) The revival of geopolitics. *Political Geography Quarterly*, **5**: S21–S36.

Hepple, L. W. (2000) *Géopolitiques de Gauche*: Yves Lacoste, *Hérodote* and French radical politics, in **K. Dodds and D. Atkinson** (eds), *Geopolitical Traditions: A Century of Geopolitical Thought.* London: Routledge.

Hobsbawm, E. J. (1990) *Nations and Nationalism since 1780: Programme, Myth and Reality.* Cambridge: Cambridge University Press.

Homer-Dixon, T. and J. Blitt (eds) (1998) *Ecoviolence: Links Among Environment, Population, and Security.* Lanham, MD: Rowman & Littlefield.

Howitt, R. (2002) Scale, in **J. Agnew, G. Ó. Tuathail, and K. Mitchell** (eds), *A Companion to Political Geography.* Oxford: Blackwell.

Hudson, A. C. (1998) Reshaping the regulatory landscape: border skirmishes around the Bahamas and Cayman offshore financial centers. *Review of International Political Economy*, **5**: 534–64.

Hudson, A. C. (2001) NGOs' transnational advocacy networks: from legitimacy to political responsibility? *Global Networks*, **1**: 331–52.

Humphrey, S. (1997) Exemplars and rules: aspects of the discourse of moralities in Mongolia, in **S. Howell** (ed.), *The Ethnography of Moralities.* London: Routledge.

Huntington, S. P. (1993) The clash of civilizations? *Foreign Affairs*, **72**: 22–49.

Ignatieff, M. (1993) *Blood and Belonging: Journeys into the New Nationalism.* New York: Noonday Press.

Jacobson-Widding, A. (1997) 'I lied, I farted, I stole ...': Dignity and morality in African discourse on personhood, in **S. Howell** (ed.), *The Ethnography of Moralities.* London: Routledge.

Johnson, C. (2000) *Blowback: The Costs and Consequences of American Empire*. New York: Henry Holt.

Johnson, N. (1995) Cast in stone: monuments, geography, and nationalism. *Environment and Planning D: Society and Space*, **13**: 51–65.

Jones, S. B. (1954) A unified field theory of political geography. *Annals of the Association of American Geographers*, **44**: 111–23.

Kaldor, M. (1999) *New and Old Wars: Organized Violence in the Global Era*. Cambridge: Polity Press.

Karanian, M. (2000) The Karabagh story. *American Philatelist*, March: 264–8.

Kasperson, R. E. and J. V. Minghi (eds) (1969) *The Structure of Political Geography*. Chicago: Aldine.

Kaufmann, C. D. (1998) When all else fails: ethnic population transfers in the twentieth century. *International Security*, **23**: 120–56.

Kennedy, P. (1986) *The Rise and Fall of the Great Powers: Economic Change and Military Conflict from 1500 to 2000*. New York: Random House.

Kern, S. (1983) *The Culture of Time and Space, 1880–1918*. Cambridge MA: Harvard University Press.

Kirby, A. (1994) What did you do in the war, Daddy? in **A. Godlewska and N. Smith** (eds), *Geography and Empire*. Oxford: Blackwell.

Klare, M. (2001) The new geography of conflict. *Foreign Affairs*, **80**(3): 49–72.

Kobrin, S. J. (1997) Electronic cash and the end of national markets. *Foreign Policy*, **107**: 65–77.

Krishna, S. (1993) The importance of being ironic: a postcolonial view of international relations theory. *Alternatives*, **18**: 385–417.

Krishna, S. (1994) Cartographic anxiety: mapping the body politic in India. *Alternatives*, **19**: 507–21.

Kühl, S. (1994) *The Nazi Connection: Eugenics, American Racism, and German National Socialism*. New York: Oxford University Press.

Kürti, L. (2001) *The Remote Borderland: Transylvania in the Hungarian Imagination*. Albany, NY: SUNY Press.

Lacoste, Y. (2001) Rivalries for territory, in **J. Lévy** (ed.), *From Geopolitics to Global Politics: A French Connection*. London: Frank Cass.

Landes, D. (1998) *The Wealth and Poverty of Nations*. Cambridge, MA: Harvard University Press.

Lattimore, O. (1940) *Inner Asian Frontiers of China*. New York: American Geographical Society.

Lattimore, O. (1945) *Solution in Asia*. Boston: Little, Brown.

Lattimore, O. (1949) *The Situation in Asia*. Boston: Little, Brown.

Levin, P. S. and D. A. Levin (2002) The Real Biodiversity Crisis. *American Scientist*, **90**(1): 6–8.

Lévy, J. (2001) A user's guide to world-spaces, in **J. Lévy** (ed.), *From Geopolitics to Global Politics: A French Connection*. London: Frank Cass.

Lilla, M. (2001) *The Reckless Mind: Intellectuals in Politics*. New York: New York Review of Books.

Livingstone, D. N. (1992) *The Geographical Tradition: Episodes in the History of a Contested Enterprise*. Oxford: Blackwell.

Lovell, N. (ed.) (1998) *Locality and Belonging*. London: Routledge.

Lowi, M. R. and B. R. Shaw (eds.) (2000) *Environment and Security: Discourses and Practices*. London: Macmillan.

Luke, T. W. (2000a) Toward a green geopolitics: politicizing ecology at the Worldwatch Institute, in **K. Dodds and D. Atkinson** (eds), *Geopolitical Traditions: A Century of Geopolitical Thought*. London: Routledge.

Luke, T. W. (2000b) The discipline as disciplinary normalization: networks of research, in **R. Sil and E. M. Doherty** (eds), *Beyond Boundaries? Disciplines, Paradigms, and Theoretical Integration in International Studies*. Albany, NY: SUNY Press.

Mackenzie, W. J. M. (1976) *Political Identity*. London: Penguin.

Mackinder, H. J. (1887) The Scope and Methods of Geography. *Proceedings of the Royal Geographical Society,* new series, **9**: 141–60.

Mackinder, H. J. (1904) The geographical pivot of history. *Geographical Journal* **23**: 421–37.

Mackinder, H. J. (1919) *Democratic Ideals and Reality: A Study in the Politics of Reconstruction*. London: Constable.

MacLeod, G. and M. Goodwin (1999) Reconstructing an urban and regional political economy: on the state, politics, scale, and explanation. *Political Geography*, **18**: 697–730.

Malley, R. and H. Agha (2001) Camp David: The Tragedy of Errors. *New York Review of Books*, 9 August: 59–65.

Manin, B. (1987) On legitimacy and political deliberation. *Political Theory*, **15**: 338–68.

Mann, M. (1984) The autonomous power of the state. *European Journal of Sociology*, **25**: 185–213.

Margalit, A. (2001) Settling Scores. *New York Review of Books*, 20 September: 20–24.

Marston, S. (2000) The social construction of scale. *Progress in Human Geography*, **24**: 219–42.

McMichael, P. (1993) World food system restructuring under a GATT regime. *Political Geography*, **12**: 198–214.

Menand, L. (2001) College: the end of the Golden Age. *New York Review of Books*, 18 October: 44–7.

Miller, B. A. (2000) *Geography and Social Movements: Comparing Antinuclear Activism in the Boston Area*. Minneapolis: University of Minnesota Press.

Miller, D. (1986) Peter Kropotkin (1842–1921): mutual aid and anarcho-communism, in **J. A. Hall** (ed.), *Rediscoveries*. Oxford: Clarendon Press.

Miller, D. and S. H. Hashmi (eds) (2001) *Boundaries and Justice: Ethical Perspectives.* Princeton: Princeton University Press.

Mishra, P. (2002) The Afghan tragedy. *New York Review of Books*, 17 January: 43–9.

Mofson, P. (1999) Global Ecopolitics, in **G. J. Demko and W. B. Wood** (eds), *Reordering the World: Geopolitical Perspectives on the Twenty-first Century*, 2nd edn. Boulder, CO: Westview Press.

Moisy, C. (1997) Myths of the global information village. *Foreign Policy*, **107**: 78–87.

Mohanty, C. T. (1991) Cartographies of struggle, in **C. T. Mohanty** et al. (eds), *Third World Women and the Politics of Feminism.* Bloomington, IN: Indiana University Press.

Morley, D. and K. Robins (1995) *Spaces of Identity: Global Media, Electronic Landscapes and Cultural Boundaries.* London: Routledge.

Murphy, A. B. (1993) Linguistic regionalism and the social construction of space in Belgium. *International Journal for the Sociology of Language*, **104**: 49–64.

Muscarà, L. (1998) Jean Gottmann's Atlantic 'transhumance' and the development of his spatial theory. *Finisterra: Revista Portuguesa de Geografia*, **33**: 159–72.

Myers, N., R. A. Mittermeier, C. G. Mittermeier, G. A. da Fonseca, J. Kent (2000) Biodiversity hotspots for conservation priorities. *Nature*, **403** (23 February): 853–8.

Nagel, T. (1986) *The View from Nowhere.* New York: Oxford University Press.

Newman, D. (2001) Boundaries, borders, and barriers: changing geographic perspectives on territorial lines, in **M. Albert** et al. (eds), *Identities, Borders, Orders: Rethinking International Relations Theory.* Minneapolis: University of Minnesota Press.

Nijman, J. (1992) The limits of superpower: the United States and the Soviet Union since World War II. *Annals of the Association of American Geographers*, **82**: 681–95.

Novotny, P. (2000) *Where We Live, Work, and Play: The Environmental Justice Movement and the Struggle for a New Environmentalism.* Westport, CT: Praeger.

Nuttall, S. et al. (eds) (1996) *Text, Theory, Space: Postcolonial Representations and Identity.* London: Routledge.

O'Hagan, A. (2001) The end of British farming. *London Review of Books*, 22 March: 3, 5–16.

O'Hagan, J. (2000) A 'clash of civilizations'? in **G. Fry and J. O'Hagan** (eds), *Contending Images of World Politics.* London: Macmillan.

O'Hanlon, M. (1998-9) Can high technology bring US troops home? *Foreign Policy*, **113**: 72–86.

O' Lear, S. (2001) Azerbaijan: territorial issues and internal challenges in mid-2001. *Post-Soviet Geography and Economics*, **42**: 305–12.

O'Loughlin, J. (1986) Spatial models of international conflict: extending current theories of war behavior. *Annals of the Association of American Geographers*,**76**: 63–80.

O'Loughlin, J. and H. Van der Wusten (1990) Political geography of pan-regions. *Geographical Review*, **80**: 1–20.

Osei-Kwame, P. and P. J. Taylor (1984) A politics of failure: the political geography of Ghanaian elections, 1954–1979. *Annals of the Association of American Geographers*, **74**: 574–89.

O'Sullivan, P. (1986) *Geopolitics.* New York: St Martin's Press.

Ó Tuathail, G. (1993) The effacement of place? US foreign policy and the Gulf crisis. *Antipode,* **25**: 4–31.

Ó Tuathail, G. (1996) *Critical Geopolitics.* Minneapolis: University of Minnesota Press.

Ó Tuathail, G. (2000a) Spiritual geopolitics: Fr Edmund Walsh and Jesuit anti-communism, in **K. Dodds and D. Atkinson** (eds), *Geopolitical Traditions: A Century of Geopolitical Thought.* London: Routledge.

Ó Tuathail, G. (2000b) The postmodern geopolitical condition: states, statecraft, and security at the millennium. *Annals of the Association of American Geographers,* **90**: 166–78.

Ó Tuathail, G. and J. A. Agnew (1992) Geopolitics and discourse: practical geopolitical reasoning in American Foreign Policy. *Political Geography Quarterly,* **11**: 190–204.

Paasi, A. (1995) *Territories, Boundaries, and Consciousness: The Changing Geographies of the Finnish–Russian Border.* Chichester: John Wiley.

Paddison, R. (1983) *The Fragmented State: The Political Geography of Power.* Oxford: Blackwell.

Parker, G. (2001) Ratzel, the French school and the birth of alternative geopolitics, in **M. Antonsich** *et al.* (eds), *On the Centenary of Ratzel's* Politische Geographie: *Europe between Political Geography and Geopolitics.* Rome: Memorie della Società Geografica Italiana. Also in **G. Parker** (2000) Ratzel, the French school and the birth of alternative geopolitics. *Political Geography,* **19**: 957–69.

Parker, W. H. (1982) *Mackinder: Geography as an Aid to Statecraft.* Oxford: Oxford University Press.

Pearcy, G. E., R. H. Fifield *et al.* (1948) *Political Geography.* New York: Crowell.

Peet, R. and M. Watts (eds) (1996) *Liberation Ecologies: Environment, Development, Social Movements.* London: Routledge.

Penck, A. (1916) Der Krieg und das Studium der Geographie. *Zeitschrift der Gesellschaft für Erdkunde zu Berlin*: 159–76 and 222–48.

Perlmutter, A. (1997) *Making the World Safe for Democracy: A Century of Wilsonianism and its Totalitarian Challengers.* Chapel Hill: University of North Carolina Press.

Perrin, N. (1979) *Giving Up the Gun: Japan's Reversion to the Sword, 1543–1879.* Boulder, CO: Shambahla.

Pettis, M. (2001) *The Volatility Machine: Emerging Economies and the Threat of Financial Collapse.* New York: Oxford University Press.

Piore, M. and C. Sabel (1984) *The Second Industrial Divide.* New York: Basic Books.

Pred, A. (1990) *Making Histories and Transforming Human Geographies: The Local Transformation of Practice, Power Relations and Consciousness.* Boulder, CO: Westview Press.

Price, M. D. (1999) Nongovernmental organizations on the geopolitical front line, in **G. J. Demko and W. B. Wood** (eds), *Reordering the World: Geopolitical Perspectives on the Twenty-first Century*, 2nd edn. Boulder, CO: Westview Press.

Princen, T. and M. Finger (1994) *Environmental NGOs in World Politics: Linking the Local and the Global.* New York: Routledge.

Pulido, L. (2000) Rethinking environmental racism: white privilege and urban development. *Annals of the Association of American Geographers*, **90**: 12–40.

Quinn, D. (1997) The correlates of change in international financial regulation. *American Political Science Review*, **91**: 531–51.

Raffestin, C. (2001) From text to image, in **J. Lévy** (ed.), *From Geopolitics to Global Politics: A French Connection.* London: Frank Cass.

Rashid, A. (2000) *Taliban: Militant Islam, Oil and Fundamentalism in Central Asia.* New Haven: Yale University Press.

Ratzel, F. (1896) Die Gesetze des räumlichen Wachstums der Staaten. *Petermanns Mitteilungen*, XLII: 97–107.

Ratzel, F. (1897) *Politische Geographie.* Munich: R. Oldenbourg.

Ratzel, F. (1923) *Politische Geographie*, 3rd edn. Munich: R. Oldenbourg.

Ratzel, F. (1969) The laws of the spatial growth of states, in **R. E. Kasperson and J. V. Minghi** (eds), *The Structure of Political Geography.* Chicago: Aldine.

Rawls, J. (1971) *A Theory of Justice.* Cambridge, MA: Harvard University Press.

Reclus, E. (1905–08) *L'homme et la terre.* Paris: Librairie Universelle.

Retaillé, D. (2001) Geopolitics in history, in **J. Lévy** (ed.), *From Geopolitics to Global Politics.* London: Frank Cass.

Robic, M.-C. (1994) National identity in Vidal's *Tableau de la géographie de la France*: From political geography to human geography, in **D. Hooson** (ed.), *Geography and National Identity.* Oxford: Blackwell.

Robin, R. (2001) *The Making of the Cold War Enemy: Culture and Politics in the Military–Intellectual Complex.* Princeton: Princeton University Press.

Robinson, F. (1999) *Globalizing Care: Ethics, Feminist Theory, and International Relations.* Boulder, CO: Westview Press.

Rogers, P. (2000) Resource issues, in **T. C. Salmon** (eds), *Issues in International Relations.* London: Routledge.

Rokkan, S. (1980) Territories, centres, and peripheries: toward a geoethnic-geoeconomic-geopolitical model of differentiation within western Europe, in **J. Gottmann** (ed.), *Centre and Periphery: Spatial Variation in Politics.* London: Sage.

Rosenberg, E. S. (1982) *Spreading the American Dream: American Economic and Cultural Expansion, 1890–1945.* New York: Hill & Wang.

Routledge, P. (1992) Putting politics in its place. Baliapal, India as a terrain of resistance. *Political Geography*, **11**: 588–611.

Routledge, P. (1994) *Terrains of Resistance: Non-Violent Social Movements and the Contestation of Place in India.* Westport, CT: Praeger.

Rubin, C. T. (1998) *The Green Crusade: Rethinking the Roots of Environmentalism.* Lanham, MD: Rowman & Littlefield.

Sachs, J. D. (2000) Tropical underdevelopment. Paper presented at the Economic History Association, Annual Meeting, Los Angeles, 8 September.

Sack, R. D. (1986) *Human Territoriality: Its Theory and History.* Cambridge: Cambridge University Press.

Sahlins, P. (1989) *Boundaries: The Making of France and Spain in the Pyrenees.* Berkeley and Los Angeles: University of California Press.

Said, E. (1978) *Orientalism.* New York: Vintage.

Said, E. (2000) Palestinians under siege. *London Review of Books,* 14 December: 9–14.

Saikal, A. (2000) 'Islam and the West'? in **G. Fry and J. O'Hagan** (eds), *Contending Images of World Politics.* London: Macmillan.

Sandner, G. (1994) In search of identity: German nationalism and geography, 1871–1910, in **D. Hooson** (ed.), *Geography and National Identity.* Oxford: Blackwell.

Sassen, S. (1991) *The Global City.* Princeton: Princeton University Press.

Schmitt, C. (1996) *The Concept of the Political.* Chicago: University of Chicago Press.

Scott, A. J. (1998) *Regions and the World Economy: The Coming Shape of Global Production, Competition, and Political Order.* Oxford: Oxford University Press.

Scott, J. W. (1992) Experience, in **J. Butler and J. W. Scott** (eds), *Feminists Theorize the Political.* New York: Routledge.

Shapiro, M. J. (1999) Samuel Huntington's Moral Geography. *Theory and Event,* 2(4): 1–11.

Sharp, J. P. (2000) *Condensing the Cold War: Reader's Digest and American Identity.* Minneapolis: University of Minnesota Press.

Sharp, J. P. (2002) Gender in a political and patriarchal world, in **K. Anderson** *et al.* (eds), *Handbook of Cultural Geography.* London: Sage.

Siegfried, A. (1913) *Tableau de la France de l'ouest sous la troisième république.* Paris: Armand Colin.

Silvern, S. E. (1999) Scales of justice: law, Indian treaty rights and the political construction of scale. *Political Geography,* **18**: 639–68.

Skocpol, T. (1994) *Social Revolutions in the Modern World.* Cambridge: Cambridge University Press.

Slater, D. (1999) Situating geopolitical representations: inside/outside and the power of imperial interventions, in **D. Massey** *et al.* (eds), *Human Geography Today.* Cambridge: Polity Press.

Smith, D. M. (1999) Geography and ethics. How far should we go? *Progress in Human Geography,* **23**: 119–25.

Smith, N. (1994) Shaking loose the colonies: Isaiah Bowman and the 'decolonisation' of the British Empire, in **A. Godlewska and N. Smith** (eds), *Geography and Empire.* Oxford: Blackwell.

Sontag, D. (2001) Quest for Mideast peace: how and why it failed. *New York Times,* 26 July: A1–12.

Soros, G. (1998–9) Capitalism's last chance? *Foreign Policy,* **113**: 55–66.

Sprout, H. and M. Sprout (1939) *The Rise of American Naval Power.* Princeton: Princeton University Press.

Sprout, H. and M. Sprout (1943) *Toward a New Order of Seapower.* Princeton: Princeton University Press.

Sprout, H. and M. Sprout (1962) *Foundations of International Politics.* New York: Van Nostrand.

Sprout, H. and M. Sprout (1965) *The Ecological Perspective on Human Affairs, with Special Reference to International Politics.* Princeton: Princeton University Press.

Sprout, H. and M. Sprout (1978) *The Context of Environmental Politics: Unfinished Business for America's Third Century.* Lexington, KT: University Press of Kentucky.

Spykman, N. J. (1944) *The Geography of the Peace.* New York: Harcourt Brace.

Staeheli, L. (1994) Empowering political struggle: spaces and scales of resistance. *Political Geography,* **13**: 387–91.

Stanley, M. (1978) *The Technological Conscience: Survival and Dignity in an Age of Expertise.* Chicago: University of Chicago Press.

Stern, A. (1975) Political legitimacy in local politics: the Communist Party in north-eastern Italy, in **D. Blackmer and S. Tarrow** (eds), *Communism in Italy and France.* Princeton: Princeton University Press.

Stewart, J. Y. (2001) Our Town: Life in the Killing Zone. *Los Angeles Times Magazine,* 7 January: 10–17, 35.

Sutherland, J. (2000) An 'endangered planet'? in **G. Fry and J. O'Hagan** (eds), *Contending Images of World Politics.* London: Macmillan.

Tarrow, S. (1994) *Power in Movement: Social Movements, Collective Action and Politics.* Cambridge: Cambridge University Press.

Taylor, P. J. (1989) *Political Geography: World-Economy, Nation-State and Locality.* London: Longman.

Taylor, P. J. (1994) The state as container: territoriality in the modern world-system. *Progress in Human Geography,* **18**: 151–62.

Tesini, M. (1986) *Oltre la città rossa. L'alternativa mancata di Dossetti a Bologna (1956–58).* Bologna: Il Mulino.

Thaa, W. (2001) 'Lean citizenship': the fading away of the political in transnational democracy. *European Journal of International Relations,* **7**: 503–23.

Thomson, J. E. (1994) *Mercenaries, Pirates, and Sovereigns: State-Building and Extra-Territorial Violence in Early Modern Europe.* Princeton: Princeton University Press.

Thrift, N. (2000) It's the little things, in **K. Dodds and D. Atkinson** (eds), *Geopolitical Traditions: A Century of Geopolitical Thought.* London: Routledge.

Thrift, N. and Pile, S. (eds) (1995) *Mapping the Subject: Geographies of Cultural Transformation.* London: Routledge.

Tilly, C. (1986) *The Contentious French.* Cambridge, MA: Harvard University Press.

Tilly, C. (1990) *Coercion, Capital and European States: AD 990–1992.* Oxford: Blackwell.

197

Tilly, C. and W. P. Blockmans (eds) (1994) *Cities and the Rise of States in Europe, A.D. 1000 to 1800*. Boulder, CO: Westview Press.

Tollefson, J. W. (1993) *The Strength Not to Fight*. Boston: Little, Brown.

UNDCP (1997) *World Drugs Report*. Oxford: Oxford University Press.

Van Creveld, M. (1999) *The Rise and Decline of the State*. Cambridge: Cambridge University Press.

Van Valkenburg, S. (1939) *Elements of Political Geography*. New York: Prentice-Hall.

Vidal de la Blache, P. (1903) *Tableau de la géographie de la France*. Paris: Hachette.

Vidal de la Blache, P. (1917) *La France de l'Est: Lorraine-Alsace*. Paris: Armand Colin.

Viroli, M. (1995) *For Love of Country: An Essay on Patriotism and Nationalism*. Oxford: Oxford University Press.

Wacquant, L. J. D. (1994) The new urban color line: the state and the fate of the ghetto in PostFordist America, in **C. Calhoun** (ed.), *Social Theory and the Politics of Identity*. Oxford: Blackwell.

Wade, R. (1998–99) The coming fight over capital flows. *Foreign Policy*, **113**: 41–54.

Wallerstein, I. (1974) *The Modern World-System: Capitalist Agriculture and the Origins of the European World-Economy in the Sixteenth Century*. New York: Academic Press.

Wallerstein, I. (1993) *Geopolitics and Geoculture*. Cambridge: Cambridge University Press.

Walzer, M. (1997) *On Toleration*. New Haven, CT: Yale University Press.

Watts, M. J. (1999) Collective Wish Images: Geographical Imaginaries and the Crisis of National Development, in **D. Massey** et al. (eds), *Human Geography Today*. Cambridge: Polity Press.

Weber, E. (1976) *Peasants into Frenchmen: The Modernization of Rural France, 1870–1914*. Stanford, CA: Stanford University Press.

Weigert, H. J. et al. (1957) *Principles of Political Geography*. New York: Appleton Century Crofts.

Whittlesey, D. S. (1939) *The Earth and the State*. New York: Henry Holt.

Williams, C. H. (1989) The Question of National Congruence, in **R. J. Johnston and P. J. Taylor** (eds), *A World in Crisis? Geographical Perspectives*. Oxford: Blackwell.

Williams, R. W. (1999) Environmental Injustice in America and its Politics of Scale. *Political Geography*, **18**: 49–73.

Wilson, E. O. (2002) Hotspots: preserving pieces of a fragile biosphere. *National Geographic*, January: 86–9.

Wittfogel, K. (1929) Geopolitik, geographischer Materialismus und Marxismus. *Unter den Banner des Marxismus* **3**, nos 1, 4, 5. Translated as (1985) Geopolitics, geographical materialism and Marxism. *Antipode*, **17**(1): 21–72.

Wittfogel, K. (1957) *Oriental Despotism: A Comparative Study of Total Power*. New Haven: Yale University Press.

Wittfogel, K. (1985) Geopolitics, geographical materialism, and Marxism. *Antipode*, **17**: 21–72.

Wokler, R. (1987) Saint Simon and the passage from political to social science, in **A. Pagden** (ed.), *The Languages of Political Theory in Early-Modern Europe.* Cambridge: Cambridge University Press.

Wolf, A.T. and J. H. Hamner (2000) Trends in transboundary water disputes and dispute resolution, in **M. R. Lowi and B. R. Shaw** (eds), *Environment and Security: Discourses and Practices.* London: Macmillan.

Wolf, E. R. (1982) *Europe and the People Without History.* Berkeley and Los Angeles: University of California Press.

Yack, B. (2001) Popular sovereignty and nationalism. *Political Theory,* **29**: 517–36.

Young, I. M. (1987) Impartiality and the civic public: some implications of feminist critiques of moral and political theory, in **S. Benhabib and D. Cornell** (eds), *Feminism as Critique: On the Politics of Gender.* Oxford: Blackwell.

Young, I. M. (1990) *Justice and the Politics of Difference.* Princeton: Princeton University Press.

INDEX

QM LIBRARY
(MILE END)